THE ILLUSTRATED DIRECTORY OF
A Century of
Flight

THE ILLUSTRATED DIRECTORY OF
A Century of Flight

RAY BONDS

SALAMANDER

A Salamander Book

Published by
Salamander Books Ltd.
The Chrysalis Building
Bramley Road
London W10 6SP

© Salamander Books Ltd., 2003

An imprint of **Chrysalis** Books Group plc

ISBN 1-84065-494-5

Credits

Project Manager: Ray Bonds
Designers: Hardlines Ltd
Artifact photography: Don Eiler
Reproduction: Anorax Imaging Ltd
Printed and bound in: Italy

The Editor

Ray Bonds has been a defense journalist, editor, and publisher during a career spanning over thirty-five years, covering subjects and periods as wide-ranging as the the history of flight, the American Civil War, anti-ballistic missile systems, stealth warfare, and modern military intelligence gathering. He has written and edited scores of well-respected titles on the world's major armed forces, their battles, weapons, and organization, with a specialism in the armed services of the United States. His works have included well-thumbed books on the shelves of official military education centers throughout the United States, Europe, and Asia, and have included the important trilogy The U.S. War Machine, The Soviet War Machine, and The Chinese War Machine and, most recently, America's Special Forces.

Acknowledgments

The publishers thank the many manufacturers, international armed forces, and private individuals for providing illustrations for this book, in particular Philip Jarrett, who made very many available from his collection.

Contents

Introduction

Aviation today is truly awe-inspiring. Given the money and a modicum of planning, any one of us can girdle the Earth in a matter of days as a fare-paying passenger using scheduled air routes. Alternatively, we can learn to fly and pilot our privately owned or hired aircraft over the countryside, or even visit other countries. Large airliners carry 500 passengers at a time, while Concorde has routinely crossed the Atlantic at twice the speed of sound.

Aviation has shrunk the world in which we live; not in miles, but in time. Journeys which only 100 years ago took many weeks to accomplish are now measured in hours. Peoples on the far side of the globe are now near neighbors.

While this has obvious advantages in terms of transport and trade, it has also had other effects. Warfare has been revolutionized. A single aircraft can carry enough weaponry to devastate an entire city. Others can destroy opponents from scores of miles away, or hunt and kill submarines far below the surface of the sea. Bombers based in the USA can strike at targets thousands of miles away in the Middle East and return nonstop. Whole armies can be transported thousands of miles in a matter of days. The implications are enormous. Aggressive nations must now think twice when confronted with air power, which has thus paradoxically become a potent force for peace.

Above: Sir George Cayley described his "governable parachute" in 1852, and this faithful reproduction was flown (under tow) in 1973. The sole means of control was the tiller-operated "influencer" projecting behind the nacelle.

Right: The boxkite invented by Australian Lawrence Hargrave in 1893 was influential in establishing the biplane layout, but Hargrave's own experiments with numerous powered model flying machines brought no real success.

Above: In Germany, Otto Lilienthal made countless flights in his monoplane and biplane hang gliders during the 1890s, but finally lost his life in August 1896 when one of his monoplanes stalled and crashed.

Below: E. P. Frost of Cambridge, England, was convinced that the birds had the answer, and spent a great deal of time and money on elaborate experimental ornithopters. This example was tested in 1906–7.

Above: Lilienthal's greatest disciple was Englishman Percy Pilcher, seen here in the Hawk glider with which he made his most successful flights. He sustained fatal injuries following an in-flight structural failure of this machine on September 30, 1899.

Nor is this all. Aviation has pushed back the frontiers of science and technology to the point where they are barely comprehensible to the layman. Speeds exceeding 2,000mph (3,200kph) and altitudes of over 80,000ft (24km) are attainable, and fighters can maneuver hard enough to make the pilot feel he weighs nine times his normal body weight. Clever navigational systems tell pilots where they are to an accuracy of a few meters' distance and a fraction of a second in time. Aircraft can land in visibility so poor that the pilot is virtually blind. Computers can be programmed to allow an aircraft to fly at the very edges of its performance envelope without straying into the area of lost control. To quote Ben Rich of Lockheed, "We could even make the Statue of Liberty fly!"

All this has come about in the space of a mere ten decades packed

Right: There appears to be nothing new in aviation. Europe's latest fighters all feature canard foreplanes, as does this Bristol Boxkite of 1910 vintage, used as a trainer by both the RFC and RNAS.

with incident. This book focuses on the evolution of manned flight, spotlighting many of the most the significant happenings; the events which led ever onwards; the milestones along the way, even to the extent of opening up the new frontier – space. For our purposes, manned flight is defined as controlled flight in a powered, heavier-than-air machine. This immediately eliminates gliders (bar those of the Wrights' early work), balloons and airships.

To present a wide-ranging picture it has been necessary to strike a balance among experimental, military, and civilian aviation; between noteworthy "firsts" and pioneering flights; between human endeavor and technology; and among superlatives such as biggest, fastest, etc.

The first decade of this century saw the birth of true manned aviation when the Wright brothers made their first flights at Kitty Hawk, North Carolina. Before this, several pioneers had succeeded in making short powered hops, but these either used take-off aids such as ramps or the machines were inadequately controlled. The same applied to Paul Cornu's first helicopter flight three years later; it was not the first, but it was the only one to meet the stringent conditions of unassisted controlled flight.

Initially, progress was slow. Not until the latter half of 1908 was real progress observable. Various endurance and distance marks were set, but in the main these were flown over closed circuits, where engine failure would be a disappointment rather than a disaster. It is in this context that Blériot's epic Channel crossing in 1909 must be seen. Both the distance and endurance had frequently been exceeded, but his flight

Right: When John Alcock and Arthur Whitten Brown made the first nonstop crossing of the Atlantic in 1919, they used a modified Vickers Vimy bomber.

over the open sea, in poor visibility, was a true milestone of manned aviation, and was the forerunner of all trailblazing flights that followed.

By now the military were showing interest in the potential of the airplane, and, from 1910 until the end of the First World War in 1918, in innovations. Two events stand out from this period, both of which were to have significant effects on the future of military aviation. The first was the birth of naval aviation, typified by Eugene Ely's ship take-off and landing in 1910/11. The second event was the service introduction of the Fokker Eindecker, which was for all practical purposes the world's first fighter aircraft. As an interesting aside, the Eindecker was also the subject of the

Above: The Russian Polikarpov I-16 was first flown on November 31, 1933, some 18 months earlier than Germany's Messerschmitt Bf 109; by 1939 the I-16 Type 17 was the world's most powerfully armed fighter.

Above: The early Boeing 747s, now often referred to as the 'Classic', have shown themselves to be particularly suited to the carriage of cargo, and many were produced both as pure freighters and as passenger/cargo combis. Europe's major all-cargo operator Cargolux flies an all 747 fleet including these 747-200Cs.

first operational experiments in stealth when, in 1916, one or two machines were clad in transparent material in an attempt to reduce their "visual signature."

Enormous technical advances were made during the "Great War." How great these were was quickly shown in the year following the Armistice. On November 27, 1918, a Curtiss NC-1 flying boat took off with no fewer than 51 people aboard, and in the following month an RAF Handley Page 0/400 completed the final stages of a flight from England to India. Then, in May 1919, three US Navy NC flying boats set out from the United States to cross the Atlantic, staging via Newfoundland and the Azores, although only one made it to Lisbon. Barely three weeks later, in the greatest flight of all, Alcock and Brown made the first nonstop transatlantic crossing in a converted Vickers Vimy, from Newfoundland to Galway in Ireland.

This ushered in an era of long-distance flights, England to Australia and nonstop across the United States, to name but two. While every successful long-distance flight, and many of the unsuccessful ones also, were in many ways remarkable, the ultimate was the first circumnavigation of the globe, or more correctly, the northern hemisphere, by Douglas DWCs of the US Army Air Service, between April 6 and September 28, 1924. Given the reliability of the aircraft at this time, the huge logistics organization set up to support the flight does not detract from it one iota.

Further epic flights followed: a formation flight of six Soviet aircraft from Moscow to Beijing in 1925; England to Australia and back in 1926; and then the flight that caught the imagination of the world – New York to Paris solo by Charles Lindbergh. Kingsford Smith crossed the Pacific from San Francisco to Brisbane in June 1928, staging through Hawaii

Above: In the 1960s and 1970s Boeing proposed a variable-sweep supersonic transport (SST) shown here in high-speed (wings swept back) and low-speed (wings forward) configurations. The idea was not taken up.

and Fiji, and Richard Byrd reached the South Pole in November, 1929. The first solo circumnavigation was made by Mrs. Victor Bruce in a Blackburn Bluebird between September 15, 1930, and February 20, 1931, although the Atlantic and Pacific legs were made by ship. The next circumnavigation was made by Wiley Post and Harold Gatty in the Lockheed Vega *Winnie Mae* between June 23 and July 1, 1931. This flight was of tremendous importance for two reasons. It was completed in a little over eight days, and it had none of the enormous logistic backup needed by the DWCs several years earlier. Just to prove that it was no fluke, Post went around again solo two years later, using the same course but with fewer stages.

Long-distance flying was hazardous, but provided that the engine kept running, the fuel lasted out, the pilot stayed awake, and no gross navigational errors were made, marvelous journeys could be achieved. Rather different was the flight over Everest on April 3, 1933. One of the last unexplored places on the surface of the globe, the Himalayas were notorious for very high winds, rapidly

changing weather, icing conditions, and extreme up- and downdraughts. In the event of engine failure there was no possibility of a safe landing.

Meanwhile, other events had been taking place. Cierva flew his Autogiro in Madrid on January 9, 1923, and a few months later the first practical experiment in flight refueling, a technology which, many years later, changed the face of military aviation, occurred.

By the mid-1930s war was once again looming. Fighter design had arrived at the monoplane with enclosed cockpit and retractable undercarriage, typified by the Bf 109, first flown in May 1935, although Russia's I-16 was rather earlier. Another event in 1935 was the first flight of the Douglas DC-3, also known as the C-47 and Dakota. It has few claims to be the first of anything, but its sheer persistence (around 400 remain in service today, and many of these are candidates for re-engining with turboprops) makes it the most enduring aircraft of all time.

For 30 years after Cornu's first flight, helicopter development had languished, but in 1937 the first practical machine, the Focke-Achgelis Fa

61, was flown in Germany. Two years later, and also in Germany, the first turbojet-powered aircraft took to the skies, an event of the first magnitude.

Equally important was the development of airborne radar in England. This came to fruition in July 1940, when the first AI-assisted night victory was scored. As in the First World War, technology moved at a breathtaking rate, and it is impossible to do justice to many innovations of the period, such as radar-aided bombing.

The Second World War saw the first application of carrier-borne air power, a factor which looms large in modern defense considerations. There had to be a turning point here, but which one? The first carrier-versus-carrier battle was Coral Sea, in May 1942. The first decisive carrier battle was Midway, just weeks later. One of the most notorious uses of carrier aircraft was at Pearl Harbor in December 1941, but this was preceded by the crippling of the Italian fleet at Taranto

Above: Harriers and Sea Harriers on their way to the Falklands, May 1982. One fully fueled and armed Sea Harrier is parked ready for action at the bow of *Atlantic Conveyor*.

in November 1940, which had actually influenced Japanese thinking. Therefore the watershed in naval aviation had to be Taranto.

Concentration of force is a cardinal rule of warfare, and the Second World War showed two significant examples of this. The first was the 1,000-bomber raid on Cologne in May 1942, of which one of the participants said, "This was the first big bomber battle, and the bombers were winning!" The second was the nuclear attacks on Japan, in which unbelievable force was concentrated in single weapons, with results so dreadful that they have never been used since, though their menace has persisted.

High spots of the immediate post-war years were the introduction of swept wings, which changed the shape of almost every high speed aircraft, and the breaking of the so-called "sound barrier" by Chuck Yeager in 1947. Other achievements worthy of mention are the development of global reach, notably by the Boeing B-52,

first flown in 1952 and still in service more than fifty years later, and the introduction of increasing degrees of automation in fighter aircraft (today unmanned aerial vehicles frequently take to the skies, and have been involved in combat, but they are beyond the scope of this book).

On the transport side, the Berlin Airlift demonstrated an unsuspected aspect of air power; that it could be used peacefully to defeat an intransigent, if not overt, enemy. Airliners benefited from the new technology also. The first turboprop airliner flew in July 1948, and the first jet airliner one year later. Both were significant milestones pointing the way to modern air travel.

Technology ran wild in the 1960s. The X-15 attained speeds and altitudes never since equaled, swing-wing technology finally matured and entered service, and the Lockheed SR-71 proved to be an uninterceptable reconnaissance vehicle. Other advances took place in close air support. Before this the helicopter had been very much a

utility machine which could carry weapons for certain roles. With the advent of the HueyCobra it took on a new lease of life as a dedicated attack machine which changed the face of the battlefield. Meanwhile, the VTOL or STOVL Harrier entered service, thus fulfilling a long-held dream of a fighting machine that was not dependent on fixed (and vulnerable bases). The US Marines' reaction was, "Great. Park one outside my foxhole!"

The close of the 1960s saw two innovations on the civil side. The first widebody transport, the Boeing 747, made its maiden flight in February 1969, setting a design trend that other manufacturers have since followed and revolutionizing air travel at the same time. And one month later it was followed into the air by Concorde, the only successful supersonic transport.

At the Paris Air Show at Le Bourget in 1975 a small fighter piloted by Neil Anderson put on a breathtaking display of agility which made even hardened observers gape in disbelief. It was of course the F-16 Fighting Fal-

con which, using relaxed stability and fly-by-wire, set standards of maneuverability by which even the latest fighters are still judged. Another standard-setter, first flown in 1979, was the F/A-18 Hornet, which with its "glass cockpit" and automated displays provided a new benchmark for man-machine symbiosis.

The 1980s started on a quieter note. Just one of mankind's many dreams had been to have a limitless source of power, and the sun was an obvious choice. While as yet it does not seem to have brought any practical benefits, the dream came true in November 1980, with the first flight of Solar Challenger. Meanwhile it seemed that one last challenge remained for the aviation pioneer; to circumnavigate the globe nonstop without refueling. The purpose-designed Voyager was a rather fragile, "this side up" sort of airplane. It was not easy to fly, and its accommodation for the two-person crew was smaller than some dog kennels. This remarkable flight has rightly become one of the great epics of sheer endurance.

The low-speed demonstration of the Airbus A320, the world's first fly-by-wire and "glass cockpit" airliner, at Farnborough Air Show in 1990, was breathtaking, as had been the piggybacking of a space shuttle on a 747 more than a decade earlier. The sheer size of the An-225, the world's largest and heaviest aircraft, was equally impressive. The stealthy F-117A Nighthawk became the belated maturation of a very ancient idea, and actually went to war, accompanied by its big stealthy brother, the B-2A Spirit. Meanwhile, the Lockheed Martin Advanced Tactical Fighter, the F-22A Raptor, a stealthy and highly maneuverable air superiority fighter that has taken more than twenty years to develop, is expected to remain the trend-setter among fighters for many years to come.

Left: The super-agile, stealthy YF-22 Raptor test-launches one of six "cropped" AIM-120C air-to-air missiles it can carry in its weapons bay.

The First Flights

England, France, Russia and later the United States of America were the countries in which the greatest efforts were made to achieve manned, powered flight during the 19th century. Early experiments with scale models led only to full-scale approximation of what was intended. In France, Félix du Temple de la Croix built a model monoplane that made short hops in 1857, first driven by clockwork and later by steam. In 1874 a full-size airplane of similar design but with a hot air engine, took off downhill and flew a short, unrecorded distance; but this did not count, as it could not become airborne from a run along level ground. In Russia twelve years later, an airplane designed by Alexander Feodorovich Mozhaiski and fitted with two English steam engines made a hop of 65-100ft (20-30m) from a ramp. It had made the same kind of assisted take-off, so also failed to comply with the parameters.

Clément Ader, a French electrical engineer, claimed that he had made a hop on October 9, 1890, after taking off from a level surface in a machine powered by steam, with a tractor airscrew (propeller). Although there was no eye witness confirmation of this, and Ader could not say how long the flight had been, the French Army gave him financial help for further development of the aircraft. This was the first instance of practical military interest in aeroplanes: a logical progression from the various armies' use of balloons, with an interim attraction to airships. Eventually the subsidy ceased, Ader exhausted his own funds and that was the end of another false start – even, perhaps, a myth.

In 1894 an American electrical engineer who lived in England, Hiram Maxim, inventor of the eponymous machine gun, came close to being the first man to fly a powered aeroplane. His creation was an enormous biplane with two 180hp lightweight steam engines, two propellers 17ft 10in (5.44m) in diameter and an all-up weight of 3.5 tons (3,556kg). To ensure that it could not make a free flight, it was run along rails with guard rails to restrain it. It did lift, but an axle failed and fouled the rails; Maxim's trials with it ceased.

The man who made the greatest progress towards the feat that everyone knows was at last accomplished by Orville and Wilbur Wright was a German engineer named Otto Lilienthal. Reasoning with what appeared to be indisputable logic that birds

Above: In the USA, Professor Samuel Langley launched his man-carrying "Aerodrome" from a catapult atop a houseboat on the Potomac River in December 1903, but it was underpowered and suffered a structural failure, plunging into the water.

should be taken as the perfect model for the technique of flight, Lilienthal had a fascination with ornithopters –

Below: Hiram Maxim's massive steam-powered test rig suffered severe damage when it broke free of its restraining rails during a trial in July 1894, and was thereafter relegated to giving strictly earthbound joyrides.

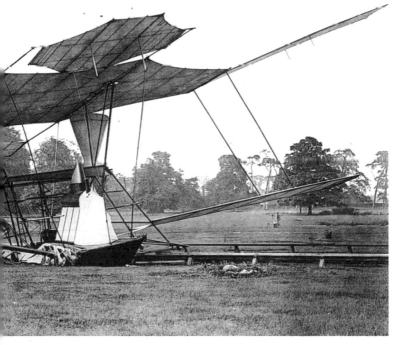

Left: Santos-Dumont's diminutive Demoiselle could only be flown by small, light pilots. This one, being flown by Swiss pilot Audemars at a British meeting in 1910, was nicknamed the "infuriated grasshopper."

wing-flapping aircraft. In 1889 he published a book, *Bird Flight As The Basis Of Aviation*, which is a classic of aeronautical literature and provided the Wright brothers with inspiration. Intending always to return to ornithopters, in the interim Lilienthal built a fixed-wing hang glider in 1891 and, in the next five years, five more variants of monoplane gliders and two biplanes were built.

He first launched himself aloft from a springboard, but soon gave this up in favour of running downhill. He was supported by his arms, his legs dangling so that he could swing his torso in order to balance and control the craft. Next, he fitted a means of working a rear elevator by body movement; altering the center of gravity in this way, he was able to rise and descend. He was fatally injured when he crashed in August 1896, but remains admired as the leading contributor to the science of airplane design in the pre-Wright era.

AMERICAN PIONEERS

Versatility was a gift given to many of those who designed aircraft of all types: kites, balloons, gliders, airplanes and helicopters. Professor Samuel Langley, an American, clearly had the gift. A railway surveyor, engineer and distinguished astronomer, he was employed on aeronautical experiments at the Smithsonian Institution in Washington, D.C. In 1891 he began concentrating on steam-driven model airplanes. After four failures, his fifth and sixth constructions, launched by catapult from a barge on the Potomac River, made many flights, of which the longest was 4,200ft (1,280m). The models were metal, with two sets of dihedral wings in tandem. A steam engine drove two propellers.

He had intended to abandon experimenting with flight, but, as could be expected, his country's president offered him a government sub-

Below: American Glenn Curtiss produced a line of successful and fast (for their time) pusher biplanes. Seen here is a Model D flown by celebrated display pilot Lincoln Beachey, during 1911.

sidy to build a full-size airplane that could be developed for military use. His opening move, in 1901, was to make a quarter-scale model with a petrol engine: the first aircraft of any type or size to have one. Two years later Langley and his assistant, C. M. Manly, presented a full-size airplane. It had a petrol engine designed by Manly that was extraordinarily efficient and light – from which radial engines were developed.

Manly was the pilot when the aircraft, in which so much hope and so many dollars were invested, was tried out. Two trials were attempted and both were failures. This contraption suffered a structural failure and flopped into the river, but Manly suffered no injury. Not only did Langley's experiments end there, but so also did the government subsidy.

Octave Chanute, an American of French extraction, was another railway engineer and builder of successful gliders. In 1894 several articles he had written were published as a volume titled *Progress In Flying Machines*. It was largely the influence of Chanute, and of course the work of the aviation experimenters, notably including Lilienthal, that encouraged the two bicycle makers, Wilbur and Orville Wright, in their own many experiments that led to these broth-

Above: The "Venetian blind" multiplanes built by Horatio Phillips in the late 1890s to early 1900s were distinctive but unsuccessful. This is his 1904 model.

ers achieving the historic feat of building a powered machine capable of sustaining flight.

Alberto Santos-Dumont was Brazilian and a flamboyant extrovert. He sometimes moored his airship outside his club in Paris and, once, at his house on the Champs Elysées. He was a sprightly little man not short of courage, determination and intelligence, essential qualities in all pioneers of flight.

On September 13, 1906, he made the first successful airplane flight in Europe. He called his machine the 14bis (14 modified) because he had first tested it by carrying it slung beneath his No14 airship. It was an unattractive contraption, a boxkite of the type usually called tail-first or canard. The aircraft flew only 23ft (7m) before returning to earth with a crunch. He then fitted an octagonal aileron to each outboard wing box. These were connected to a harness he wore, so that he could control them by leaning left or right.

Hitherto the early airplanes, with few exceptions, had been biplanes. Trajan Vuia, a Romanian who lived in Paris, designed and built two monoplanes that had a great influence on the development of this type. Both were bat-like in shape and had tractor propellers. The first was controlled by

Above: Alliott Verdon Roe's first full-size aeroplane was this tail-first biplane, which eventually achieved limited hop-flights at Brooklands, Surrey, England, in June 1908.

wing warping, with a forward fin and rear rudder. A heavy landing in it persuaded Vuia to add a rear elevator and a framework under the wing, with a four-wheel undercarriage, from which he operated the controls. In 1906 and 1907 he made several short hops after taking off from level ground. Trajan Vuia's second machine, flown in 1907 with a 24hp Antoinette engine, achieved only two short hops.

The next year Santos-Dumont made another biplane, but it did not fly; so in November he started testing a monoplane that did, the No 19. In 1909 he made an improved version, the Demoiselle (Dragonfly), with a 20hp two-cylinder engine and 18ft (5.5m) wingspan. Three bamboo poles formed the framework and the pilot sat on a canvas sheet stretched

between two of these, under the wing on which the engine was mounted. The moveable tail was on a ball-and-socket joint. It was difficult to fly but has an exalted place in airplane history. It was the first design that was in the public domain, free for anyone to copy and build: deliberately, its inventor did not patent it.

As well as the famous names of the Wright brothers, Santos-Dumont and Louis Blériot (of whom more later), in the first decade of the 20th century there was a plethora of other daring men in their flying machines deserving of mention. A

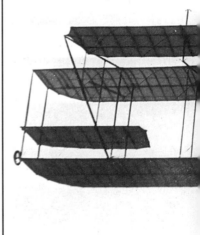

Right: "Colonel" S. F. Cody made the first officially recognised powered flight in Great Britain on October 16, 1908, in his British Army Aeroplane No 1. This is one of his later products, the biplane on which he won the Michelin Cup on December 31, 1910, for a 4hr 47min flight that covered just over 185 miles (296km) and established new British records for duration and distance over a closed circuit. It had a 60hp ENV "F" engine, spanned 46ft (14m) and weighed 2,950lb (1,338kg) loaded.

Above: Based on the Farman design, the Bristol Boxkite of 1910 was used by both civilian and military operators. Powered by a 50hp Gnome engine, it spanned 34ft 6in (10.5m), had an all-up weight of 1,050lb (476kg) and flew at 40mph (64kph).

prize for the weirdest-looking aircraft would perhaps go to Horatio Phillips. His research into aerofoils (wing sections) was fundamental to the theory of flight. His experiments with aerofoils that differed greatly in shape brought him to the correct deduction that the low pressure on top of a wing contributes more to lifting it than the high pressure below. In 1907 he constructed a multiplane aircraft that had four banks of wings, arranged in tandem, which were dubbed "Venetian blinds." It made a flight of 500ft (152m), but was too cumbersome to be a practical proposition. Such trials showed that one long, narrow wing would give as much lift as multiplane wings of similar ratio.

In 1906 a national British newspaper, the *Daily Mail*, encouraged aircraft constructors and pilots by offering money prizes for the best model aircraft. A. V. Roe, who became famous as Sir Alliott Verdon Roe, founder of

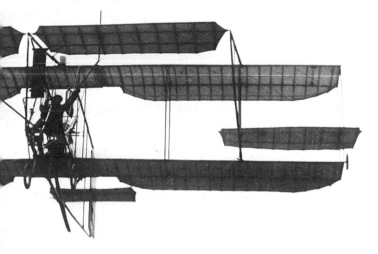

Above: French-domiciled Englishman Henry Farman bought an early Voisin, removed the "side-curtains" between the wings and later added ailerons to produce a controllable aeroplane in which he made the first official kilometer circular flight in Europe, on January 13, 1908.

Avro, one of the earliest airplane manufacturers, won $365 (£75).

In the USA, Glenn Curtiss designed and flew the "June Bug." On July 4, 1908, he won a magazine prize for the first officially recorded flight of 1km to be made in that country.

The first airplane flight in Britain was made at Farnborough on October 16, 1908, over a distance of 1,390ft (424m), and ended in a crash landing. The pilot was a colorful, extrovert American ex-patriate, Samuel Franklin Cody, who later

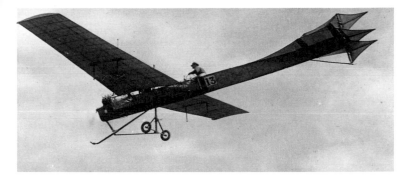

became a British citizen, but not for long: he was killed in a flying accident in 1913, aged 52. He designed and built the aircraft, which was named British Army Airplane No 1.

It was a Frenchman, Louis Blériot, who was the most influential designer of monoplanes. His No VII, built in 1907, had a 50hp Antoinette engine, a tractor airscrew and an enclosed fuselage. His concentration on mono-

Above: The Antoinette VII of 1909 had wing warping instead of ailerons, but lateral control was still exercised by means of handwheels on either side of the pilot. Its improved 60hp Antoinette engine gave it a speed of 52mph (84kph).

planes won him a place in aviation history that is second only to that of the Wright brothers in the annals of the early days.

Italy lagged behind the other European nations in developing an aircraft industry, but Gianni Caproni was emerging as their best designer. His first powered machine was the Ca 1, which appeared in 1910.

TECHNOLOGY FORGES AHEAD

On January 26, 1910, Glenn Curtiss made the first three seaplane take-offs, from California's San Diego Bay in a machine of his own design. The eight-cylinder engine drove a pusher propeller and the aircraft had a broad main float for hydroplaning. A later product was a flying boat whose wooden hull replaced the seaplane's floats and outriggers. On March 28, 1910, Henri Fabre made the first take-

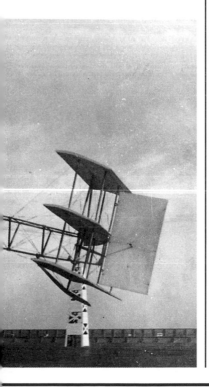

Left: By 1910 A. V. Roe was making successful flights in the latest of a series of triplanes. Here, he takes a passenger (back to the radiator) for a flight in the Roe III. This machine had a 35hp Green engine, spanned 31ft (9.45m) and had an all-up weight of only 750lb (340kg).

off from water in his float plane (Hydravion) and was credited with a hop of 1,640ft (500m) at about 37mph (60kph). The first seaplane to take off and land safely was the Lakes Flying Co.'s Waterbird biplane, on Lake Windermere in the northwest of England. The first amphibian was the Sopwith Bat Boat, which won the £500 Mortimer Singer Prize for being the first all-British aircraft to make twelve landings alternately on land and water, within five hours. The first flight over the Alps was accomplished on September 23, 1910, by the Portuguese, George Chavez, in a Blériot monoplane, though he crashed to his death at the end of the flight.

Year by year astonishing feats were being performed by pilots whose small number of flying hours made their accomplishments all the more remarkable. In 1913 Roland Garros made the first crossing of the Mediterranean. On January 1, 1914, the world's first scheduled passenger-carrying service by airplane was inaugurated. A Benoist flying boat, carrying one passenger, now plied between two Florida towns, Tampa and St Petersburg. On July 30, 1914, a Norwegian, Tryggve Gran, in a Blériot monoplane, became the first to cross the North Sea.

Above: An evocative study of a Paumier biplane making a sunset flight at France's celebrated flying ground at Issy-le-Moulineaux.

Above: The celebrated pilot Hubert Latham taxies out in his Antoinette IV monoplane, 1908. This aileron-equipped machine spanned 12.80m (42ft), weighed 460kg (1,014lb) and was powered by a 50hp Antoinette engine driving a two-bladed metal propeller.

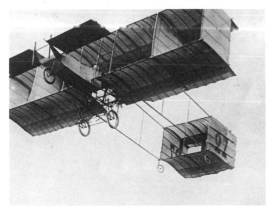

Left: British designer J. W. Dunne produced a succession of inherently stable, tailless swept-wing aircraft. This D.8 flown by the French military in 1913–14 was powered by an 80hp Gnome rotary engine, had a span of 46ft (14m), weighed 1,900lb (862kg) loaded and could attain 56mph (90kph).

Below left: The primitive Voisin boxkites of 1909–10 had no lateral control, and could only be turned in flat, wide, skidding curves to avoid sideslipping.

The Wright Flyer

> '*Success four flights thursday morning all against twenty one mile wind started from Level with engine power alone average speed through air thirty one miles longest 57 [sic] seconds inform Press home Christmas. Orevelle [sic] Wright.*'
>
> ORVILLE WRIGHT

Thus was an historic moment announced. In previous years, and even days, others had tried. Some had even accomplished short hops, but with these, flying speed was achieved only by taking off down a sloping ramp; with no form of control the man on board was a mere passenger, and flight was not sustained.

By contrast, the first flight by Wilbur Wright at Kitty Hawk was made from level ground, the

Right: A series of glider trials to perfect the control system and piloting techniques had preceded the first powered flight. This is the No 3 glider in modified form being launched with Orville aboard in 1902.

machine took off under its own power, sustained controlled flight for a short period, then landed at a point at the same height at which it had started. These factors, and in particular the fact that the Flyer was under control at all times, made this the first true powered manned flight by a heavier-than-air machine.

Wilbur and Orville Wright were fascinated by flight from their youth. They built their first glider in 1900, and when this was less successful than hoped, embarked on an extensive research program, building among other things a wind tunnel. Other problems were gradually solved; lateral control in flight using moveable rudder surfaces coupled with wing warping; a suitable lightweight petrol engine; and the precise design of the propellers. Gliding also allowed them to learn to fly before the event; something that most of their predecessors had not bothered to do.

Finally, the Wright Flyer was ready for the attempt. The brothers flipped a coin to decide who was to make the first trial, and Wilbur won. Few spectators were present; it was very cold and blowing hard as the motor was started. Orville later described the scene as follows:

Above: Probably the most famous aviation photograph ever taken, this is the momentous instant on December 17, 1903, when the first powered "Flyer" lifted from its launch rail and made a 12 second flight covering a distance of 120ft (37m) over the ground. The fourth and last flight that day lasted 59 seconds and covered 852ft (260m).

"With a short dash down the runway [actually a wooden monorail track], the machine lifted into the air and was flying. It was only a flight of twelve seconds, and it was an uncertain, wavy, creeping sort of flight at best; but it was a real flight at last and not a glide."

The airplane had covered a mere 120ft (36.5m), less than two-thirds of the length of the cabin of a jumbo jet, but it was a start. Then it was Orville's turn. He later recalled:

"...I found the machine pointing upwards and downwards in jerky undulations. This erratic course was due in part to my utter lack of experience in controlling a flying machine and in part to a new system of controls we had adopted, whereby a slight touch accomplished what a hard jerk or tug made necessary in the past. Naturally I overdid everything."

On the fourth and final flight of the day, Orville remained airborne for

59 seconds (the "57 seconds" cited in the telegraph message was a transcription error) and covered 852ft (260m). From these modest beginnings, the first manned powered flights by a heavier-than-air machine, came aviation as we know it today.

Right: The brothers Orville (left) and Wilbur Wright carry out repairs to one of their earlier aircraft. In 1909 they delivered the first military aircraft to the US Army – and by so doing ensured that warfare would never be the same again.

Left: Harry Atwood takes off from the
White House lawn in a two-seat version of
the Wright Type B in June 1911. It was a
magnificent sight for President Taft who
was in office at the time.

Straight Up

> '*The way to fly is to go straight up... Such a machine (the helicopter) will never compete with the aeroplane, though it will have specialized uses, and in these it will surpass the aeroplane. The fact that you can land at your front door is the reason you can't carry heavy loads efficiently.*'
>
> EMILE BERLINER

A strange contraption sat in the middle of a field near Lisieux, France. Mounted on four flimsy wheels, it consisted of a framework of steel tubes and bracing wires. In the center was an Antoinette aero engine of 24hp, from both ends of which a thicker steel tube projected upwards at about 30 degrees. At each end of this was a large spoked pulley wheel, driven by a belt from a central point above the engine. Projecting from each pulley wheel were two arms with paddle-shaped blades at their extremities. These were the rotors, designed to turn in opposite directions to each other. Below these, on cantilevered frames suspended fore and aft beneath the rotor axes, were control surfaces; moveable planes, the angle of each controlled from levers set on either side of the engine. Uncomfortably close behind the motor was a seat for the pilot, Paul Cornu.

Cornu was a French bicycle maker who, like so many other men of his time, had become fascinated by powered flight. Unlike the Wright brothers, he sought to build a machine that could rise vertically, a helicopter. In 1906 he built his first working model. Powered by a 2hp petrol engine, it weighed only 28lb (12.7kg). It was successful, and he went on to build the full-scale machine, which he completed in August 1907. On September 27, ballasted with a 110lb (50kg) bag of soot, Cornu's helicopter lifted briefly off the ground in an unmanned flight. Further trials followed, until at last Cornu was ready.

The first attempt at manned flight, made on November 9, ended in failure when a drive belt broke. Four days later, on November 13, Cornu squeezed into the pilot's seat, slipped his feet into the stirrups provided, and started the Antoinette engine. Slowly he opened the throt-

tle; the engine revolutions built up, and the rotors turned at ever increasing speed. With the rotors spinning at 90 revolutions per minute, the contraption shuddered, then lifted its wheels to about 12in (30cm) above the ground, sustaining this position for about 20 seconds.

That afternoon a further flight was made. At takeoff, Cornu's brother was standing on the frame and, failing to dismount in time, he was lifted rapidly to a height of about 5ft (1.5m). Several more flights followed, the longest lasting about 60 seconds, and a forward speed of roughly 7mph. (11kph)) was achieved. On some of these a passenger was carried. After this promising beginning,

however, Cornu's resources were exhausted, and the project lapsed.

Other French pioneers of the era were the Breguet brothers, Louis and Jacques, and Professor Richet who flew the four-rotor Breguet Richet # 1 on September 29, 1907, at Douai. It was stabilized by four men on the ground, making the man on board little more than a passenger. The # 2 was flown with little more success in 1908.

Below: Frenchman Paul Cornu's strange, tandem-rotor machine is credited with having been the first "helicopter" that made a free flight carrying a man.

Across the Channel

> '*I headed for this white mountain, but was caught in the wind and the mist... I followed the cliff from north to south, but the wind, against which I was fighting, got even stronger. A break in the coast appeared to my right, just before Dover Castle. I was madly happy. I headed for it. I rushed for it. I was above ground!*'
>
> LOUIS BLÉRIOT

In 1909 Lord Northcliffe, proprietor of the *Daily Mail* newspaper, offered a prize of £1,000 to the first pilot to fly an airplane across the English Channel. During the summer of that year three entrants estab-lished bases on or near the coast of France; Louis Blériot with his Blériot Type XI monoplane at Les Baracques (literally "shanties") just south of Calais; Hubert Latham, with an Antoinette monoplane just down the

Above: The cross-Channel machine on display after its epoch-making flight. Its Chauvière propeller was one of the most advanced designs for its time.

road at Sangatte; and Charles, Comte de Lambert, with a Wright biplane at Wissant, between Caps Blanc Nez and Gris-Nez.

Latham was the first to try. Taking off in perfect weather at 06.42 on July 19, he coaxed his little Antoinette to the then exceptional altitude of 1,000ft (305m) and set course for Dover, only to suffer an engine failure and ditch just short of half way. He was picked up by his escort, the boat *Harpon,* and returned to Calais, where he immediately ordered another machine.

Within days, all three contenders were ready, waiting only for favorable weather conditions. These duly arrived on the morning of July 25. After a short trial flight, Blériot set off at 04.35, preceded by his

Left: Louis Blériot poses in the No XI monoplane in which he made his celebrated cross-Channel flight in 1909, under the power of a small 25hp three-cylinder Anzani engine.

escort, the French destroyer *Escopette*. The day was misty, and the English coast invisible. With no compass, Blériot, flying at between 150 and 300ft (45 and 90m), at first steered by following the destroyer, but soon passed her and bored on into the mist. He later recalled the moment:

"For about ten minutes I was on my own, isolated, lost in the middle of the foaming sea, seeing no point on the horizon, perceiving no boat. Also my eyes were fixed on the oil distributor and on the level of fuel consumption. These ten minutes seemed long and, truly, I was happy to glimpse... a grey line which broke away from the sea... It was the English coast."

A freshening wind had blown Blériot to the north, and he was off St. Margaret's Bay. Dover was nowhere in sight, but he could see three boats which appeared to be making for a port. Following their course, he at last saw an opening in the cliffs, where by arrangement waited M. Fontaine, a French journalist, waving a Tricolore.

The wind had strengthened, and Blériot was forced to put down where he could, on a downward slope in Northfall Meadow. The landing was heavy, breaking the propeller and both main wheels, but Blériot suffered only minor injuries. The time was 05.12. He had flown 24 miles (36.5km) in 37 minutes.

Just 12 minutes earlier Latham had woken, and, finding conditions favorable he determined also to try, but before he could take off, the wind got up and the attempt was abandoned. He tried again two days later, but once again engine failure forced him to ditch barely half a mile from Dover. The Comte de Lambert, with his Wright biplane, did not attempt the crossing.

Above: Blériot prepares to depart from Les Baraques on July 25, 1909. He was walking on crutches at the time, owing to a mishap at a flying meeting shortly before.

Below: The widespread adoption of the Blériot No XI following the Channel crossing is typified by this study of one such aircraft in use in Russia.

Aircraft Go To Sea

> *'Ely has proved that an airplane can leave a ship and return to it, even with crude preparations. Others have demonstrated that an airplane can remain in flight for a long time, from five to eight hours or more, that observations can be made from great altitudes, that photographs can be taken, that reconnaissance can be made, that messages can be sent and received by wireless telegraph, that passengers can be carried, that the airplane may be stowed on board... and readily assembled for use in less than one hour...'*
>
> CAPTAIN W. I. CHAMBERS, USN

US Navy officials were present at Fort Myer in September 1908 when the Wright Model A was first demonstrated to the US Army. They were enthusiastic about the potential of aircraft for naval purposes, but first the problems of shipboard operations had to be overcome. The task fell to Eugene Ely, a Curtiss demonstration pilot. A wooden flying platform 83ft (25m) long by 28ft (8.5m) wide was rigged over the bow of the light cruiser USS *Birmingham*, and Ely was to have taken off when the ship was steaming at 20kt. But before the ship could gather way, Ely opened the throttle of his Curtiss pusher biplane and rolled forward,

off the end of the deck. With insufficient flying speed, the Curtiss dropped toward the water, slowly accelerating as it went. For a second, disaster seemed imminent as it brushed the waves, but the little biplane staggered back into the air, its engine vibrating badly because the propeller had been damaged by the impact. Seeking safety, Ely headed for the fogshrouded shore, landing five minutes later on Willoughby Spit, near what is now Naval Air Station Norfolk, Virginia.

Above: Eugene B. Ely takes off from the deck of USS *Birmingham*, November 4, 1910.

Below: Seaplane carrier HMS *Ark Royal* in 1914–15, with a Sopwith Type 807 seaplane on deck.

A few weeks later Ely resumed shipboard trials. This time a flying platform 119ft 4in (36.4m) long had been built over the stern of the armored cruiser USS *Pennsylvania*, a much larger ship than *Birmingham*. Primitive arrester gear was provided by a series of ropes weighted with sandbags, which were laid across the flight deck and raised slightly above it by two wooden rails, also intended as guide strips for the air-craft's wheels. Safety rails lined the edges, with canvas nets outboard of these to guard against a mishap.

Taking off from Selfridge Field, California, on January 18, 1911, Ely flew his flimsy Curtiss, now fitted with a spring-loaded hook, out over San Francisco Bay to rendezvous with the cruiser. It had originally been planned that the landing would be made with the ship under way,

Below: Frenchman Henri Fabre's Hydravion seaplane was powered by rear-mounted Gnome engine driving a pusher propeller. Never having flown before, he lifted his seaplane off the water, the first to do so, on March 28, 1910.

Above: The Short S.27 being hoisted aboard HMS *Hibernia*. It was in this aircraft that Cdr R. Samson made the first British flight from a ship under way, on May 2, 1912. Takeoff was along a down-sloping ramp. The S.27 was fitted with pontoon floats to enable it to land alongside the ship.

but her captain considered that there was insufficient searoom for maneuver, and had anchored.

It was now a matter of precision flying. Too short an approach would result in hitting the stern of the cruiser; too long and Ely might easily overrun and collide with the superstructure. His approach was well judged; he touched down about a third of the way along the weighted ropes, and came to a halt in just 30ft (9m), at precisely 10.01.

After an early lunch on board, Ely took off from the platform, this time without incident, and flew back to Selfridge Field. He had proved that aircraft could be operated from ships, but he was not to enjoy his triumph for long. He was killed in a flying accident later that year.

Henri Fabre's Hydravion had made the first takeoff from, and landing on, water on March 28, 1910, but deck landings were deemed preferable for naval operations.

The Pace Quickens

The Air Battalion of Britain's Royal Engineers had been created on April 1, 1911, to equip with both airships and airplanes. The following year, the Royal Flying Corps (RFC) came into being. France and Germany also formed air forces and airplanes figured in war for the first time. The Italian Army had acquired its first airplanes in 1910, and in 1911, when the Italo-Turkish War erupted in Libya,

Italy sent seven airplanes by sea to Tripoli: two Blériots, two Etrichs and three Nieuports. She also possessed a few Farmans. Belligerence and colonial ambition had been quick to put the most advanced method of locomotion to destructive use.

In 1912, Bulgaria, Serbia, Greece and Montenegro had formed an alliance to free Macedonia from Turkish rule. The Bulgars, having few air-

Below: Eddie Rickenbacker was the USA's First World War ace of aces, with 21 aircraft and four observation balloons to his credit. Here he poses in France with his SPAD XIII fighter bearing the hat-in-the-ring emblem of the 94th Sqn, 1st Pursuit Group, the unit he commanded.

planes or pilots, hired mercenaries who brought their own aircraft. An American pilot, Riley Scott, had already invented a bomb sight and bomb rack, a great convenience: hitherto, the pro-Bulgaria pilots had tied a bomb loosely to one foot and simply kicked it off over the target.

When the First World War began, the RFC's only airship squadron, No 1, was in the process of re-equipping entirely with airplanes. Henceforth there would be no more airships on the Battle Order. Four airplane squadrons already existed, numbered from 2 to 5, and there were 110 air-

planes on the strength. Nos 6 and 7 Squadrons were being formed. The squadron establishment was 12 aircraft and 12 pilots. They flew a variety of types with maximum speeds of 65 to 75mph (120kph). There were Blériot No XIs like the one that first flew the Channel, and four makes of biplane: the Farman Shorthorn, which had a 75hp Renault engine and a speed of 66mph (106kph); the Martinsyde, with an 80hp Gnome or a Le Rhône engine; the Bristol Scout, with a Le Rhône; and the BE2c, most favored because its 90hp engine was made, like the airframe, in the Royal Aircraft

Above: An early attempt to fire through the propeller arc. This French Morane Type N monoplane, flown by pre-war pilot Jules Vedrines, has an unsynchronized Hotchkiss machine gun with 25-cartridge strip feed. Steel deflector wedges have been attached to the wooden propeller blades to deflect mistimed bullets.

Above: Another way to avoid propeller damage was to mount the gun to fire clear of it. This Nieuport 27 of 1 Sqn, RFC, in France in the winter of 1917, has a Lewis gun on a Foster mount, aimed through an Aldis sight.

factory at Farn-
borough, Hamp-
shire, in south-
ern England.

The RFC's
greatest handi-
cap was that the
other British
engine manufac-
turers, of whom
the leaders
were Wolseley,
Beardmore and
Rolls-Royce,
were producing
very small quan-
tities. All aircraft
constructors had
to depend most-
ly on small
rotary air-cooled
French engines,
Le Rhône, Cler-
get and Renault.
Later that year
the Avro 504, a
biplane that was

Above: A German pilot poses with his Fokker D VII, armed with a pair of synchronized Spandau machine guns. The controlability and responsiveness of the D VII, which entered service in the spring of 1918, made it an excellent fighter.

the first modern-looking military type, with an enclosed fuselage and clean lines, came into service. With a 110hp Le Rhône nine-cylinder engine that gave it a speed of 95mph (153kph), it could climb to 18,000ft (5,486m). Improvements were made over the next four years, including the addition of a Lewis gun mounted on the upper mainplane.

The Royal Naval Air Service (RNAS) faced the same equipment problems.

France entered the war with a total of 160 airplanes in 25 Escadrilles, each established for six airplanes. Some were flying Farman Longhorns. Other types were: Farman F20 with a Gnome or Le Rhône 80hp engine that gave a maximum speed of 65mph (105kph); Voisin LA with a 130hp Salmson engine and speeds up to 65mph; Caudron G III with a Gnome engine and 65mph speed; Morane-Saulnier L, Le Rhône-engined, capable of 72mph (116kph). Only the Voisin was armed with a machine gun.

Germany had 246 airplanes, of which 198 were sent to the Front in 33 Field Service Units, each with six airplanes. Ten Home Defence Units of four airplanes each remained in the Fatherland. The Germans enjoyed high-volume production of two excellent makes of engine, Mercedes and Benz, both of which were heavy, in-line and water-cooled. The German Military Aviation Service was flying two-seater biplanes capable of 65 to 76mph (105 to 122kph), the Albatros and AEG, and two single-seater monoplanes: the Taube, which was made by the Albatros works, and Fokker.

Russia had 300 airplanes in her air force, Belgium 25 and Austro-Hungary 35.

DEADLY RACE

The function of airplanes was at first limited to reconnaissance and artillery spotting – reporting to the gunners the fall of shells in relation to the target. Air fighting had not been serious-ly contemplated by any of the air forces. The first type that could defend itself and attack enemy air-craft was the Voisin: a machine gun was mounted in its cockpit. Because

Above: A German DFW C.V two-seat reconnaissance aircraft goes about its business over the Western Front. Powered by a 200hp Benz Bz VI water-cooled engine, the C.V served in large numbers from the end of 1916.

the pilot and observer sat side-by-side instead of in the usual tandem seating and the propeller was a pusher type, there was no obstruction to the field of fire. The British, French and Germans often carried bombs of roughly 20lb (9kg), which they dropped by hand.

The deadly race to dominate the world in air power began in Europe at a rate and on a scale of progress that demanded total application to military

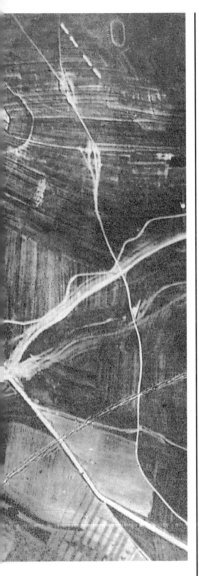

over Mesopotamia (now Iraq). The Austro-Hungarians, allied to Germany, equipped themselves with German aircraft. In the words of Generale Felice Porro, the Italian air arm was "in an embryonic state": it had only 58 airplanes. By 1915 Britain had 161, France 1,150 and Germany 764.

The Italian Macchi factory was manufacturing the French Nieuport under licence, but the Italians designed and built their own bomber, the Caproni, with three 190hp Isotta-Fraschini engines, giving it a maximum speed of 85mph (137kph). By early 1918 the Caproni C4 triplane, which had three 270hp water-cooled V-type Isotta-Fraschini engines, was operational. Its wingspan was 98ft 1in (29.9m), length 49ft 6in (15m); it had a maximum speed of 87mph (140kph) and seven hours' endurance. By the summer, a development from it, the Ca5, had entered the air battles. This had three 30hp Fiat A-12bis water-cooled engines, its wingspan was 76ft 9in (23.4m), length 41ft 5in (12.65m) and its maximum speed was 94.4mph (152kph). The endurance was four hours.

In the same year a fighter of Italian design and build, the Ansaldo SVA5, joined the Battle Order. With a water-cooled engine, it attained 136.7mph (220kph).

Not all designs incorporated the latest improvements. The ultimate purpose of a warplane designer is to achieve maximum lethality: armament and bomb load, high speed and ceiling are the priorities, coupled with the shortest possible production time. Esthetically pleasing form is secondary. The French Morane-Saulnier Type L parasol monoplane, the British B.E.2 and Avro 504, and German Fokker E III of 1914–16 had enclosed fuselages and tractor propellers. However, the British Vickers FB5 Gunbus, the Royal Aircraft Factory FE8 and de Havilland DH2 all had booms between the nacelle and tail unit, and a pusher propeller.

A young Dutchman, Anthony Fokker, was establishing himself as a brilliant aviation engineer. He was also an aircraft designer, but above all,

aviation requirements. Only in the USA could development in the civil – essentially commercial – sector be pursued.

The Italian Military Air Service had been formed on January 7, 1915, and Italy declared war on Austro-Hungary on May 24 that year. Turkey had by now declared itself on the German side, so Britain's RFC was in action

he was an outstanding businessman. Although he was educated in Holland, he studied aeronautics in Germany and in 1912, when aged 22, set up a company there. His first airplane (though there is an unresolved argument that attributes the design to another Dutchman, Jacob Goedekker) was the Spin – which means spider in Dutch (in German it is Spinne). This monoplane had first flown in 1911. Its wingspan was 36ft 1in (11m), and length 25ft 2in (7.70m). Powered by a 25hp Argus engine, it reached a maximum speed of 56mph (90kph). A German named Rheinhold Platz was Fokker's chief designer; he was responsible in 1917 for the Fokker Triplane, based on the British Sopwith Triplane.

The latter, which first flew in 1916, was the most interesting and innovative airplane of the mid-war period. Its three wings imparted superb maneuverability and a ceiling of 20,000ft (6,096m), with a top speed of 120mph (192kph). Unfortunately for many German fighter pilots, the Fokker imitation initially had a fatal defect: structural weakness caused a number of in-flight failures of the top wing.

Above: A Henry Farman F27 used by 30 Sqn RFC in Mesopotamia for supply dropping and reconnaissance. Wingspan 53ft (16.15m), length 30ft (9.1m), height 12ft (3.65m), engine Salmson 140hp or 160hp 9-cylinder radial water-cooled, maximum speed 92mph (148kph), endurance 2hr 40min, crew 2.

Left: Although slow, the Vickers FB5 was an extremely sturdy machine. Nicknamed "Gunbus" by its crew, it served well until the Germans introduced proper Fokker scouts armed with forward-firing synchronised machine guns.

DIVERSITY IN DESIGN

The most handsome and streamlined airplanes that began to appear in 1916 were the Morane-Saulnier Type N and, even more pleasing to the eye, Germany's Albatros DV with its sleek torpedo shape. The Albatros DIII was powered by a Mercedes 160hp engine and had a top speed of 110mph (177kph). By the end of the war the French SPAD XIII (acronym for La Société pour l'Aviation et ses Derives) had attained 133mph (214kph), the Fokker DVII 130mph (209kph), the Sopwith Dolphin and French Nieuport 28 128mph (206kph).

Those who were interested in the use of airplanes for commercial purposes looked to the biggest. Multi-engine bombers had attained formidable dimensions and good speeds. By 1918 there was a rich diversity of makes. In Russia, Igor Sikorsky's Il'ya Murometz variant, IM-G3, was powered by two 220hp Renault inner engines and two 150hp RBZ-6 outers. It carried a bombload of 2,000lb (907kg) and there were three machine gun positions. In Italy, when the Caproni Ca42 entered service in 1918, its bombload was 3,000lb (1,360kg).

Germany operated two behemoths. The Friedrichshafen G.III had 260hp Mercedes engines, pusher propellers, a maximum speed of 87mph (140kph) and five hours' endurance. Its bombload was 2,200lb (998kg). The twin-engine Gotha G.V. had the same power units, bombload and pusher airscrews, a top speed of 87mph (140kph) and six hours' endurance.

Right: Soldiers examine an Albatros DV that has made a forced landing in the British lines. This aircraft was subsequently test flown in Britain to enable its performance and handling to be assessed and compared with its Allied counterparts.

In 1917 the massive bulk of the Handley Page O/100 heaved itself into the air and set about pulverising the enemy with the 2,000lb (907kg) bombload it carried. With twin Rolls-Royce Eagle engines, it could make 95mph (153kph) and had six hours' endurance. The following year the O/400 entered squadron service with the same engines and bombload, of the same dimensions, but was credited with 2mph (3kph) greater speed, 22lb (10kg) greater gross weight and four hours' endurance.

Seaplanes and the design of flying boats also benefited from the hothouse of war. The Felixstowe F.2A flying boat of 1917, a much refined development of the Curtiss America series and powered by Rolls-Royce Eagle 375hp motors, carried a crew of four to six, according to its armament. It had a Lewis gun in the nose and on either side at the waist, plus either a 13in (33cm) torpedo or two

230lb (104kg) flat-nosed anti-submarine bombs.

The type still most ahead of its time was the Junkers J1, which not only had a metal airframe covered with thin sheet iron, but also, being a cantilever monoplane, was much stronger than biplanes with wooden airframes and fabric-covered wooden wings. It was not until the mid 1920s, however, that other manufacturers began to design for all-metal construction.

The airplanes that attracted the greatest interest were the Fokker E I-E III Eindeckers, which cost the RFC and French Air Force heavy losses in 1916, and the de Havilland DH2, which was the first to turn the tables. The Albatros DI, which appeared in late 1915, was steadily improved and the Fokker D VII was capable of 130mph (209kph) by the end of the following year. The Bristol Fighter had a maximum speed of 120mph (193kph). The Sopwith Camel could attain 115mph (185kph) and had the most remarkable agility. The SE5 was another great fighter and was 5mph (8kph) faster than its contemporaries. The DH4 and DH9 were two-seater light bombers. Rolls-Royce engines were the best in the world, closely followed by the Mercedes; Wolseley and Armstrong Siddeley engines were also giving good service.

However, the British still relied mostly on French engines. France's outstanding airplanes were the Nieuport 17, whose top speed was 103mph (166kph), Spad VII with 120mph (193kph) and the Spad XIII with a speed of 133mph (214kph). Italy was engaged mostly on bombing, but manufactured French fighters under licence: Nieuport in 1915, Caudron in 1916, SPAD in 1917–18. By the time the armistice was declared, every aspect of aeronautics had made unprecedented progress.

The Age of the Fighter

> '*... my pilot pointed to his left front and above,*
> *and looking in the direction he pointed, I saw a*
> *long dark brown form fairly streaking across the sky.*
> *We could see that it was a German machine, and when*
> *it got above and behind our middle machine, it dived*
> *on it for all the world like a huge hawk on a hapless sparrow.*'
>
> JAMES McCUDDEN

The period known as the "Fokker scourge" started with the introduction into service of the Fokker Eindecker. A single-seat monoplane with at first one, and then two fixed machine guns firing through the propeller arc, the Eindecker can be said to have been the first true fighter airplane, and for several months it cut a deadly swathe through its British and French opponents.

The idea of fixed forward-firing guns, aimed by pointing the airplane, dated from before the war. These could easily be fitted to an aircraft with a pusher layout, but the aerodynamically more efficient tractor configuration meant that the gun had to be fired through the propeller arc. The problem then became how to fire the gun while not hitting the propeller blades. The answer was synchronization gear which fired the gun when the blades were not in line with the muzzle. This was invented before the war, but technical problems delayed its entry into service.

A crude solution adopted by Frenchman Roland Garros was to fit steel wedges to the propeller of his Morane Saulnier L to deflect any bullets which might otherwise have hit it. Success came quickly, with four victories in 19 days, but he was then

Right: A fine take-off study of a Royal Aircraft Factory BE2e two-seat reconnaissance aircraft of 1916. Wingspan 40ft 9in (12.4m), length 27ft 3in (8.3m), height 12ft (3.6m), weight 1,430lb (650kg), engine RAF 1a, 90hp 8-cylinder vee air-cooled, maximum speed 90 mph (145 kph), endurance 4 hr, crew 2.

Above: The Farman F40 entered service with the French in 1915 as an army and artillery co-operation aircraft. Wingspan 58ft (17.69m), length 30ft (9.1m), height 13ft (3.96m), weight 1,650lb (748kg), engine Renault 8C, 130hp 8-cylinder vee air-cooled, maximum speed 84mph (135 kph), range 263 miles (423km), crew 2.

brought down and his aircraft captured. It was examined by Dutch aircraft designer Anthony Fokker, and a synchronization gear developed by Fokker engineers, based on several earlier schemes, was fitted to one of his own designs, the M5K, later to become the E 1 Eindecker.

So far as is known, the first operational flight on an Eindecker was made by Oswald Boelcke on June 24, 1915, and the first combat success was by Leutnant Kurt Wintgens on July 1, although his opponent, a French Morane, came down in the French lines and this victory was unconfirmed. The first confirmed victory came on August 1. It was a Sunday morning, with low cloud, when

Below: Leutnant Walter von Bülow with his Fokker E III Eindecker escort fighting scout in 1916. Wingspan 31ft 3in (9.52m), length 23ft 8in (7.2m), height 7ft 11in (2.4m), weight 1,342lb (610kg), engine Oberursel UI9 100hp 9-cylinder rotary air-cooled, maximum speed 81mph (130kph), endurance 1hr 30min, crew 1.

Above: This Nieuport XI fighter of 1916 is fitted with launching tubes for eight Le Prieur rockets for use against enemy observation balloons. Wingspan 25ft (7.6m), length 18ft (5.5m), height 8ft (2.4m), weight 705lb (320kg), engine Le Rhône 9C 80hp 9-cylinder rotary air-cooled, maximum speed 100mph (161kph), range 156 miles (250km), crew 1.

B.E.2cs of the Royal Flying Corps raided the German airfield at Douai. Boelcke took off still in his nightshirt, only to have his gun jam. Max Immelmann, who had flown the Eindecker for the first time only three days earlier, was more fortunate. Catching up with a B.E. near Vitry, he fired about sixty rounds before his gun jammed. The sole occupant of

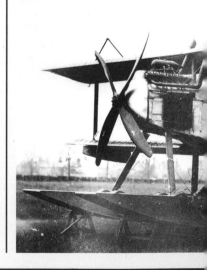

Above: The Airco DH2 scout, produced to counter Fokker's Eindecker, entered service on the Western Front early in 1916. Wingspan 28ft 3in (8.6m), length 25ft 3in (7.7m), height 9ft 6in (2.9m), weight 943lb (428kg), engine Gnome Monosoupape 100hp or Le Rhône 110hp 9-cylinder rotary air-cooled, maximum speed 90mph (145kph), endurance 3hr, crew 1.

Right: The Fairey Campania of 1917 was a carrier-borne patrol seaplane for the RNAS. Wingspan 61ft 7in (18.77m), length 43ft 4in (13.21m), height 15ft 1in (4.59m), weight 3,725lb (1,690kg), engine Rolls-Royce Mk IV 250hp 12-cylinder vee water-cooled, maximum speed 80mph (129kph), endurance 6hr 30min, crew 2.

the British aircraft, Lieutenant Reid, who had left his observer behind in order to carry a bomb load, sustained a bullet in his elbow and was forced to land his airplane on the German side of the lines.

In February 1916 the first British fighters, D.H.2s and F.E.2bs, started to arrive at the front, and from that time the Eindecker's days were numbered. Immelmann was killed in action on June 18, 1916, with his score at fifteen. Boelcke went on to become the greatest fighter leader of the war before falling on October 28, his final score standing at forty.

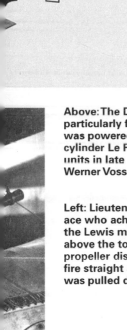

Above: The Dr I single-seat fighter triplane, although not particularly fast, was very agile and had a high rate of climb. It was powered by the 110hp Oberursel Ur II copy of the nine-cylinder Le Rhône rotary engine. It began to equip German units in late 1917, and among the many aces who flew it were Werner Voss and Manfred von Richthofen.

Left: Lieutenant-Colonel W. A. "Billy" Bishop, VC (a Canadian ace who achieved 72 "kills" during the First World War) tests the Lewis machine gun in a Nieuport Scout. Mounting the gun above the top plane from where it could fire above the propeller disk was an early method of allowing an airplane to fire straight ahead. To change the ammunition drum, the gun was pulled down the curved slide.

The Giant Bombers

The first heavy bomber in history was the Il'ya Muromets Type V, built in 1914, a variant of Igor Sikorsky's design for the first four-engine passenger aircraft, which had made its entrance in 1913: *Le Grand* (it was fashionable in Russia to speak French), was much the biggest airplane then in existence. The Type Vs, of which between seventy and eighty were built, equipped the world's first heavy bomber unit, the EVK Squadron. Ultimately there were seven versions, all with ski or multiple-wheel landing gear. They operated by night and day, making sorties of up to six hours. The later ones had the first self-sealing fuel tanks. Only one was shot down, after having downed three fighters.

Germany's Gotha G IV and V, which began bombing London in June 1917 by day and night, had the advantages of speed and height. Britain's RFC and RNAS had no fighters with a fast enough rate of climb

or maximum speed to intercept them, until SE5a squadrons entered the scene. The biggest German bomber was the Staaken R VI, which appeared in June 1917. Each of four 260hp Mercedes D IVa engines in tandem pairs drove one tractor propeller and one pusher propeller.

Italy, which entered the war on the Allies' side in May 1915, manufactured two types of heavy bomber for its Military Air Corps, the Caproni Ca5 biplane and Ca42 triplane. The latter was delivered in 1918 and sold also to Britain's Royal Naval Air Service in the same year.

In April 1918 the RAF formed the Independent Force, a bomber unit based in Northern France and devoted to the destruction of targets in Germany, France and Belgium. The unit comprised five night squadrons and four day squadrons. Operating the Handley Page O/100 and O/400, as well as the de Havilland DH4, it flew a total of 650 raids.

Above: The DFW RI, one of a number of extraordinary Riesenflugzeug (giant aircraft, or R-planes) built and flown in Germany, had four 220hp Mercedes D IV engines and spanned 97ft (29m).

Below: The Handley Page O/400 night bomber, which entered service with the RAF Independent Force in 1918, was used to deliver the 1,650lb (748kg) bombs which were the "blockbusters" of their day.

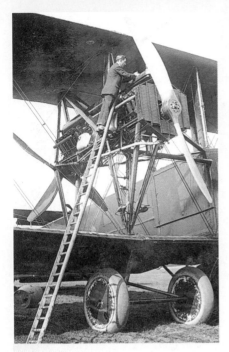

Left: Ministering to one of the four 375hp Rolls-Royce Eagle VIII engines of a Handley Page V/1500, intended to bomb Berlin but rendered unnecessary by the Armistice.

Right: The giant Sikorsky Il'ya Muromets bomber had four 150hp engines, could fly at 80mph (128kph) at sea level, had a ceiling of 11,500ft (3,505m) and an endurance of over five hours, was armed with three machine guns and could deliver up to 1,870lb (850kg) of bombs.

Below: No fewer than six 160hp Mercedes D IIIs powered the Staaken VGO III, which spanned 138ft 5in (42m) and had a duration of 6hr. It carried its seven-man crew on some seven bombing missions against railway installations, troop encampments and depots in the vicinity of Riga, Latvia.

Peace Returns

The ceasefire on November 11, 1918, did not mean a total cessation of activity by Britain's Royal Air Force (formed by the amalgamation of the RFC and RNAS on April 1,1918). Even before the war had ended, the RFC started long-distance flights for the ultimate benefit of civilians. The first was made by a Handley Page O/400, which took off from England on July 28, 1918, and landed in Egypt on August 7. On November 29, 1918, an O/400 left from Cairo for Baghdad, with a night stop at Damascus. On January 13, 1919, an HP V/1500, Britain's biggest bomber, which was about to enter squadron service when peace was declared, set off from Britain for India. It arrived thirty-two days later after frequent engine trouble.

On December 14, 1918, the RAF, at the request of the Foreign Office, began two daily courier flights by DH9s (two-seater bombers) between London and Paris. Up to seven passengers were also carried in an HP O/400.

On July 27, 1919, No 1 (Communications) Squadron was formed for long-distance trips – A Flight was equipped with DH4s, two-seater bombers, while B Flight flew two Avro 504s and two B.E.2es. On December 13 that year an entire Communications wing came into being with two squadrons, each operating one HP O/400 carrying eight passengers, and four DH4s that carried two.

Britain, France, Italy and, to a lesser extent, the USA had been distracted from applying progress to commercial aviation. Now they could resume. Instead of merely taking people up for short pleasure flips, companies were acquiring bombers converted to carry passengers and baggage, or purpose-built passenger aircraft. In the immediate aftermath of

Above: An array of civil aircraft on display at the Olympia Aero Show in London in 1920. Most new designs failed to gain a foothold in the market, owing to the ready availability of huge numbers of cheap war-surplus aircraft.

war, however, RAF types were much used. One of the passenger carriers, Aircraft Transport and Travel, used

DH9Bs in 1919 and 1920. It equipped its passengers with thick coats, helmets, goggles and gloves, and, in the fall and winter, hot-water bottles.

In Germany all military flying came to a dead stop: the peace treaty compelled her to disband her air force.

In the USA the design and production of military aircraft languished during the war years. When the USA entered the war on the Allies' side in April 1917, her air force had to be equipped with the SPAD XIII and DH4. Civil flying had been able to advance without interruption and on May 15, 1918, the first regular airmail service was introduced. Curtiss JN4s flown by Army pilots plied between Washington, Philadelphia and New York until the Post Office took over on August 12, 1918, with purpose-built Standard JR1B mailplanes. By December 31 the US Aerial Mail Service was operating with 91 percent regularity.

Left: This Fairey IIIC seaplane, carried by HMS *Nairana*, served with the expeditionary Syren Force sent by the British to North Russia in 1919 to support the Imperial Powers in their unsuccessful struggle against the Bolsheviks.

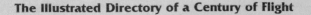

Above: France's first real passenger carrier was the Farman Goliath, which began life as a bomber design but was quickly given a passenger cabin. Wingspan 86ft 10in (26.45m), length 47ft (14.33m), height 16ft 4¾in (5m), weight 10,515lb (4,769kg), engines two 260hp Salmson 9-cylinder radial liquid-cooled, cruising speed 75mph (120kph), range 250 miles (402km), crew 2, passengers 12.

Right: An Airco DH4A of Aircraft Transport and Travel is made ready to depart Heathrow on an early postwar cross-Channel flight. Like many early commercial aircraft, it was a converted bomber.

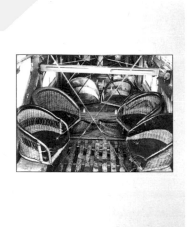

Immediately after the armistice the US Post Office bought war-surplus airplanes that included one hundred US-built DH4Bs with 400hp Liberty engines, which made it possible to begin a coast-to-coast service on May 15, 1919. The first experiment with flying part of the cross-continental route from San Francisco to New York by night was made when two airplanes took off from each terminal city on February 22, 1921. One of the eastbound pilots crashed in Nevada and was fatally injured, and bad weather forced one westbound pilot to abandon his flight at Chicago. The flight to New York was ultimately completed in 33 hours 20 minutes.

PASSENGER FLIGHTS

Civil flying was permitted to resume in Britain on May 1, 1919. However, it had already resumed in Germany. In February 1919 Deutsche Luft-Reederei (German Airline) instituted a daily service between Berlin and Weimar. In March, the manufacturers of Junkers aircraft began a service between Dessau and Weimar with J10 all-metal monoplanes. The same month, scheduled Berlin-Hamburg flights were started, and soon after, Nuremberg-Leipzig-Berlin and Augsburg-Munich. In 1926 the companies still in business joined to form Deutsche Luft Hansa.

In Britain, the first flights to take advantage of this commercial oppor-

Above: Passengers line up to board a Handley Page O/10 at Croydon in 1920, for a flight to the Continent. The inset picture shows the spartan interior of an earlier passenger conversion of the O/400 bomber.

Right: The Zeppelin-Staaken E.4/20 of 1919 was an amazingly advanced all-metal commercial transport weighing 18,740lb (8,500kg) and powered by four 245hp Maybach engines, which gave it a cruising speed of 125mph (200kph). Intended for Friedrichshafen–Berlin services, it was broken up in late 1922 after the Control Commission ordered suspension of test flying.

tunity were not between the capital and major provincial cities. On May 24, Avro Civil Aviation Service started daily flights between Manchester, Southport and Blackpool. Again, the Avro 504 was the chosen aircraft. This service, which had received no subsidy, ended eighteen weeks later.

On August 25, 1919, Aircraft Transport and Travel began a daily service between London and Paris. At 12.30pm a DH16 left the airfield at Hounslow and arrived at 2.50pm at Le Bourget. A DH4A bound for London also took off at 12.30pm – from the airfield at Le Bourget and bound for London. It landed at 2.40pm. Both pilots were RAF officers.

On the same day, an HPO/7 of Handley Page Transport made the same flight between London and Paris. On September 2 it began its scheduled service between the two capitals.

In March 1919 the Farman Line began a weekly passenger flight between Paris and Brussels. In the following month, Cie des Messageries Aeriennes (CMA) launched a Paris-Lille cargo operation. A daily Paris-London service opened in co-operation with Handley Page Transport in September.

Such cautious beginnings were not the style of another French company set up in the same year and based at Montaudran, near Toulouse: Lignes Aerienne Latécoère (soon known simply as La Ligne). It was the creation of Pierre Latécoère, an armament manufacturer who had ventured into the field of aircraft construction. By July he was running an experimental mail service between Toulouse and Rabat, in Morocco. A

year later, with Gallic dash, he had stretched the operation to Casablanca. He recruited wartime aircrew, as did all the growing airlines in the former Allied countries. By 1925 La Ligne was running a scheduled operation between Toulouse and Dakar, in French West Africa.

While the war had dominated the attention of Britain and her allies, two important innovations unconnected with the conflict were introduced. On March 11, 1918, the first regular international airmail service began: between Vienna and Kiev. On June 24, 1918, the first domestic airmail service was started; this time, between Montreal and Toronto in Canada. It is indicative of the dearth of civilian pilots that the aircraft was flown by an RAF officer. On August 12 that year, the USA's first airmail route opened, between New York and Washington, D.C. The first USA-Canada airmail service was established on March 3, 1919, between Seattle and Victoria.

PRIZE FLIGHTS

The ending of the war incited an abundance of ambitious ventures. In 1913 the British newspaper, the *Daily Mail*, had offered a £10,000 prize for the first crossing of the North Atlantic by air. Contestants would be displaying a confidence that, only three or four years previously, would have seemed absurd. Even the two first flights to India, only a few months

earlier, had not covered such a distance on any of the refueling stages – and they were across land, with only a comparatively short crossing of the Mediterranean. Those in search of fortune and fame needed to be the greatest of optimists. In the spring of 1919 some twelve crews were

Below: The prototype Vickers Vimy Commercial arrives at Amsterdam for the First International Air Transport Exhibition, held in July and August 1919. A mating of the Vimy's engines, wings and tail unit with a new monocoque fuselage to accommodate passengers, the Commercial was not an oustanding success, but a military version, the Vernon, became the RAF's first troop carrier.

Above: A classic small airliner of the 1920s, the Junkers F13 employed the all-metal structure developed by the German manufacturer in the First World War, with characteristic corrugated aluminum skinning. This one was operated by Swedish Airlines.

departure, Frederick Raynham and William Morgan, in a Martinsyde, crashed on takeoff.

On June 14 two ex-RAF officers, John Alcock as pilot and Arthur Whitten Brown as navigator, made their start in a Vickers Vimy bomber with extra fuel tanks. With a great quantity of petrol aboard, the aircraft was barely able to leave the ground, but became airborne at 4.28pm. Electricity for the radio was provided by a wind-driven propeller, which soon fell off. Overcoming various difficulties, after just short of sixteen and a half hours later

preparing in Newfoundland to make the attempt.

The first Atlantic crossing was made by a US Navy crew in a Curtiss NC4 flying boat. Three boats (the usual way of referring to this type of aircraft), each with a crew of six, left Trepassey Bay, Newfoundland, on May 8. US Navy destroyers stationed every 50 miles (80km) marked their route. Two of the NC4s were wrecked. The route took the surviving aircraft via the Azores, where it refueled, and Lisbon, where it fueled again. On May 31 it arrived in England, having covered 3,925 miles (6,317km) in 57hr 16min, at an average speed of 78mph (126kph). This was a fine achievement, although it was neither nonstop nor across the North Atlantic.

The weather delayed the competitors for the *Daily Mail* prize until May 18, when Harry Hawker and Mackenzie-Grieve set out in a Sopwith Atlantic. They had to make a forced landing on the sea, about halfway across, near a Danish steamer, which rescued them. An hour after the first

Right: Handley Page W8b G-EBBH of Imperial Airways runs up its two uncowled 360hp Rolls-Royce Eagle VIII engines. Carrying 12 passengers, the W8b first flew in August 1921.

they landed in Ireland, and claimed the record and a knighthood each. Tragically, Alcock was killed in an accident when flying over France on December 19.

The next to share a £10,000 prize were the Australians Ross and Keith Smith. It was their government that offered it, for a flight from England to Australia, a distance of 11,290 miles (18,170km), to

Above: The US Navy Curtiss NC4 flying boat, the first aircraft to cross the Atlantic, accomplished in stages, lands gently in Lisbon harbor for refueling.

be completed within 30 days. They took off from Hounslow, near London, in a Vickers Vimy on November 12, 1919, and landed at Fanny Bay, Darwin, on December 10 with 52 hours to spare. Only one other crew completed the trip.

In the same month as the maiden England to Australia flight, Britain's Air Ministry announced the RAF's completion of its survey of a route to South Africa. On February 4, 1920, yet another Vickers Vimy, this time in the hands of Lieutenant Colonel Pierre van Ryneveld and Squadron Leader Christopher Quintin Brand, was airborne from Brooklands in southern England on its way to the

Cape of Good Hope, South Africa. Both men were South Africans and the venture was financed by their government. Their aircraft, named Silver Queen, did not behave as regally as hoped: she crashed at Wadi Haifa when making an emergency landing in the dark, and was written off. The government replaced her with another of the same type, which was optimistically christened Silver Queen II. This one crashed at Bulawayo, in Southern Rhodesia (Zimbabwe), and was succeeded by a war surplus DH9 bearing the name Voortrekker (Pioneer), with which they resumed their flight on March 17. They landed at Cape Town three days later.

LIGHT AIRCRAFT
The category of aircraft that has introduced a wide variety of men and women to the pleasure that can be obtained by the acquisition of a pilot's license is the light aeroplane. One of the earliest was the Sopwith Dove, evolved from the famous Pup fighter. In 1923 the English Electric Wren made a great impression by flying 85 miles (137km) on one gallon (4.5 liters) of fuel with a 3.5hp engine that also powered motorcycles and managed 50mph (80.5kph). The Cygnet,

first flown in 1924, was the first aircraft that Sidney Camm, designer of the Hurricane, designed for Hawker.

The definitive light aircraft that set the standard for this genre was the DH60 Moth, powered by a 60hp ADC Cirrus engine, which first flew on February 22, 1925. With a replacement Gipsy engine it became known as the Gipsy Moth. On October 26, 1931, the Tiger Moth made its first flight. It differed from its predecessor in three ways: it had staggered and swept-back wings, to aid egress from the front cockpit when wearing a parachute; and an inverted engine to improve the forward view. Its 120hp Gipsy III engine was replaced by a 130hp Gipsy Major in the second production batch. Britain's Air Ministry ordered it after its first flight, to be the RAF's *ab initio* trainer.

MILITARY AIRCRAFT
While civil aviation was thrusting ahead all over the globe, military aircraft were developing more slowly. In 1924 the Vickers Virginia bomber entered squadron service with the RAF. The US Army Air Corps flew the Martin MB-2 bomber. It had two 420hp Liberty engines and carried 2,000lb (907kg) of bombs. Light day

Above: A relic of the war years, the Sopwith Snipe served in RAF fighter squadrons until 1926. Wingspan 31ft 1in (9.49m), length 19ft 10in (6.09m), height 8ft 3in (2.51m), weight 2,020lb (916kg), engine one 234hp Bentley BR2 9-cylinder rotary air-cooled, maximum speed 121mph (195kph), range 310 miles (499km), crew 1.

Above: Dutch manufacturer Anthony Fokker produced the aerodynamically clean FIII, which first flew in the early months of 1921. This is one of 12 of the type to serve with KLM. Wingspan 57ft 9½in (17.62m), length 36ft 3¾in (11.07m), height 12ft (3.65m), weight 4,188lb (1,900kg), engine one 240hp Armstrong Siddeley Puma 6-cylinder inline water-cooled, cruising speed 84mph (135kph), range 420 miles (676km), crew 1, passengers 5.

bombers still had their uses. The first new type built for the RAF was the two-seater Fairey Fawn, which had a top speed of 114mph (183kph) and a 460lb (209kg) bombload.

Japan's first indigenously built light bomber, a Mitsubishi, appeared in 1927. Concurrently, the Italian Air Force received the Fiat BR1 two-seater, whose top speed was 153mph (246kph) and bombload 1,000 (454kg)

The RAF's last biplane heavy night bomber, the Handley Page HP 38 Heyford, first flew in June 1930.

The first postwar fighter ordered in quantity for the RAF was the Gloster Grebe, which entered service in October 1926. It had two Vickers machine guns and a maximum speed of 152mph (245kph). The Armstrong-Whitworth Siskin had also been ordered, and joined its first squadron in May 1924; its maximum speed was 134mph (215.6kph), and it had two Vickers guns. It was flown by Bomber Command until mid-1939, when it was withdrawn from front-line service.

Below: This four-passenger Blériot Spad 33, with a 230hp Salmson radial engine, was operated by Cie des Messageries Aériennes on its London-to-Paris service in the early 1920s.

Atlantic Nonstop

> '*Snow was still falling, and the top sides of the plane were covered completely by a crusting of frozen sleet. The sleet embedded itself in the hinges of the ailerons and jammed them, so that for about an hour the machine had scarcely any lateral control. Fortunately the Vimy possesses plenty of inherent lateral stability; and as the rudder controls were never clogged by sleet, we were able to hold to the right direction.*'
>
> SIR ARTHUR WHITTEN BROWN

In 1913 the *Daily Mail* offered a prize of £10,000 for the first direct transatlantic crossing by air, but owing to the outbreak of war, there were no attempts to win it until 1919. A west-to-east crossing, utilizing the prevailing winds, offered the best chance of success. Three competitors assembled at St. John's in Newfoundland, the nearest start point: the Martinsyde Raymor, flown by Raynham and Morgan; the Sopwith Atlantic, flown by Hawker and Mackenzie-Grieve; and a Vickers Vimy flown by Alcock and Brown, this being the only twin-engined aircraft.

The first away, on May 18, was the Sopwith. The Martinsyde attempted to follow an hour later, but crashed on takeoff. Meanwhile, Hawker and Mackenzie-Grieve were plodding eastwards, but two-thirds of the way across a radiator failure forced them to ditch alongside a Danish steamer.

At last the Vimy was ready, and on Saturday June 14, laden with 1,033 US gallons of fuel, bumped across the field, scraped over the boundary and vanished into a dip on the far side. Disaster looked imminent, but with both Rolls-Royce Eagle engines at full throttle it finally lumbered into the air.

On a transoceanic flight of this length, provided that the engines kept going, navigation was the big problem. The US Navy Curtiss flying boats which made a staged crossing via the Azores a month before had had 55 warships spaced across the ocean at 50-mile (80km) intervals, marking the course with searchlights and starshells. The Vimy had no such aid, and Brown, the navigator, was forced to rely on "shooting" the sun or stars with a sextant for position, and taking drift sightings for course variations. Heavy cloud across most of the Atlantic meant that the Vimy had to climb above it to enable the sun and stars to be seen, then descend beneath it for drift sightings to be taken. At one point in the flight Alcock and Brown were at 11,000ft (3,350m); at another they were almost skimming the waves.

The Vimy was not immune to mechanical troubles. The inner exhaust pipe split away from an engine casing, fortunately causing no other damage. The radio and intercom both failed. The air speed indicator froze, giving a constant reading of 90mph. (145kph). This last nearly

Right: John Alcock (left, with camera) and Arthur Whitten Brown flew a modified Vockers Vimy long-range bomber when they made the first nonstop crossing of the Atlantic Ocean in 1919, a truly remarkable achievement just 16 years after the Wrights' first powered flights.

led to disaster, as the Vimy stalled, dropped a wing, and spiraled down through thick cloud. Just when all looked lost, it emerged into clear air with sufficient height for Alcock to recover control, barely 60ft (18.5m) above the water. After a further hour passed flying in clear air, they were assailed by hail, sleet and snow, and another hazard emerged – icing. Brown several times knelt on fuselage topdecking to chip ice away from the petrol overflow gauge on a centersection strut.

At last, with a misfiring starboard engine, they crossed the Irish coast and landed in a bog near Clifflen in Galway, the heavy ground tipped the airplane on to its nose but did not do much damage. They had been airborne for 16 hours 27 minutes, their average speed had been 121mph (195kph), and they had covered 1,890 miles (3,024km).

Right: The Vickers Vimy
flown by British pilot
Captain John Alcock and
navigator Lieutenant
Arthur Whitten Brown
on their epic
transatlantic nonstop
voyage, seen taking off
from St. John's,
Newfoundland, at
4.13pm GMT, June 14,
1919. The momentous
1,890-mile (3,042km)
flight lasted 16 hours
and 27 minutes and
ended in a bog at
Derrygimla, County
Galway, Ireland, where
the aircraft tipped up on
its nose.

Left: Alcock and Brown's Vimy at Brooklands, England, shortly after the record-breaking flight. While the flight started a brilliant new chapter in aviation history, the Vimy had originally been intended to make history of a different kind. A long-range, twin-engined bomber powered by Rolls-Royce Eagle engines of 360hp each, it was designed to carry a war load to Berlin in reprisal against the German bombing of London, but the armistice intervened before the type could be produced in quantity.

Ross and Keith Smith

Every aspect of aviation had made a great advance during the First World War, which enabled pilots to embark with confidence on long-distance flights that would have been impossible four years earlier. The *Daily Mail*'s offer of a £10,000 prize in 1913 for the first crossing of the North Atlantic by air was won on June 14/15. This prompted the Australian Government to offer the same amount for a flight from England to Australia, to be completed in 30 days.

Six crews entered. The winners – the only ones to meet the time limit – were two ex-officers, Ross Smith,

Below: The refueling of big aircraft was not a simple process under the best of circumstances, but in primitive conditions the fuel for the Smiths' Vimy had to be poured into the aircraft's tanks can-by-can through a large funnel with a chamois leather filter.

aircraft captain, who had been in the Royal Australian Air Force during the war, and his elder brother Keith, navigator and second pilot, who had served in the wartime RFC/RAF. Their mechanics, still serving in the RAF, were Sergeant J. M. Bennett and Sergeant W. H. Shiers. Their aircraft was a Vickers Vimy bomber, a type that had first flown on November 30, 1917; it had two 360hp Rolls-Royce Eagle VIII engines driving four-bladed propellers. Its maximum speed was 103mph (166kph) at sea level – hardly a relevant altitude for any major journey.

They took off from Hounslow, on the western outskirts of London, for their 11,290 mile (18,170km) venture on November 12, 1919. Their route took them via Taranto, Cairo, Ramadie, Bandar Abbas, Karachi, Delhi, Muttra, Allahabad, Calcutta, Akyab, Moulmien, Bangkok, Singora, Singapore, Soerabaya, Bima and Atamboes to Darwin. They had expected to cover 600 miles (966km) a day, but storms over the Mediterranean, in the Middle East and in south-east Asia reduced their average to a daily 400 miles (644km). They landed at Fanny Bay, Darwin, Australia, on December 10, 1919, two days and four hours within the time limit. They flew on to Adelaide, their home town, via Melbourne and Sydney, among other places. Both were knighted.

Only one other crew completed the journey, well outside the time limit.

Ross Smith was killed in 1922 when flying a Vickers amphibian with which he planned to make a flight round the world.

Below: Ross and Keith Smith pose in the snow at Hounslow Aerodrome with their Vimy, G-EAOU, on November 12, 1919, shortly before embarking on their epic adventure. They jokingly said that the aeroplane's registration letters stood for "God 'elp all of us".

Above: Approaching the end of their 27-day flight, members of the Vimy's crew enjoy a cup of tea near a small Australian town. Owing to the dearth of prepared landing grounds en route, the aircraft often had to be put down in rough fields.

Rotary Wings

> '*Demonstrated publicly at the Cuatro Vientos airport in Spain, the craft amazed and fascinated the whole aeronautical world. It was safe. Once... it climbed too steeply and lost all its forward motion, which, for the conventional aeroplane, would have meant plummeting to earth. This did not occur.*'
>
> COLONEL H. F. GREGORY, USAAF

The rapid development of the airplane following the Wright brothers' first flight was not paraleled by the helicopter. The complexity of the latter, coupled with its inherent propulsive inefficiency, retarded development for many years. But the potential to operate from very small areas and to fly very slowly remained desirable.

To achieve this, Juan de la Cierva attempted to combine the advantages of the rotary wing with the propulsion system of the fixed-wing aircraft in the "Autogiro." This differed from the helicopter in that the engine drove a propeller in the nose, and was not connected to the rotor, which was driven by the airflow in forward flight. In Madrid in 1920 he built the Cierva C.1, based on a Deperdussin monoplane fuselage. This was unsuccessful, as were the next two machines.

The main problem was that, as with helicopters, while individual rotor blades gave an equal amount of lift when the machine was hovering, in forward flight the advancing blade created more lift than the retreating blade, thus causing an unstable rolling moment which became worse as forward speed increased. Cierva's solution was ingenious. He semi-articulated the root of each rotor blade, allowing it to flap up and down and also to "advance and retreat." The changing angle of attack of each blade thus balanced out the lift around the rotor disc.

Cierva's first successful machine was the C.4 It used a modified Hanriot fuselage with an 80hp Le Rhône engine, and had a four-bladed rotor of 33ft (10m) diameter and stub wings on outriggers both to increase stability and to offload the rotor in forward flight. On January 9, 1923, the C.4 made its first official flight at Cuatro Vientos airport, near Madrid, piloted by Lieutenant Alejandro Gomez Spencer. It covered a circular

Right: An Avro-built Cierva C.19 MkIV "Autogyro" being test-flown at Brooklands, England.

**ove: Juan de la Cierva's C.4 "Autogiro" at Cuatro Vientos airport, near
**drid. The concept was that the rotor was not driven by the engine, but
ted itself as the aircraft was drawn along by its propeller – autorotating.

course of 2½ miles (4km) in 3 minutes 30 seconds, at an altitude of

82ft (25m). Later it demonstrated that it could maneuver freely, and that it could land safely after losing virtually all forward motion. At this stage a moderate takeoff run was still needed, but the landing roll was very short. The fixed-wing hazard of stalling on the landing approach had been eliminated.

Further developments followed: the C.6A in May 1924, and the two-seater C.6D on July 29, 1927. Then on September 18, 1928, Cierva, by now based in England, flew across the Channel in his C.8L-III with a passenger aboard. The final development was a system whereby the rotor was initially turned by the engine, then decoupled when flying revolutions were reached, allowing a "jump-start" to be made.

Cierva C-30As were license-built by Avro for the RAF, and served from 1934 to 1945 as the Rota MkI, mainly on radar calibration duties. De la Cierva died in an airliner crash in England in 1936.

The Barnstormers

The word "barnstormer" evokes high jinks and daring. It was coined for the touring theatrical companies in late 19th-century USA, who had to make do with barns in which to set up stage. The aerial barnstormers were also entertainers, but their calling involved an element that did not threaten actors – the risk of injury and death.

Today's aerobatic displays by fighters emitting coloured smoke evolved from the early-day daring men, mostly British and American, in their primitive flying machines. Effectively, they were also the first test pilots, and provided aircraft designers with valuable information. Moreover, from the First World War onward fighter pilots have benefited from the antics they initiated, which are the basis of all the manoeuvres for attack and defence used in air fighting.

Lincoln Beachey is considered the best of the first generation. Flying a Curtiss biplane, his repertoire included vertical power dives and scooping up a scarf or handkerchief with a wingtip. When he flew low over the Niagara Falls and under the suspension bridge below them, he provided valuable evidence of how to contend with severe air turbulence. He gave up his death-defying avocation in 1913, but was lured to resume when he heard that the outstanding French pilot, Adolphe Pégoud, on September 2, 1913, had demonstrated a loop. As communications between Russia and the Western world were slow, the USA and Europe were unaware that the

first loop had already been performed on August 20, 1913, by Lieutenant Peter Nikolaevich Nestarov of the Russian Air Service, flying a Nieuport IV. Beachey was killed in 1915 when, at 2,000ft (610m), his machine's wings folded.

An article in *Flight* magazine in 1913 spoke warily of the barnstormers. "Several accidents have resulted from the deliberate performance of tricks in the air, such as were at one time notorious in America, where several pilots have been killed in front of spectators. Catering to the sensations of the crowd, these men would display the most amazing nerve in making steep dives followed by banked turns in which the wings would approach to a vertical position. On one occasion the machine actually turned turtle through over-banking and the pilot was killed."

Right: Curtiss test pilot Roland Rholfs poses with the company's Model 18T Wasp triplane, in which he gained the world climb and altitude records on September 18, 1919, attaining 34,910ft (10,640m).

Above: The choice of aeroplane for Roland Toutain, a French daredevil of the 1920s, is a Caudron C60 biplane trainer, powered by a 130hp Clerget rotary engine.

Pégoud, an employee of the Blériot company, had also demonstrated a parachute jump. One of his aerobatics began with a bunt (outside loop), out of which he half-rolled upright at the bottom, then half-looped up, thus performing an "S." Another stunt was to stall at the top of a 45-degree climb and let the airplane slide back in a parabola. He had trained for inverted flight by having his airplane hung upside down with him in it. An ingenious innovation of his that enabled takeoffs and landings on confined and bumpy areas failed to arouse interest. It entailed flying under a cable stretched between two posts and climbing to engage a quick-release gear with a longitudinal cable, which brought him to a stop. In the First World War he was the first pilot to be dubbed an "ace" (a term invented by the French press), for having scored five

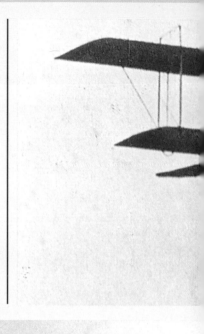

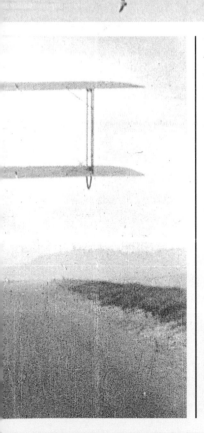

victories. He was shot down in 1915 while reloading his Lewis gun.

After the war, great numbers of young men who learned to fly in the air forces could not settle to humdrum civilian jobs, so they turned to barnstorming. There was also an abundance of surplus aircraft to be bought cheaply, of which the most popular were the Curtiss Jenny and Avro 504. They did valuable public relations work by taking people up for short, cheap flights as well as thrilling spectators with wing-walking, riding astride the tail, dangling from the undercarriage and mock combat. The first instance of flight refueling was a stunt; a pilot with a can of petrol strapped to his back moved from one aircraft to another. Many pilots graduated from barnstorming to air racing and long-distance pioneering flights.

Above and left: The slow and stable Curtiss Jenny and Standard biplane trainers made ideal mounts for US stunt pilots. The man above hangs by his teeth from a trapeze attached to the undercarriage, while the one on the left changes from aeroplane to automobile on a mercifully clear road.

Spanning the World

Britain, France, Italy, Germany and the USA, war-weary but commercially and technically ambitious, were competing to design and produce the world's most advanced airplanes. These were to be bigger, faster, safer, with greater capacity for both passengers and freight than their competitors, and capable of flying ever-increasing distances without refueling.

The US aircraft industry was slow to develop in these postwar years. Commercial airliners were either purchased or license-built from European manufacturers, although in the 1920s the famous companies such as Boeing and Curtiss began manufacturing aircraft to their own design.

The routes on which the British company Air Transport and Travel was so solicitous about its passengers' protection from the cold had multiplied rapidly. The London-Paris route was soon also being flown by Handley Page Transport and in 1922 Daimler Airway began competing with the others. In May the following year, in collaboration with the Dutch airline KLM, it began a London-Amsterdam service.

By 1924 the various British airlines were working between London and Amsterdam, Basle, Berlin, Brus-

sels, Cologne, Paris and Zurich. Several small companies were formed to carry passengers between Britain and continental Europe, and one, British Marine Air Navigation, operat-

Above: Lioré et Olivier 213s, in French airline Air Union's red and gold Golden Ray livery, prepare to leave Croydon Airport in June 1932 with celebrities bound for Reims to celebrate the 250th anniversary of the discovery of champagne.

Above: The all-metal Ford 5-AT Trimotor saw widespread use in the USA from the early 1930s. Here, an aircraft of National Air Transport, powered by Pratt & Whitney Wasp radials, takes aboard its cargo of mailbags.

Below: This British-registered Sikorsky S-38B amphibian, powered by a pair of 420hp Pratt & Whitney Wasp radials, was the private transport of millionaire Francis Francis, who bought it in 1932.

Above: The Boeing Model 40A of 1927 was designed expressly to fly with the new Boeing Air Transport Corporation on the San Francisco–Chicago portion of the transcontinental airmail route.

ed a flying boat between Southampton and Jersey. There was not enough custom to make them all financially viable: in consequence, only four were still in business by 1924, so were amalgamated as Imperial Airways on March 31 that year.

A clever and forceful man of authority, Sir Sefton Brancker had figured prominently in all aspects of aviation since 1911. At that time a captain in a cavalry regiment in India, with characteristic originality Brancker flew in a Bristol Boxkite during cavalry manoeuvres. In 1913, Brancker, having returned to England, learned to fly (officers had to do so at their own expense before joining the RFC), followed a course at the RFC's Central Flying School and was put on the RFC Reserve. He was soon appointed Deputy Director of Military Aeronautics at the Military Aeronautics Directorate. In 1915 he was given command of a wing on the Western Front and rose to the rank of Major General before leav-

ing the RAF to become Director of Civil Aviation. Priority then was given to establishing air routes for Imperial Airways between Britain and her far-flung empire.

AROUND THE WORLD

In 1921, Alan Cobham, a wartime RFC pilot, took his first big step up the lad-

Right: This Vought O2U-1 floatplane of the US Navy was attached to the cruiser USS *Raleigh* during 1928. An observation biplane, it was powered by a 450hp Pratt & Whitney air-cooled radial.

der of fame when he made a 5,000-mile (8,047km) flight around Europe.

On April 6, 1924, two US Army Air Service crews, flying two-seater Douglas World Cruisers with interchangeable wheel and float landing gear, took off from Seattle to make the first flight round the world. They landed on September 28, having flown via the Aleutians, Japan, India, Europe, Iceland and Greenland. Their flying time was 15 days, 11 hours and 7 minutes.

On November 20, 1924, Alan Cobham, with Sefton Brancker aboard, took off from Croydon, south of London, in a DH50 with a 230hp Siddeley Puma engine, on a return journey to Rangoon. They landed back at home on March 18, 1925, after flying a total of 17,000 miles (27,360km). In 1926 Cobham flew to Cape Town and back, and followed that up with a flight of 23,000 miles (37,015km) around Africa. His next trail-blazing venture was a round trip to Australia. His experience exemplified the ardors and perils suffered by flyers in the 1920s, when navigational aids were few and primitive, there was no long-range radio communication between ground and air, and searing heat in the tropics and sub-tropics caused fatigue and illness at the altitudes at which most long flights were made.

An early innovation was flight refueling, but it did not become general practice until the 1940s. It was first used by the United States Army Air Corps when a pair of DH-4Bs set a new world endurance record of 37hr 15min 43.8sec on August 27/28, 1923. None of the airlines took advantage of the facility because the methods employed were still very primitive.

Britain gave priority to establishing a regular passenger and mail air service between London and India. The route was being put together in stages. In June 1921 the RAF had begun a mail run between Baghdad and Cairo. The entire route was surveyed between December 1926 and January 1927 by Imperial Airways with a DH66 Hercules. On January 7, 1927, the company took over the first link in the chain of communication from the RAF and added Basra and Gaza to the sector. In 1920 the Compagnie Franco-Roumaine de Navigation Aérienne began running a Paris-

Above: Passengers disembark from a Blériot 165 of Air Union at Croydon about 1928. Only two of these biplanes, powered by 420hp Gnome-Rhône Jupiter 9Ab 9-cylinder air-cooled radial engines, were built. This one was named after aviation pioneer Octave Chanute.

Prague service; the following year Paris-Budapest and Paris-Stamboul were added. In 1922 another new service was flown by the USSR-German Deruluft, between Königsburg, Kowno, Smolensk and Moscow. By 1923 some airlines were even making night flights. Flying boats were being used by the Belgian line SNETA – later taken over by Sabena – on routes in the Congo.

Australia, with its 2,974,000 square miles (7,702,660sq km), was an obvious candidate for coverage by

air routes. December 1921 marked the first flights of the mail service between Geraldton and Derby, both in Western Australia but over 1,000 miles (1,600km) apart. Two years later Qantas started a passenger service between two Queensland towns, Charleville and Cloncurry.

Passenger and mail services, flown by night as well as day, proliferated all over the United States of America during the 1920s. As early as

1921 it was possible to fly from coast to coast between New York and San Francisco in 33hr 20min. Ernest Gann, a giant figure in the pantheon of air pilotage and navigation, described a typical winter's night flight carrying mail when this was a government monopoly. Flying the US Mail in an open cockpit, he said, was a job for young men already matured beyond their numbered years.

Most of the aircraft were war-surplus De Havilland DH-4s built in America under license, with a 12-cylinder Liberty engine replacing the Rolls-Royce Eagle. On a winter night the cold was intense. The exhaust pipe had not been extended beyond the cockpit, but ended 12 inches (30.5cm) or so astern of the engine block. This, Gann said ironically, gave the pilot the dubious advantage of judging his engine-fuel mixture by the color of the exhaust flame without getting a stiff neck from constantly turning to look behind him. The carbon monox-

Left: When it first appeared in 1925, the de Havilland DH60 Moth heralded a revolution in privately owned light aeroplanes. Here the prototype, G-EBKT, displays its folding wings at the company's Stag Lane Aerodrome in Middlesex, England. The engine was the specially created 60hp ADC Cirrus I 4-cylinder air-cooled inline.

Right: The French Breguet 19 general-purpose biplane was one of the most prolific and successful military aircraft of the interwar years, being used by many national air arms and for many record-breaking long-distance flights.

Below: The Armstrong Whitworth Argosy airliner entered service with Imperial Airways in 1926, carrying 20 passengers on the airline's Silver Wing service to Paris. Wingspan 90ft 8in (27.64m), length 65ft 10in (20.07m), height 19ft 10in (6.05m), weight 18,000lb (8,165kg), engines three 386hp Armstrong Siddeley Jaguar III 14-cylinder radial air-cooled, cruising speed 90mph (145kph), range 330 miles (531km), crew 2, passengers 20.

Above: Junkers' first trimotor transport, the G23, was followed in 1925 by the G24, powered by three 280/310hp Junkers-L5 inline engines. This Deutsche Luft Hansa G24 at Tempelhof, Berlin, shows the now-familiar corrugated skinning.

ide exuded was, fortunately, swept away by the slipstream. In 1926 in the course of flying two million miles (3,218,600km), two pilots were killed, fifty-nine had minor injuries, and nine airplanes were lost. By 1927 flying the mails had been completely contracted to private companies.

The HP O/100 and O/400, converted from bombers to passenger carriers, had been a boon to the nascent airlines; but, like all makeshifts, they had to be succeeded

as soon as possible by airplanes specifically designed for their function. The first of these was the twin-engine Handley Page W8, which appeared in 1921. It was quickly followed by the W8E and W8F Hamilton and W9a Hampstead, each of which had a third engine in its nose. On February 10, 1926, the HP W10, ordered by Imperial Airways, made its first flight. The reversion to twin motors proved short sighted: two out of the four that were built crashed.

Above: Despite their unconventional float-incorporating fuselages, the interwar line of Loening amphibians were successful. This OL-5 was the first aeroplane delivered to the newly established US Coast Guard Air Service in 1926.

adverse weather. At last, on April 18, they were able to depart for Fernando Po, 200 miles (320km) east of Brazil, but had to force-land at St Paul's rock, which badly damaged the aeroplane. An escorting Portuguese cruiser took the officers aboard until a replacement Fairey IIID was delivered. This one also came to grief, at Fernando de Noronha. Yet another seaplane was provided and they reached their destination on June 16.

On October 14-15, 1927, the South Atlantic was crossed non-stop by two French Air Force officers. Their aircraft was a Breguet XIX and in 19hr 50min they covered the 2,125 miles (3,420km) between St. Louis, in Senegal, and Natal, in Brazil.

Two resounding triumphs in the second decade of the 20th century caught the world's attention probably more than any other feat of aviation during those ten years. Twenty-five-year-old Charles A. Lindbergh, a native of Detroit, won the $25,000 prize offered for the first non-stop flight between New York and Paris. He made the takeoff run in his purpose-built Ryan NYP (Ryan New York–Paris), named Spirit of St Louis, from Long Island on 20 May 1927, not sure that the 237hp Wright Whirlwind engine would lift it into the air with the weight of 450 US gallons (1,705 liters) of fuel in the fuselage and

SPIRIT OF ADVENTURE

Countries with smaller populations were also contributing to the conquest of the air. Portugal, with only some six million inhabitants, showed the spirit of adventure that had lured Vasco da Gama to make his great sea voyages in the late 15th and early 16th centuries. Two Portuguese naval officers took off from Lisbon on March 30, 1922, in a Fairey IIID floatplane to cross the South Atlantic against the prevailing wind. They staged through Las Palmas, the Cape Verde Islands and Porto Praia, delayed at each by

Below: Probably the most inelegant transport aircraft of the interwar years were the Farman Jabirus. This is the first production F-3X, built in 1924, which had four 180hp Hispano-Suiza 8Ac engines.

Above: The Fokker line continued with the F VII. This one, powered by a water-cooled 450hp Napier Lion, was used by Fokker for demonstrations in England.

wings. However, he landed safely at Le Bourget, the Paris airfield, on May 21 after a flight of 33hr 39min that had covered 3,590 miles (5,776km).

The other of the two greatest triumphs in aviation during the 1920s was Charles Kingsford Smith's flight with his co-pilot, C. T. P. Ulm, from San Francisco to Brisbane, Australia, between May 31 and June 9, 1928 – the first full crossing of the Pacific Ocean. Both men were Australians, and their aircraft was a Fokker F VIIB/3M, named Southern Cross. The flight began at Oakland, California, and ended at Brisbane, having covered 7,389 miles (11,890km) in 83hr 38min flying time, via Honolulu and Fiji.

Britain's *Daily Mail* newspaper, which had been so generous in awarding prizes for feats that advanced man's mastery of the air, introduced a remarkable innovation in August 1928. This not only exploited the rapid advances that aircraft design and performance had made, but was also a masterstroke of journalistic genius. In August 1928 the newspaper bought a DH61 Giant Moth, a cabin biplane that was an airborne extension of its London Fleet Street headquarters. A dark-

Left: Although it originated in the First World War, the doughty DH9A served with the RAF into the early 1930s. These aircraft, built from reconditioned stored fuselages, belong to 39 Squadron, based at Spittlegate, Yorkshire, England, in the mid-1920s.

Above: The Boeing FB-1 shore-based fighter equipped US Marine squadrons from the mid-1920s. A 435hp Curtiss D-12 12-cylinder water-cooled inline engine gave it very clean lines and a top speed of 159mph (256kph).

room was fitted out, an office desk installed and, most ingenious of all its features, a motorcycle was carried. Photographs of events in the news could now be developed and printed, and the stories typed, in flight. On landing, the motorcyclist aboard would then make a speedy delivery of the whole package to head office.

Two years earlier, this newspaper had also, in unforeseen circumstances, initiated the delivery of bulk air freight. In 1926 there was a general strike in Britain during which coal miners, printers and many others ceased work and neither trains nor buses ran. The *Daily Mail* was the only British paper that had an office in

Paris. The British editions were therefore printed there, flown to the airfields near London and taken thence by car to newsagents. No such quantity of cargo had previously been carried by aircraft, and this initiative introduced a type of service that spread quickly for all manner of goods.

POLAR FLIGHTS

Such was the grip that flying had on men and women of adventurous spirit, not least on those for whom exploration was an irresistible lure, that it seemed inevitable that someone would want to fly over the North and South Poles. In 1897 three Swedes had made a foolhardy attempt to fly

Right: The Armstrong Whitworth Siskin single-seat fighter served with the RAF in various marks from 1924 to 1932. Here, mechanics and riggers tend to Siskin III J7758 and its 325hp Armstrong Siddeley Jaguar III 9-cylinder air-cooled radial engine.

Above: Four Focke-Wulf A38 Möwe (Seagull) ten-passenger aircraft were built for Luft Hansa in 1931. Wingspan 65ft 7¼in (20m), length 48ft 0in (14.63m), height 13ft 1in (3.99m), weight 8,818lb (4,000kg), engine one 480hp Siemens Jupiter VI 9-cylinder radial air-cooled, range 500 miles (805km), crew 2, passengers 8.

over the North Pole in a balloon, which vanished without trace until its wreckage was found in 1930. By then both poles had been reached on foot. Veteran Norwegian explorer Roald Amundsen, who had been the first to trudge to the South Pole, tried to make it to the North Pole three times in an airplane during 1925. His companions were an American, who financed him, and two Norwegian pilots.

The first flight over the North Pole was made by Amundsen and an Italian crew in the airship *Norge* on May 11-14, 1926. US Commander Richard Byrd made the first crossing of the South Pole in a Ford 4-AT Trimotor on November 28, 1929.

One typical instance will convey the ingenuity and toughness demanded of bush pilots who flew over "The Frozen North." One of the best known

was "Punch" Dickins, who set off from Edmonton, Alberta, one morning in 1929 to deliver mail on a 1,500-mile (2,414km) trip following the Mackenzie River to Aklavik. En route, landing on frozen snow, an undercarriage strut broke and the tips of the propeller were bent. Dickins and the mechanic who accompanied him repaired them. A wrecked boat yielded piping to replace the strut and they sawed 6in (152mm) off the propeller blades.

Above: The ubiquitous Avro 504 was given a new lease of life when it was modified and re-engined with an Armstrong Siddeley Lynx radial to become the 504N trainer, which remained in production until 1933. This one belonged to the Cambridge University Air Squadron.

The aircraft that were flown over the huge, uncharted wilderness of northern Canada were fitted with wheels that could be interchanged with skis or floats, and had to be high-winged for stability and for convenience when loading and unloading. A typical one was the Fairchild 71, which made its maiden flight in 1929. Wingspan was 50ft (15.24m), length 32ft 10in (10m), and its 430hp Pratt & Whitney engine gave a top speed of 129mph (208kph). The pilot flew solo and the cabin had capacity for six passengers or the same weight in mail or freight.

On November 6, 1929, the Junkers G-38 took to the air for the first time. It was a typical Dr. Hugo Junkers design: he believed fervently in a "flying wing" shape, which enabled most of the fuel and payload to be carried within the wing structure. In this instance, six passengers were seated in the wing center-section, which had windows forward, and twenty-eight passengers in the fuselage. Only two of this type were built; they operated with Deutsche Luft Hansa until one crashed in 1936, and RAF bombs destroyed the other in 1940.

Left: From April 1926 three 420hp Bristol Jupiter 9-cylinder air-cooled radial engines formed the powerplant of the Handley Page W9 Hampstead, which carried 14 passengers in a heated cabin. Only one was built, but the Jupiter was used to power the next generation of Imperial Airways airliners.

World Circumnavigation

> *'Midway in Yokohama Bay we passed the volcano 0 Shima which was putting out great clouds of steam, and soon afterwards thru a rift in the clouds we could see Japan's famous Fujiyama with the sun shining on its snow capped dome some 12,400 feet above sea level – a truly beautiful sight.'*
>
> LT. LESLIE ARNOLD

Early in 1923 the US Army Air Service became increasingly interested in making a circumnavigation of the globe. Aware that failure would be worse than not making the attempt, the Air Service started planning, virtually on a succeed-at-all-costs basis. The first step was to acquire suitable aircraft, and the choice settled on a Navy torpedo bomber, the Douglas DT-2. Suitably modified, this became the Douglas

World Cruiser, or DWC.

A two-seater biplane, the DWC was perhaps an odd choice for a long-distance flight, as it had only one engine. On the other hand it was sturdy and reliable by the standards of the day, pleasant to fly, and the landing gear could be quickly switched from wheels to floats. The DWC differed from the DT-2 mainly in a vastly increased fuel capacity, from 96 to 773 US gallons. A new radiator arrangement was adopted, allowing different sizes for different climates. Oak propellers were provided for the floatplane configuration and walnut propellers for flights with a wheeled undercarriage. Four aircraft, named *Seattle, Cbicago, Boston* and *New Orleans,* were made ready.

The flight started on April 6, 1924, when the four DWCs, fitted with floats, departed Prince Rupert, Seattle, heading for Sitka in Alaska. From here they followed the line of the Aleutians as far as Attu. Already they were one short; *Seattle* crashed

Below: Three Douglas World Cruisers in floatplane configuration at Seward, Alaska, at an early stage of the flight, attract a gaggle of spectators. One aircraft, *Seattle*, had already been lost.

Above: The World Cruisers as landplanes, running up their engines at the RAF aerodrome at Drigh Road, Karachi, India.

in fog in Alaska, although Major Frederick Martin and Staff Sgt. Alva Harvey survived. The next stage involved refueling at sea off Nikolski in Siberia, then on in easy stages down Japan. Crossing to the mainland, they then followed the coast past Hong Kong, Saigon, and Rangoon, before arriving at Calcutta on June 26, where they swapped floats for wheels and changed propellers.

Their course then took the DWCs across the Indian sub-continent to Karachi, on to Baghdad and eventually through into Europe, calling at Paris and London en route, and arriving at Brough, Yorkshire, on July 17, where they again reverted to floats. Their course now took them northward, to the Orkneys and Faeroes, then on to Reykjavik. It was at this point that *Boston* lost power and alighted on the sea. The thorough American organization paid off; USS *Ricbmond* was at hand and the crew were saved, although the aircraft was lost.

The two survivors, *Chicago*, flown by Lowell Smith and Leslie

Arnold, and *New Orleans,* flown by Erick Nelson and John Harding, carried on via Greenland and Canada, arriving in Boston on September 8, where they swapped their floats for wheels. The transcontinental flight was flown in easy stages, and they arrived back at Seattle on September 28, an elapsed time of 175 days. They had flown a total of 73 legs, over mountains, oceans, freezing ice and baking deserts, covering a total of 26,503 miles (42,405km). It had been an epic journey.

Below: The American airmen pose in front of *Chicago* at Karachi.

Sir Alan Cobham

Long-distance flights with all their dangers clearly gave Alan Cobham a simultaneously seductive and menacing challenge. In the 1920s he made more long flights than any other of the pioneer pilots and was the best-known Briton among them.

Cobham began his flying career in the Royal Air Force. After demobilisation he joined the ebullient fraternity of barnstormers in 1919, aged 25: not to hurl an aircraft about the sky, but to give staid joy rides to an eager public. In 1932 he formed a flying circus which gave displays and short flights on what he called his National Aviation Day Campaign, from April to October every year from 1932 to 1936. It put on over 12,000 performances and carried nearly a million passengers.

His greatest interest was in promoting civil aviation. Between his civilian debut and the outbreak of the Second World War on September 3, 1939, he gave it outstanding service. His main concern was not in speed or altitude records, but to demonstrate that long distances could be flown safely in several stages and that it would be possible to carry passengers to any part of the British Empire if airfields with fuel and servicing facilities were established at suitable intervals along the routes.

In 1921 he made a 5,000-mile (8,047km) circuit of Europe. His shortest international flight, demonstrating the diminutive new de Havilland DH53 Humming Bird in 1923, was from Lymne to Brussels to advertise its economical engine. With

Above: Alan Cobham (with case) poses with his mechanic beside the DH50 at Karachi during the England to Australia return flight.

his mechanic A. B. Elliott, he took the Director of Civil Aviation, Sir Sefton Brancker, on a survey flight to Rangoon that began on November 20, 1924, and ended on March 17, 1925. On November 16 he was off again, bound for Cape Town some 16,100 miles (25,750km) away. He flew in a de Havilland DH50 which had been re-engined with a 385hp Armstrong Siddeley Jaguar III, accompanied by Elliott and B. W. Emmott, a photographer. They landed back in England on March 13, 1926.

Cobham's next flight, with Elliott, was his most celebrated. The DH50 had been converted to a floatplane. A forced landing on forested or mountainous terrain would have been disas-

Left: Cobham's DH50 on the Nile. When he arrived back in London from Australia he was within seconds of his stated ETA!

trous, so he had chosen a route along which there was an abundance of sheltered bays and creeks on which to alight. His book about the journey says: "Ninety in every hundred people we met at the various landing places between London [he actually took off, just after dawn, from Rochester on June 30, 1926] and Australia had never seen a seaplane before, and an even greater percentage knew little or nothing about aircraft and what was required for the safe landing, mooring-up and taking off again in a seaplane." He had to depend on the co-operation of the authorities at each landing place, to whom he sent the relevant information and instructions.

After refueling at Marseilles, Naples was the first overnight stop. The hard work of many weeks' preparation had tired him. Awakened next morning at 4.30am, he postponed departure till 11.00am. Athens was the next stop; and there, "The doctor advised rest, for I was suffering from exhaustion."

Next stop Alexandretta, then Baghdad. They left there before dawn next day and soon met a sandstorm that forced them to fly at 50ft (15m) in a temperature of 110 degrees in the shade. Basra was 100 miles (160km) away when there was a loud explosion and Elliott began to bleed copiously. There was nowhere to land. At Basra he was rushed to hospital, but died that night. He had been hit by a bullet fired from the ground.

An RAF sergeant who knew the Jaguar engine volunteered to take his place. With five stops on the Indian sub-continent and eleven more in Burma, Malaya and the East Indies, they landed at Port Darwin on August 5. On August 29 they started back and landed on the Thames near the Houses of Parliament at 2pm on October 1, 1926. Cobham was knighted. In 1927 he flew a flying boat round Africa.

Below: Cobham (left) with A. B. Elliott (right) and photographer B. W. Emmett, and DH50 with Armstrong Siddeley Jaguar engine.

Atlantic Solo

> *These phantoms speak with human voices... able to vanish or appear at will, to pass in and out through the walls of the fuselage as though no walls were there... familiar voices, conversing and advising on my flight, discussing problems of my navigation, reassuring me, giving me messages of importance unattainable in ordinary life.*
>
> CHARLES AUGUSTUS LINDBERGH

In 1919, New York hotel owner Raymond Orteig offered a prize of $25,000 for the first nonstop flight between New York and Paris. This was a far more formidable undertaking than Alcock and Brown's transatlantic flight in 1919, not least because the distance between New York and Paris was much greater. Reliability thus became a primary requirement, and at that time no suitable aero engine existed.

Progress over the next few years meant that, by 1926, the prize appeared to be within reach. On September 21 that year, French fighter ace René Fonck failed to coax his overloaded Sikorsky S-35 trimotor off the ground at Roosevelt Field and crashed, killing two of the four-man crew. Then on April 26, 1927, the

Right: A sailor mounts guard on Lindbergh's aeroplane after its return to the USA.

Below: Lindbergh's Ryan NYP (New York–Paris) monoplane during the tour of the USA following his momentous flight. The lack of forward view for the pilot is evident.

Above: A candid shot of Charles Lindbergh in the UK in 1937.

Keystone Pathfinder of Noel Davis and Stanton Wooster crashed on takeoff with fatal results. The next attempt was made on May 8 that year, when another French fighter ace, Charles Nungesser, and his copilot Francois Coli took off from Le Bourget in *L'Oiseau Blanc*, a single-engined Levasseur PL.8 biplane. After crossing the French coast north of Le Havre they were never seen again. It began to appear that the task was impossible.

However, a US Mail pilot, Charles Lindbergh, had decided to attempt the feat. He was used to flying at night and in poor weather. His planning for the transatlantic attempt was meticulous. Foremost was the aircraft. He wanted a monoplane for

minimum drag, a single engine to minimise fuel consumption (another and rather perverse reason was that with a trimotor there was three times as much to go wrong), and an enclosed cabin. Unlike the other competitors, he proposed to fly alone.

His first choice was a Bellanca, but, unable to acquire one, he turned to the Ryan M-1. Following a downpayment on February 25, 1927, Ryan began building a modified version for the flight. The NYP, as it was called for obvious reasons, was fitted with a 237hp Wright J-5C Whirlwind radial engine. The wing span was increased, the latest navigational aids were fitted, and fuel capacity was increased to 376 US gallons. To

Right: Lindbergh's modified Ryan M-1 on the Potomac, Washington, D.C., following its return to the US after his historic solo flight from New York to Paris, May 20, 1927.

keep the center of gravity within limits, a large fuel tank was fitted in front of the cockpit, completely blocking the windscreen, and the only forward view was through a periscope. The airplane was named *Spirit of St Louis* after the city in which Lindbergh's financial backers were based.

Taking advantage of a brief break in the poor weather, Lindbergh took off from Roosevelt Field, New York, at 07.54 on May 20. Shortly after 22.00 on the following day, *Spirit of St Louis* touched down at Le Bourget after a flight lasting 33 hours, 30 minutes and 29.8 seconds. He had overcome fog, icing, storms, fatigue and disorientation to get there. Just over two weeks later, Clarence Chamberlin and Charles Levine flew non-stop from New York to Eisleben in Germany. Lindbergh's triumph had been a close-run thing.

Left: Shortly before the war, Lindbergh paid several visits to Germany to see the nation's growing aerial might. He is seen here at an international flying meeting in Berlin in 1936. The aircraft in the background is a Czechoslovakian Avia BH122 aerobatic aircraft.

Above: Lindbergh's Ryan NYP, named *Spirit of St Louis* (after the city of its sponsors), was taken on a grand tour after his triumphant return to the United States. Thousands came to see the pilot and the monoplane, and a host of honors were feted upon the pioneer,

AIR PHOTO
BY—

luding the first peacetime Congressional Medal of Honor and the first
tinguished Flying Cross. He was a hero to a generation of Americans
ed to seeking their heroes on the sports field.

More Records Fall

It is generally agreed that the greatest of all the long-distance pilots of the 1930s was Wiley Post, a famous barnstorming American Indian who had only one eye, and was distinguished for wearing a black patch. With a navigator, Harold Gatty, he took off in Lockheed 5C Vega from New York on June 23, 1931 and landed back there after making a circuit of the globe in 8 days, 15 hours and 51 minutes. The distance flown was nearly 15,500 miles (24,945km). Two years later Wiley Post set off again to repeat the flight, this time on his own and in less time.

In Italy, in 1931, the Air Minister, General Italo Balbo, was only 35 years old. He attracted worldwide attention to himself and his service in January that year by leading a formation of ten Savoia S55 twin-hulled flying boats from Portuguese Guinea to Natal (Brazil). On July 1, 1933, he led off a formation of twenty-four of the same aircraft from Orbetello, in Italy, to Chicago. They flew via Iceland and landed at their destination on the 15th. The formation took off for home on July 25, lost an aircraft in the Azores, and arrived back in Italy on August 12.

The first east-west Atlantic crossing was made by Hermann Köhl, Captain J. Fitzmaurice and Baron von Hunefeld in the Junkers-W33 Bremen on April 12-13, 1928. James Mollison first attracted public attention when he flew his Puss Moth from England to Australia in under nine days, a record. On May 20-21, 1932, he made the first solo east-west Atlantic crossing, as well as setting a London-Cape Town record. His wife (the renowned Amy Johnson) broke this record later in the year. In July 1933 both Mollisons flew a DH84 Dragon from Pendine, in Wales, to Bridgeport, Connecticut, where they were both injured in a crash landing.

Record flights dominated the aviation scene in the 1930s, and one of the most useful was the flight over Mount Everest on April 3, 1933, because it yielded valuable information about the problems in flying at very high altitude, buffeted by swirling winds. The two aircraft were a Westland PV3, flown by the Mar-

Right: The Hawker Fury, powered by a water-cooled 525hp Rolls-Royce Kestrel 12-cylinder vee, was the epitome of the elegant, high-speed biplane fighter of the 1930s. These are aircraft of No 1 Squadron, RAF, in 1936.

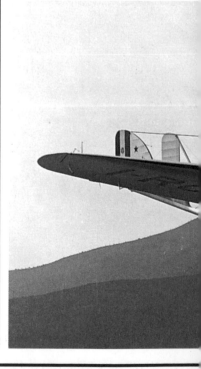

Right: A pair of Italian Savoia-Marchetti S55X flying boats which took part in General Balbo's second mass Atlantic crossing to visit the 1933 Chicago World's Fair. They were powered by two 850hp Isotta-Fraschini 18-cylinder water-cooled inline engines mounted in tandem.

Above: Jimmy Doolittle poses with Shell Oil's Lockheed 9C Orion Shellightning in 1932. Wingspan 42ft 10in (13.05m), length 27ft 10in (8.48m), height 9ft 8in (2.95m), weight 3,325lb (1,508kg), engine óne 550hp Pratt & Whitney Wasp 9-cylinder radial air-cooled, cruising speed 200mph (322kph), range 750 miles (1,207km), crew 1, passengers 6.

quess of Clydesdale, and a Westland Wallace flown by Flight Lieutenant D. F. McIntyre.

AIR RACES

The Schneider Trophy race of 1931 was a welcome antidote, in Europe and the USA, to the Depression that had afflicted the world for the previous two years. Jacques Schneider, a Frenchman born in 1879, was a racing driver who learned to fly in 1911. In 1913 he instituted a trophy for the winner of a seaplane race – an event that was to have a significant influence over the design of high-speed aircraft.

The first contest was held in Monaco in 1913: 28 laps of a 10km (6.2 miles) course. It was won by a Frenchman in a Deperdussin monotype at an average speed of 45.75 mph (73.63kph). The following year a British pilot won with a Sopwith Tabloid at 86.78mph (139.66kph). In 1923 a US Army Air Corps team won

at 177mph (285kph). The USA won again in 1925 at Baltimore with 233mph (375kph). Three wins in succession would gain permanent possession of the trophy. The Americans were regarded as certain winners in 1924, but their competitors were obliged to withdraw and they sportingly canceled the event.

In 1925 Britain entered a Supermarine S4, designed by R. J. Mitchell and flown by an RAF officer, but it crashed. A Gloster biplane that also competed was easily beaten. The Americans won again. In 1926 Italy won with a Macchi M29. In 1927, at Venice, the RAF team won with Mitchell's Supermarine S5, and again in England in 1929 with the S6. In 1931 the RAF's S6B triumphed at

340.08mph (547.29kph), flown by Flight Lieutenant J. N. Boothman, thus retaining the trophy in perpetuity. The Rolls-Royce 2,300hp engine was then boosted to 2,550hp and the aircraft set a new world seaplane record of 407.5mph (655.8kph) later that year. Mitchell based the design for the Spitfire on these three seaplanes.

The Italian seaplanes that had competed in the 1929 race had many differences between them. The Macchi M67 had a 1800hp Isotta-Fraschini engine. The Fiat C29 was very small, with a lightweight 1,000hp AS5 engine. Some of the aircraft were quaintly unconventional. The SM65 was a monoplane with twin floats and twin booms, and had a 1,000hp

Isotta-Fraschini engine driving a tractor propeller at the front of the central nacelle and a similar engine at the rear, driving a pusher propeller.

Air races saw increasingly better times set by the competitors, which in turn brought forth faster fighters and bombers. One of the great heroes of military and civil aviation is an American, James (Jimmy) Doolittle. As a fighter pilot, he won the Schneider Trophy in 1925. In 1930 he joined the Shell Company and in 1932 won an annual air race in the USA, the Thomson Trophy, flying a closed circuit around pylons. In the same year he set a new landplane record of 296.287mph (476.815kph), flying a Gee Bee R-1 Super Sportster. He rejoined the US Army Air Corps in 1940 as a major, flew bombers and rose to lieutenant-general. In 1942 he led a hazardous but morale-boosting raid on Japan by sixteen B-25 Mitchell bombers flying from a carrier.

The many annual races held in the USA bred several racing airplanes, most of which were one-offs. The Travel Air "Mystery" of 1929 had a top speed of 235mph (378kph). The Wedell-Williams achieved a speed of 266.674 mph (429.158kph) in 1932. In 1939 the Crosby CR-4 recorded 263mph (423kph) with a 350hp engine.

In Britain the King's Cup Air Race was graced by royal patronage. It was meant to be held annually over a 700-750 mile (1,120-1,200km) course, but the distance was considerably shortened as years went by. The first was flown in 1922, and in 1930 it was won by a woman, Miss Winifred Brown. The race encouraged the design of racing aircraft such as the Mew Gull and Miles Hawk Speed Six.

One of the fastest seaplanes ever built was the Macchi MC72, which in 1934 set a world seaplane record of 440.681mph (709.188kph).

By 1930, military aircraft had attained a streamlined beauty. The Hawker Hart, a two-seater day bomber first delivered to the RAF in

Above: Hawker Hart light day bombers of No 57 Squadron, RAF. The Hart served from 1930 to 1939. Wingspan 37ft 3in (11.35m), length 29ft 4in (8.9m), height 10ft 5in (3.18m), weight 2,530lb 1,148kg), engine one 525hp Rolls-Royce Kestrel 12-cylinder vee watercooled, maximum speed 184mph (296kph), range 470 miles (756km), crew 2.

Above: An assortment of aircraft line up for the start of the 1938 King's Cup Air Race. Front to rear: de Havilland Technical School TK2, Miles M2L Hawk Speed Six, de Havilland DH88 Comet racer, and two Percival P6 New Gulls, the nearer of which won the race.

January, was both fast and manœuverable. Steel-structured but fabric-covered, it was capable of a maximum speed of 184mph (296kph), faster than contemporary British fighters. The Hawker Demon two-seat fighter that joined its first squadron three years later was 3mph (5kph) slower. The Hawker Fury single-seat fighter, however, could make 223mph (357kph), and a batch sold to Yugoslavia were 10mph (16kph) faster. The Hawker Hurricane MkI, which first flew in 1935, attained 316mph (509kph), while the Spitfire I of 1937 clocked 355mph (571kph).

In the USA the Boeing P-26A of 1933 achieved 234mph (377kph) and the Curtiss P-36 302mph (486kph). In Germany the pretty Ar 68E flew at 202mph (324kph), and the Messerschmitt Bf 109B-2, 280mph (450kph). In the USSR the 1933 Polikarpov I-15 attained 224mph (360kph), while the 1934 Polikarpov I-16 flew at 362mph (582kph). In Italy the mid-1930s biplane Fiat CR42 had a top speed of 221mph (355kph). In Japan the 1932

Mitsubichi A5M could reach 265mph (426kph).

In 1937 the British company Napier had started development of a 24-cylinder engine, the Sabre, in which high hopes were invested by both the company and the Air Ministry. It turned out to be a compendium of imperfections when installed in the Typhoon fighter a few years later, but one of the lesser-known airplane constructors, Heston Aircraft, welcomed it in its early days as the power unit for its Heston Racer, which was judged to be capable of 520mph (837kph). Unluckily for the firm, it suffered an accident on its first flight, and the outbreak of war compelled Heston to abandon it.

COMMERCIAL AIRCRAFT DEVELOPMENTS

In the USA, Douglas, Boeing and Lockheed were all making great strides in a totally different sector of aircraft construction, the design and production of airliners.

In Europe rapid growth in passenger air traffic spawned a bewildering variety of commercial airplanes. The earliest Imperial Airways type to establish itself in the favor of British travelers was the Handley Page HP42, which made its first flight on November 17, 1930. A useful feature was the short takeoff and landing run, which enabled it to use relatively small grass airfields. The crew numbered three and there was room for thirty-eight passengers.

One of the most elegant types was an improved version of the DH Dragon, the Dragon Rapide, which accommodated ten passengers and was first seen in 1934. The RAF bought 521, renamed the type Dominie, and used them for communications and as a radio trainer at Electrical and Wireless Schools.

Some very odd military and civil aircraft were on offer in the 1930s.

The Handley Page HP47 general-purpose military monoplane was on with its pod and boom fuselage th allowed a rear gunner the widest possible field of fire. The Blériot 125 ha a twin-boom fuselage, in each which six passengers were seate and the two-man crew occupied cockpit above the fuselage. Th British Burnelli monoplane, with i aerofoil-shape fuselage tha increased lift and improved efficienc carried fifteen passengers and ha two 750hp Perseus engines. Th type was also built in the USA.

FLIGHT REFUELING

Refueling in flight was of great inte est to airlines. In July 1935 two Ame icans, Al and Fred Key, spent 653h 34min flying around the airport Meridian, Mississippi, in a Curtis Robin that was refueled in the air. Thi

d to the founding in 1936 of a company in Britain, called Flight Refuelling Ltd., to develop this procedure. The company had two Vickers Virginias, an Armstrong Whitworth AW23, a Handley Page HP51, a Vickers B19/27 and Boulton Paul Overstrand converted to carry the fuel.

The Imperial Airways technical adviser, Major Robert Mayo, proposed an alternative method to refueling in flight, in which a small, heavily loaded airplane would be placed on top of a big one that would fly it off the ground and release it at cruising height and speed. In 1938 Imperial Airways agreed to provide a Southampton-New York flying boat service, to be refueled in the air, after practice had been carried out with a Short C Class flying boat, the Cambria. Two Short flying boats, Cabot and Caribou, were to be refueled by

HP Harrows that had been converted to tankers. *Caribou* took off on the first flight on August 5, 1939, landed at Shannon on the west coast of Ireland to refuel and was refueled again over the Atlantic by a Harrow. On the return journey the boat was refueled off Newfoundland.

Transatlantic services also attracted France and Germany, both of which operated over the south Atlantic. Aéropostale flew between Paris and Dakar, in West Africa, and along the South American east coast from Natal to Buenos Aires. Mail was taken only part of the way by air. From Dakar to Natal, Brazil, it was taken by sea. In 1936, after Air France took on the mail, it was flown all the way.

From 1930 to 1932 the German air line Deutsche Luft Hansa was also assisted by ships that took mail from the Canary Islands to Fernando do Noronha, in Brazil.

In 1932 a fleet of seaplane/flying boat depot ships made their first appearance and refueled Dornier Wal flying boats in mid-ocean. The aircraft would alight alongside the steamer, which hoisted it aboard, refueled and serviced it, then shot it into the air by catapult. As this last ministration imposed a 4.5g acceleration, the method was confined to cargo carriers. Mail flights also crossed the North Atlantic in the same manner, using Heinkel He 12 seaplanes launched when 300 miles from New York. Next, Dornier Do 18 flying boats replaced them and refueled alongside a liner, *Schwabenland*, halfway across.

Left: Even before his solo Atlantic flight, Charles A. Lindbergh had achieved fame and respect as a professional pilot, here seen helping the U.S. Mail to open up South American air routes. After the Atlantic flight he made several others over the Caribbean and Central America, and from Alaska to Japan, and around the Atlantic, surveying potential airline routes.

LONG DISTANCES

The year 1934 was a momentous one for flying: it saw the longest air race ever held before or since (England to Australia). Sir William MacPherson MacRobertson donated the prizes. Two trophies were to be competed for concurrently: an open one for sheer speed and the other a handicap contest. The destination, Melbourne, had been chosen to mark the centenary of the Australian city's foundation.

Among the entries were three of a new type specially built by de Havilland, the DH88 Comet, a twin-engined, two-seater, long-range, low-wing cantilever monoplane. There was no restriction on the number of crew. Every effort had been made to ensure that the race was as safe as possible. Lifebelts and at least three days' provisions had to be taken.

Of the sixty-four airplanes originally entered in the first flush of ambition, only twenty eventually took part. The competitors started from Mildenhall, Suffolk, and were watched by a crowd of 60,000. Numbers had been drawn for starting order and Jim and Amy Mollison were off first. The Mollisons were also the first to reach Baghdad – in 12hr 40min. Next came the two other Comets.

The Mollisons arrived at Karachi in record time, 22hr 13min, but had to retire with mechanical problems. C. W. A. Scott and T. Campbell Black won the race in 70hr 54min, a great credit to the Comet's two 230hp Gipsy 6 engines. The handicap winner was a standard Douglas DC2 airliner of KLM.

The Comet inspired many designers to use its shape as a template. The sleek Caudron C41 Typhon high-speed mail plane was one of the derivatives.

Also to put its stamp on the year 1934, with its first flight on June 19, was an aerial extravaganza that could only have been conceived in Russia – the ANT-20. This was an A. N. Tupolev

design built by TSAGI (Central Hydr[o] and Aerodynamic Institute) an[d] named *Maxim Gorki*. It had a crew [of] twenty-three and could carry for[ty] passengers. Illuminated electric signs and slogans could be displaye[d] under its wings. The wings and fuse-lage accommodated a printing pres[s], radio broadcasting unit, and cir[ema] equipment for disseminating prop[a]ganda leaflets and films.

Flying a Percival Vega Gull, C. W. A. Scott had another impressive vi[c]tory in 1936, partnered this time [by] Giles Guthrie. The event was th[e]

Right: The "St. Louis Robin" refuels in mid-air as the pilots Dale Jackson and Forrest O'Brien keep their aircraft in the air for a record-setting $17\frac{1}{2}$ days endurance flight, July 13-30, 1929.

chlesinger race from Portsmouth, ngland, to Johannesburg, South frica. They were the only competi- rs to finish the distance.

Since the Wright brothers had first own, the proprietors of the *Daily Mail* ewspaper had been generous and ar-sighted in providing financial incen- ves for the advance of aviation. In 935 Lord Rothermere, the newspa- er's owner, distressed by the British ir Ministry's lack of enterprise, had an irplane built for him that he was cer- ain would galvanise the Air Marshals to awareness that the RAF's aircraft were not keeping up with the times.

This handsome monoplane, the Bristol 142, which he named Britain First, was a four-passenger executive transport with a top speed of 307mph (494kph). As that was 100mph (161kph) faster than any British fighter, Rothermere's psychological ploy proved successful: the Air Ministry ordered a bomber that would be on much the same lines. In consequence, the Blenheim made its first flight on June 25, 1936, and entered squadron service in 1937. A night fighter variant followed it in December 1938.

The Flight of *Winnie Mae*

> '*With a good railroad to follow, I had no trouble navigating. The only time I can get lost following a railroad is when there are two of them... I rocked the plane when Irkutsk hove into sight. I knew it must be Irkutsk, because we had passed only a few isolated way stations on the line, and I hadn't heard of any other cities in those parts. In fact, I had never heard of Irkutsk until I planned a flight around the world.*'
>
> WILEY POST

Wiley Post was the personal pilot of oilman F. C. Hall, whose aircraft, a Lockheed 5C Vega, was named *Winnie Mae* after Hall's daughter, Mrs. Fain.

Aviation was Hall's abiding interest and, at a time when he had little need of a personal aircraft, he encouraged Post to look for new uses. Post did not have far to look; his imagination was fired when the airship *Graf Zeppelin* circled the world in twenty-one days. This was the record that he not only set out to beat, but to halve.

His first need was for a first-class navigator, and the man chosen was Harold Gatty, a Tasmanian who ran a navigation school. Together they began to plan the flight, while the *Winnie Mae* was modified to give greater range, with greatest care being taken to ensure that the trim would not change too much as the fuel was used. Gatty was also part of this operation; he was to shift backwards and forwards as required to balance out the load. Post also had an armchair fitted for greater comfort for long periods at the controls.

Right: Wiley Post emerges from the cockpit of his Lockheed 5C Vega high-wing monoplane, *Winnie Mae*. He was the greatest of all the American long-distance pilots of the 1930s, his round the world flight in June 1931 dramatically beating the previous record time of 21 days set up by the airship *Graf Zeppelin*.

Modifications were not confined to the Vega. Post schooled himself in irregular sleep patterns for months before the flight, to increase tolerance to fatigue, as he realized that

he would be unable to operate to a fixed schedule.

Shortly after dawn on June 23, 1931, *Winnie Mae* lifted off from Roosevelt Field, New York, and set course for Harbour Grace, Newfoundland. The next stage was the longest, a direct crossing of the North Atlantic to Sealand, near Chester in England. The weather was poor, but they made landfall with little difficulty.

The next stop was Berlin, then on to Moscow, before beginning the long haul across Russia via Novosibirsk, Irkutsk, Blagoveshchensk and Khabarovsk. The Russians had provided new maps, but these were of limited value only, and Gatty relied on the

old navigator's trick of edging constantly to the left, so that when the time came to search they could turn to the right without having to guess.

Despite bad weather, incidents were few until Irkutsk, where *Winnie Mae* bogged down in the mud on landing. Herculean efforts got her clear, and they took off again after a twelve-hour delay.

From Khabarovsk they crossed to Alaska,, landing at Solomon to refuel. Taxiing out to take off once more, near-disaster struck when *Winnie Mae* sank in soft sand and bent her propeller tips. The resourceful Post effected a temporary repair with the aid of "a wrench, a broken-handled hammer and a round

stone!" The rest of the flight was comparatively uneventful, and they touched down at Roosevelt Field just 8 days, 15 hours and 51 minutes after they had left.

Winnie Mae's adventures were not over. Two years later, flying solo, Post repeated the trip with fewer stops, setting a new record of 7 days 18 hours 49 minutes.

Above: Wiley Post (right) with navigator Harold Gatty. Their record-breaking flight was a great technical achievement, and one of great fortitude, since they and their Vega spent over 106 hours in the air covering nearly 15,500 miles (24,945km), with no chance of sleep except at stops.

Flying Boats

In the infancy of aviation airplanes were frequently damaged by heavy landings. It occurred to some pilots and constructors that to alight on water might obviate this. In 1913 an American, Glenn L. Curtiss, accordingly replaced the pontoons on one of his seaplanes by a boat-shaped hull, with which he carried out successful trials. The first European to emulate him was T. O. M. Sopwith with his amphibious Bat Boat, a year later. The First World War accelerated development. In Britain, John Porte, a squadron commander in the Royal Naval Air Service (RNAS), designed flying boats with a V-shaped hull, which was the most important improvement.

For landplanes, increasingly large airfields were needed, with all the expenses of real estate, hangars, terminal buildings and airfield lighting. The overheads for operating flying boats and floatplanes were much lower.

In 1926 the Short Singapore, the first flying boat of metal stressed-skin construction, was launched. The following year the three-engine Short Calcutta began to fly the Mediterranean sector of the Imperial Airways England to India route. The Short Kent followed, and in 1935 the same company began the production of 18 four-engine Empire class boats with four 910hp Bristol Pegasus engines, the first of which flew in July 1936. They carried twenty-four passengers, who slept aboard, and two tons of mail and freight. Cruising speed was 164mph (264kph), maximum speed 200mph (322kph) and range 810 miles (1,300km). Two years later a daily service was in operation from England to Egypt, four a week were flying from England to India, three to East Africa and two each to South Africa, Malaya and Australia.

When Pan American Airlines decided to introduce a transpacific service, starting from San Francisco, it could be done only by stages via islands. Landing facilities already

Above: A Pan American Sikorsky S-42 Clipper at Foynes, Ireland, after inaugurating an experimental transatlantic service in July 1937. These aircraft had four 700hp Pratt & Whitney Hornet 9-cylinder air-cooled radial engines, which gave them a cruising speed of 170mph (274km/h) and a range of 1,200 miles (1,930km).

Left: Pan American began operating the Martin M-130, carrying 14 passengers, on transpacific services in 1935. Powered by four 950hp Pratt & Whitney R-1830 Twin Wasp 14-cylinder air-cooled radial engines and spanning 130ft (39.6m), they remained with the airline until 1942.

existed at Honolulu and Manila and two more were created at Guam and Wake Island. The stages were: San Francisco-Hawaii 2,295 miles (3,693km), Hawaii-Wake 2,414 miles (3,885km), Wake-Guam 1,500 miles (2,414km), Guam-Manilla 1,594 miles (2,565km). The airline's specification for the necessary aircraft required a flying boat capable of flying 2,500 miles (4,020km) into a 30mph (48kph) headwind while carrying a crew of four and at least 200lb (90kg) of mail. Martin built three M-130 flying boats with four 800/950hp Pratt & Whitney Twin Wasp engines that could carry forty-one passengers: but only fourteen seats were fitted for the Pacific run. Cruising speed was 157mph (253km) and

range 3,200 miles (5,150km) – or 4,000 miles (6,440km) if carrying freight only. The boats were named *China Clipper*, *Philippine Clipper* and *Hawaii Clipper*. The mail service began on November 22, 1935, with a 59hr 40min flight. From October 21, 1936, passengers were also carried.

On June 26, 1937, Imperial Airways began a Bermuda-New York service with the C-class flying boat *Cavalier*, and Pan American followed suit with the Sikorsky S-42 *Clipper III*. On July 5-6, the long-range class *Caledonia* made Foynes, on the river Shannon in Ireland, to Botwood in Newfoundland, Canada, in 15hr 3min, then on to Montreal, while *Clipper III* flew in the reverse direction and continued to Southampton.

Above: The Short S23 C-Class Empire flying boats were introduced into service by Imperial Airways in 1936. Four 920hp Bristol Pegasus 9-cylinder air-cooled radial engines gave them a cruising speed of 165mph (265.5kph), and they carried up to 24 passengers. The cockpit is shown in the inset.

Neither of these aircraft carried enough fuel for commercial services, so, after an experimental air refueling exercise, C class flying boats were built to take-off with full payload and be refueled in flight.

The ubiquitous Sunderland was a direct development of the C-class and served throughout the Second World War in the maritime patrol and anti-submarine role.

In 1938 the Boeing 314 Clippers, flagships of Pan American Airlines, began a transatlantic service which was maintained throughout the Second World War.

During the war the development of long-range troop and cargo transport aircraft progressed far ahead of flying boats' performance and the number of airfields increased enormously. These factors, and the fact that not all big cities have expanses of water conveniently near, soon led to the disappearance of large passenger or freight flying boats.

Over Everest

> *Somewhat to my dismay Everest bore that immense snow plume which means a mighty wind tearing across the summit, lifting clouds of powdered snow and driving it with blizzard force eastward. Up went the machine into a sky of indescribable blue till we came on a level with the great peak itself. This astonishing picture of Everest, its plume now gradually lessening, its tremendous southern cliffs flanked by Makalu, was a sight which must remain in the mind all the years of one's life.*
>
> Lt. Col. L. V. Stewart Blacker

By 1932 aircraft had reached almost every corner of the globe, but one place remained unexplored. Mount Everest, at 29,030ft (8,848m), was not only the world's highest peak; it was located in a remote and inaccessible area of the Himalayas.

Attaining a greater altitude than Everest was not the problem. What was needed was an aircraft with the endurance to reach the area from a base some considerable distance away, and the ability to sustain the necessary altitude plus a significant safety margin for an extended period and operate in the teeth of some of the world's most severe and unpredictable weather. Backing came from Britain's Air Ministry, the Royal Geographical Society, and Lady Houston. The purpose of the flight was twofold: patriotic flag-waving, and a photographic survey.

The airplanes had to be two-seaters with large wing area and

Right: The Houston-Westland PV.3 approaches the highest point on Earth for the first flight over Mount Everest, on April 3, 1933, one of the greatest moments in flying history.

room for cameras and other equipment. They had to be capable of being fitted with supercharged Bristol Pegasus radial engines, and to have sufficient ground clearance to allow the use of an oversize propeller. The choice fell on a torpedo bomber, the Westland PV.3, with a Westland Wallace military general-purpose machine as backup. Both were extensively modified.

The base selected was Purnea in India, some 150 miles (241km) south of Everest, which was reached on March 22, 1933. It then became a matter of waiting for favorable conditions. Three de Havilland Moths were

in support, and on April 3 one of these reported the mountain peaks clear and wind speed at altitude 57mph. (92kph). This was stronger than desirable, but the PV.3 (by now renamed the Houston Westland), flown by Lord Clydesdale and Lt. Col. Stewart Blacker, and the Wallace with F1t. Lt. David McIntyre and cameraman Sidney Bonnet, took off at 08.25.

Not until 19,000ft (5,791m) did they clear the ground haze, to see three brilliant white peaks towering above the clouds: Makalu and Kachenjunga off to the right, and Everest straight ahead, its summit streaming a

ierce white plume of snow. On they flew, climbing steadily over huge mountains and glaciers – impossible country for a forced landing.

As they approached Everest a downdraught sent them plunging 2,000ft (610m). Clawing to regain height, they were then swept on an updraught, and at last cleared the summit of the world's highest mountain by the perilously small margin of 500ft (150m).

They circled the summit for fifteen minutes in winds gusting up to 120mph (193kph), with ice from the plume rattling against the wings. Then cameraman Bonnet collapsed

in his cockpit. This was not surprising; he had earlier trodden on his oxygen feed and repaired it with his handkerchief. The two Westlands, now turned for home, touching down after a flight lasting just three hours.

Below: The Houston-Westland PV.3 machine, one of two biplanes used in the aerial survey expedition in the Himalayas, during the course of which it made the first-ever flight over Mount Everest. It was fitted with specially supercharged Bristol Pegasus engines.

Women Pioneer Pilots

The first woman pilot to arouse international interest was Britain's Amy Johnson, who took off from Croydon on May 5, 1930, for Australia in a de Havilland Gipsy Moth that she had named *Jason*. The press paid little attention to her until she arrived at Karachi in six days, a new record: thenceforth she was in the headlines and remained there for the rest of her life. On her arrival in Australia on May 24 Britain's *Daily Mail* awarded her £10,000. In the summer of 1931 she flew *Jason II*, a de Havilland Puss Moth, to Tokyo via Moscow.

In 1932 she married Jim Mollison, a world-famous flyer. A year later, between July 22 and 24, 1933, they flew in a twin-engine de Havilland Dragon from Pendine, in Wales to Bridgeport, Connecticut – where they crash-landed. The following year they entered a de Havilland DH88 Comet in the Mildenhall-Melbourne race, but retired at Karachi with mechanical trouble.

During the Second World War Amy joined the Air Transport Auxiliary (ATA), which delivered aircraft from factories and maintenance units to squadrons. She died in a crash, flying an Airspeed Oxford, in foul weather over the Thames estuary in January 1941.

In 1934 Jean Batten, a New Zealander, became the first woman to make a return flight from Australia to England. Such was the general ignorance about flying that when she arrived at Cyprus she found the windsock tied down to its mast to protect it from wind damage. On November 11, 1935, flying a Percival Gull, she made the first South Atlantic crossing by a woman. Between October 15 and 16, 1936,

Right: Amy Johnson flew her de Havilland DH60 Gipsy Moth, *Jason*, from Croydon to Darwin in 1930 to complete the first England–Australia solo flight by a woman.

piloting the same aeroplane, she became the first woman to make the flight from Britain to New Zealand. Her time of 11 days and 45 minutes broke the record.

An American, Amelia Earhart, in a Lockheed Vega, was the first woman to fly solo across the Atlantic on May 20–21, 1932. In 1935 she achieved two more firsts: Hawaii-California, January 11–12, a flight of 18hr 16min, and Mexico City-New Jersey. In 1937, on a round-the-world attempt in a twin-engine Lockheed Electra, with Fred Noon navigating, they were both lost without trace somewhere over the Pacific.

Below: American aviatrix Amelia Earhart's choice for her 1937 attempt on a round-the-world flight was a Lockheed Model 10-E Electra Special with a pair of Pratt & Whitney R-1340 Wasp S3H1s.

Left: Jean Batten poses with the Percival Gull Six, powered by a 200hp de Havilland Gipsy Six 6-cylinder inline engine, which was her mount for her record-breaking long-distance flights in the mid-1930s.

The Short-Mayo Composite

In the late 1930s mail between Europe and the American continent went by sea. There was a great demand for an airmail service. Prompted by this, and taking into account the high cost of in-flight refueling, an ingenious alternative was conceived by Imperial Airways' Technical General Manager, Major Robert Mayo. To avoid the expense of replenishing fuel while airborne and making enough fuel available for a long journey, he suggested that a huge multi-engine flying boat should give a "lift" to a smaller, but heavily laden, seaplane. The engines of both aircraft would combine to produce the power necessary for lift-off and for the initial climb.

Short Brothers designed and built the S.21 flying boat, which had a wingspan of 114ft (34.7m), was 84ft 11in (25.9m) long and was named *Maia*. Its four 920hp Bristol Pegasus nine-cylinder radial engines gave it a maximum speed of 200mph (320kph) and it had a range of 850 miles (1,360km). *Maia* made its maiden flight on July 27, 1937. The S.20 seaplane, named *Mercury*, which first flew on September 5 the same year, had a 73ft (22.3m)

Right: A close-up of the superstructure on the flying boat *Maia*, which enabled it to carry the smaller, heavily laden seaplane *Mercury* on its back to assist it into the air.

Below: The composite at rest at Rochester. *Maia* had Bristol Pegasus radial engines, while *Mercury* had Napier Rapier inlines.

wingspan and was 50ft 11in (15.5m) long. Its engines were four 340hp Napier Rapiers, its maximum speed was 195mph (314kph) and its range 3,900 miles (6,276km).

The first composite flight of the two aircraft took place on January 20, 1938, and they made their first in-flight separation on February 6, 1938.

On July 21, 1938, *Mercury*, after becoming airborne by this unortho-dox means, made the first transat-lantic crossing by an airplane whose main cargo was mail and newspa-pers. *Maia* had taken off, carrying *Mercury*, from Shannon; *Mercury* alighted at Montreal 20 hours and 20 minutes later. From there it flew to Port Washington, New York, but made no more commercial flights. Like many other good ideas, the innovation proved not to be economi-cally viable.

Above: A dramatic study of *Mercury* leaving Southampton, southern England, for Foynes, Ireland, in July 1938, in readiness for its first transatlantic flight. After the first commercial separation, on July 21, it flew nonstop to Montreal in 20 hours 20 minutes.

Three months later *Maia* launched *Mercury* near Dundee to start it on a flight of 6,000 miles (9,656km) to the Orange River in South Africa that set a long-distance record for seaplanes.

Left: *Mercury* is carefully lowered on to its parent flying boat during airworthiness trials at the Marine Aircraft Experimental Establishment at Felixstowe, Suffolk. The last commercial separations were made on November 29, 1938, and January 12, 1939.

The Immortal DC-3

> ' ... as you approached Arnhem you got the impression
> that there wasn't wing-span room between flak bursts,
> not to mention the small-arms fire! To my right a Dakota,
> I think flown by F1t. Lt. Lord, caught fire. Having dropped
> our load, we banked and weaved as violently as possible
> to avoid fire from the ground and headed home.
> ...I never ceased to be amazed at the damage the Dakota
> could sustain and continue to fly. One came back with
> a hole in the fuselage large enough to push a chair through. '
>
> FLT. LT. ALEC BLYTHE

Arguably the most successful and certainly the longest-lived transport aircraft of all time, the Douglas Sleeper Transport, piloted by Carl Cover, made its maiden flight from Clover Field, California, on December 17, 1935. Initially configured to carry fourteen passengers in sleeping berths, or twenty-one seated, in its long career it has carried everything from mules to rolls of newsprint.

The DC-3, as it is better known, was technically advanced for its day. By 1938 it dominated the American domestic market, providing 95percent of all scheduled services, and by the following year, now used by thirty overseas airlines, the DC-3 accounted for 90percent of the world's airline traffic.

The DC-3 was soon adopted by the military, and it quickly became a mainstay of Allied transport squadrons during the Second World War as the C-53 Skytrooper and C-47 Skytrain in US service, and as the Dakota with Britain's RAF. The difference between the two US designations was that, while the C-53 was primarily a troop-carrier, the C-47 was modified to carry heavy freight.

Right: A US Army Air Force C-47 of the 9th Troop Carrier Command drops parachuting supplies to Allied forces in Bastogne, Belgium, December 23, 1944, in support of the continuing Overlord drive to eliminate German forces from Europe.

At war, DC-3s carried out many missions apart from basic cargo and troop-carrying, however. They towed gliders, dropped paratroopers, air-dropped supplies, and flew out the wounded.

The DC-3's list of Second World War battle honors is almost endless. It took part in the Allied landings in North Africa in November 1942, the invasion of Sicily, the D-Day landings, the insertion and supply of the Chindits behind Japanese lines in Burma, and flew the notorious "Hump" sup-

ply route between India and China, which involved crossing the Himalayas, often in atrocious weather conditions.

The airborne operation at Arnhem in September 1944 saw C-47s in intense action. They flew out in neat vics, low enough for the crews in their cockpits to be seen from the ground. Later they returned, here a propeller feathered, there holes in wings or tail, cowlings black with oil, often trailing ropes of thick gray smoke, but somehow still flying. Sad-

Above: A special DC-3: A US Air Force EC-47 assigned to the 360th Tactical Electronic Warfare Squadron, in a flight over the Republic of Vietnam during hostilities there, April 9, 1970.

Right: Curtains at the windows of this unpainted DC-3 confirm its peaceful role as an airliner. The DC did more than any other aircraft to develop and establish a reliable system of world airlines.

dest of all was when only two came back where three had gone out.

While only 803 civilian DC-3s were built, military requirements added another 10,123, plus about 2,700 license-built in the Soviet Union as Lisunov Li-2s. Many DC-3s flew on the Berlin Airlift of 1948/49.

Even in major air forces the C-47 soldiered on into the 1970s. In USAF service, as the EC-47, it was equipped with sensors for electronic

reconnaissance, while the AC-47 was fitted out as a gunship and used in Vietnam in the defense suppression role.

Well over 400 DC-3/C-47s have served with a total of forty-four nations. The flight regime is so benign that fatigue is almost unknown, and this has led two companies to offer turboprop conversions, remarkable for a design nearing its three score years and ten!

The Helicopter

> ' *Professor Focke and his technicians standing below grew ever smaller as I continued to rise straight up, 50 meters, 75 meters, 100 meters. Then I gently began to throttle back and the speed of ascent dwindled till I was hovering motionless in midair. This was intoxicating! I thought of the lark, so light and small of wing, hovering over the summer fields. Now Man had wrested from him his lovely secret.*'
>
> HANNA REITSCH

Hanna Reitsch, famous German woman test pilot of the 1930s was lyrical about her first helicopter flight in the latter half of 1937. Technical difficulties had delayed development of this flying machine, and it was not until twenty-nine years after Cornu's first flight that a really practical helicopter was developed.

This was the Focke-Achgelis Fa 61, powered by a 160hp Bramo, radial engine. Two shaft-driven rotors were carried on outriggers attached to each side of the fuselage, set to rotate in opposite directions. Lateral and directional control was by means of differential operation of the cyclic pitch to produce asymmetric lift.

The first flight, by test pilot Ewald Rohlfs, took place on June 26, 1937, and lasted just 28 seconds. Gradually the machine was developed, and starting the following year it set a whole series of world records.

On June 25, 1937, it reached 8,002ft (2,439m) altitude, and remained aloft for 1 hour, 20 minutes and 49 seconds. The very next day it established a distance record of 10.2 miles (16.4km) a closed-circuit distance record of 50.08 miles (80.604km), and a speed in a straight line record of 76.128mph

Right: On February 19, 1939, the world's first woman helicopter pilot, Hanna Reisch, spectacularly flew the Fa 61 inside the Deutschlandhalle, Berlin, flying in all directions and in every possible corner of the hall, and also holding the machine stationary.

(122.553kph, 66.13kt). Rohlfs was the pilot in each case.

Hanna Reitsch then entered the record arena on October 25 with a flight of 68 miles (109km) between Bremen and Berlin. In February the following year she made a well-publicized series of flights inside the Deutschlandhalle, although this was not all that well received by the public, who failed to realize the significance of what they were seeing. Two further records were set before the outbreak of war: straightline distance of 143 miles (230km) on June 20, 1938, and altitude at 11,244ft (3,427m) on January 29, 1939. The pilot in both cases was Karl Bode.

While the Fa 61 demonstrated that the helicopter was at last a practical proposition, it lacked the ability to perform a really useful role. Larger size and greater power were the answers, and it was followed by the Fa 223 Drache, first flown in August 1940.

The Drache retained the twin rotors on outriggers, was powered by a 1,000hp Bramo, and had a fully enclosed cabin. Designed for the transport, anti-submarine, rescue and reconnaissance roles, it was ordered

in quantity, but only a handful were produced, mainly owing to Allied bombing.

In September 1945 a lone Drache was flown across the English Channel for evaluation, its German crew accompanied by RAF personnel, but it was destroyed in an accident the following month.

The twin-rotor configuration of the Focke-Achgelis design was unwieldy, and American pioneers Bell and Sikorsky used the "penny-farthing" layout in their Model 30 and VS-300 machines, as did the Sikorsky R-4, which was used on operational trials in the final months of the war.

Right: The Bell Helicopter Model 30 prototype being flown by inventor Arthur Young, in about 1943. Young's aircraft was a pioneer of the "penny-farthing" configuration for helicopters, in which a vertical tail rotor was used to counter engine torque. This machine paved the way for the Model 47, the world's first commercial licensed helicopter.

Left: The Focke Achgelis Fa 223E Drache, the first helicopter to go into production, was an ambitious design intended for a variety of roles, including transport and anti-submarine duties, although very few actually entered service.

Defense and Attack

Britain and France went to war with Germany again on September 3, 1939. By then aerial photography, record-breaking long distance flights, air races, and air displays had yielded a substantial amount of information about various nations' commercial aviation and the strength and organization of their air forces and the mettle of their pilots and crews.

In 1920 the German Defence Ministry had set about secretly resuscitating the German air force. In the same year, Professor Hugo Junkers formed an aircraft company to manufacture the all-metal F13 transport and aero engines. In 1922 Ernst Heinkel and in 1924 Heinrich Focke and Georg Wulf founded aircraft manufacturing companies. In 1926 the Bayerische Flugzeugwerke (Bavarian Aircraft Factory) began manufacturing, changing its name in 1938 to Messerschmitt A.G.

A military flying training centre for German officers was established in Russia. In 1926 Germany reactivated its state airline, Deutsche Luft Hansa, with Erhard Milch, a former fighter pilot, as chairman. This led to the construction of large airfields that were secretly intended for use also by the embryonic *Luftwaffe*. Luft Hansa crews later provided training for the newly re-formed air force.

Britain's Royal Air Force maintained a higher level of training and a sharper state of operational preparedness than any other air force. It was also unsurpassed in fighting qualities. The *Luftwaffe*, however, suffered no lack of brave men or skilled senior officers; and some of the airplanes it flew were as good as, or better than, the RAF's.

At the outbreak of the Second World War, the Royal Navy's most numerous aircraft was the Fairey Swordfish, a biplane torpedo-bomber with the sluggish maximum speed of 138mph (222kph). Entering service in 1934, it was dubbed the "Stringbag," on account of its archaic appearance; but production continued until 1944.

Delivery of its successor, the Albacore, only 27mph (43kph) faster, began in December 1939.

The Fleet Air Arm's first victory of the war came on September 25, 1939, when a Blackburn Skua from HMS *Ark Royal* shot down a Dornier Do 18 flying boat on reconnaissance.

The Battle of Britain is the most famous air campaign in history, not only because the numerical odds

Above: The crew of a Douglas Boston III bomber of 107 Sqn, RAF, discuss the forthcoming operation, 1943. Powered by a pair of 1,600hp Wright Double-Row Cyclone radial engines, the Boston first entered RAF service in 1941.

were heavily in the enemy's favor, but also because it was the crucial victory of the whole war. The simple, direct language of Churchill's touching tribute to the RAF's fighter pilots after the summer-long battle stirred the emotions: "Never, in the field of human conflict, has so much been owed by so many to so few."

That succinctly expressed the essence of the skill and devotion to duty shown by the Spitfire and Hurri-

cane fighter pilots, the air gunners in two-seater Defiants, and the usually forgotten crews of Blenheim night fighters that carried a top secret "black box."

RADAR

The ace up Britain's sleeve in preparation for conflict was radar, installed on the ground and in aircraft. Originally known as "range and direction finding" and shortened to "RDF," the true nature of this facility, invented and developed in Britain, was hidden by its innocuous title: those who were not in on the secret assumed it to be a navigation aid. When Britain divulged the secret of RDF to the Americans, they renamed it "radio direction and ranging" – radar.

The Bristol Blenheim night fighter's "black box" was a radar set known as airborne interception (AI). A derivative of the Bristol 142, the Blenheim began squadron service in

Above: Messerschmitt Bf 109E-1 fighters of 8/JG2 "Richthofen" stand at readiness on a French airfield in May 1940. Powered by a 1,175hp Daimler-Benz DB 601A, this variant had four 7.9mm machine guns.

March 1937. This marked a huge advance on the RAF's then fastest bomber, the Hawker Hind, a single-engine biplane two-seater with a fixed undercarriage. The Blenheim was a twin-engine monoplane with a retractable undercarriage. AI was first fitted to Mk I Blenheim bombers.

March 1939 saw the Mk IV Blenheim's delivery begin, first to bomber and then to night fighter squadrons. It had a lengthened nose to allow the navigator better accommodation. When the Blenheim bomber first appeared on the RAF's Order of Battle, it was 13mph (21kph) faster than the

Above: Ground crew tend to a Boeing B-17E Flying Fortress of the US Eighth Air Force's 414th Bomb Squadron, 97th Bomb Group, at Grafton, Yorkshire, in September 1942.

RAF's most modern fighter, the Gloster Gladiator, a single-seat biplane with a fixed undercarriage.

The first British monoplane day fighter, the first with a retractable undercarriage and the first to exceed 300mph (482kph) was the Hawker Hurricane. This superb airplane entered squadron service in December 1937. In the winter following the Battle of Britain, it was also pressed into use as a night fighter. The Supermarine Spitfire began its squadron career in 1938, had the same armament and engine as the Hurricane, but was 40mph (64kph) faster.

Left: This Belgian-based Italian Fiat CR42 fighter was shot down by a Hurricane on November 11, 1940, and forced-landed near Orfordness, Suffolk, England. It was repaired and test flown, and now resides in the RAF Museum at Hendon.

DOGFIGHTS

The conflict that would spread around the globe began with Hitler's order to invade Poland. In opposition to the Polish Air Force and the RAF, the *Luft-waffe* put up an excellent fighter, the Messerschmitt Bf 109. The Bf 109 made its first flight in September 1935 and by September 1939 the 109E was in squadron service. It was faster than the Hurricane and Spitfire, but both could turn inside it, a greater advantage in a dogfight than sheer speed.

A fighter that also took part in the invasion of Poland was the Bf 110 (Me 110), known as the *Zerstörer* (Destroyer). Originally used as bomber escorts, Bf 110s soon themselves had to be escorted by Bf 109s. However, eventually, fitted with airborne radar, the Bf 110 became a successful night fighter.

Below: A low-flying Bristol Blenheim I light bomber turns the heads of Army personnel during operations in the Middle East in 1940. Powered by two 840hp Bristol Mercury VIII radial engines, the Blenheim first entered RAF service in March 1937.

Above: Junkers Ju 87 dive bombers – "Stukas" – prepare to take off from a field in Russia. Although the Stuka struck fear into civilian populations, it lacked agility and was easy prey to contemporary fighters.

In July 1941, RAF pilots on offensive operations over France began to encounter the radial-engined Focke-Wulf Fw 190, whose top speed with boost was 408mph (656kph).

When Germany invaded Poland on September 1, 1939, the spearhead of the air attack was the Junkers Ju 87 dive bomber (*Sturtzkampf-flugzeug*, "Stuka" for short), which first flew in 1936. During the Battle of France in 1940 the Stuka and Bf 109 created havoc on the French roads.

The Polish Air Force faced the might of the *Luftwaffe* with twelve squadrons of PZL P11c fighters, which were more than 100mph (160kph) slower than the Bf 109, and feebly armed. Nevertheless, the Poles shot down 126 German aircraft for the loss of 114.

Right: An extremely rare color photograph of Hawker Hurricane Is of No 3 Squadron, RAF, at Biggin Hill in 1939. Wingspan 40ft (12.19m), length 32ft (9.75m), height 13ft 1in (4m), weight 6,600lb (2,994kg), engine one 1,030hp Rolls-Royce Merlin 12-cylinder vee liquid-cooled, maximum cruising speed 318mph(511kph), range 460 miles (740km), crew 1.

The *Luftwaffe*'s most versatile bomber, the Junkers Ju 88, which first flew in December 1936, was made in many versions and used for day and night bombing, torpedo dropping and as a night fighter. In 1940 the Heinkel He 111 bomber became a familiar sight over France and Britain, as did the Dornier Do 17 – known to the British as the "flying pencil."

The best fighter of the French Air Force (*l'Armée de l'Air*) in the early months of the war was the Bloch ME 152C-1, delivery of which began in December 1939. Of France's twenty

Above: Hurricane IIC nightfighters of 87 Squadron on patrol in 1941. A total of 79 home based operational squadrons and 66 overseas squadrons were equipped with the type.

six combat-ready fighter squadrons on May 10, 1940, when Germany invaded Belgium and Holland and was about to cross the French frontier, nineteen flew this type. A better fighter, which began squadron service on February 1, 1940, was the Dewoitine D520S.

A good French light bomber, the Breguet 693, made its first flight on October 25, 1939. Before France gave up the fight on June 22, 1940, some 224 had been delivered to squadrons.

The RAF bomber squadrons based in France had to make do with the Fairey Battle. Introduced to frontline service in May 1937, it was slow and inadequately armed with only two machine guns. The enemy shot Battles down in droves.

RAF Bomber Command also made a valuable contribution to victory in the Battle of Britain. While the fighting over southern England was at its height, Hitler was assembling barges along the French coast in anticipation of winning the air battle and then invading Britain. The barges were bombed almost daily, which not only destroyed great numbers of them but also drew off some of the enemy fighters. In June 1940 three of the Avro Ansons involved in this task were attacked by nine Bf 109s. The Ansons had a sluggish top speed of 188mph (302kph) and modest armament of two .303

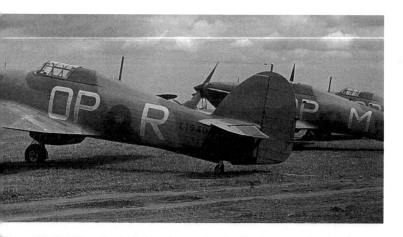

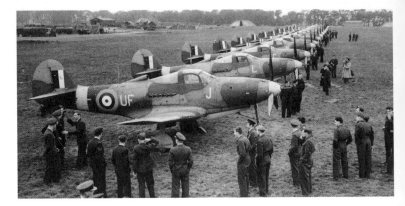

Above: Less successful was the American Bell P-39D Airacobra, which had a tricycle undercarriage, a cannon firing through the propeller boss, and a 1,150hp Allison engine mounted behind the pilot with a long driveshaft to the propeller. The only RAF Squadron to have Airacobras, No 601, soon got rid of them.

machine guns, yet incredibly they shot three of the Messerscmitts down.

BOMBERS

Bombers were used both tactically and strategically. At the outbreak of war, the RAF's heaviest bombers were the Hampden, Whitley and Wellington, all with two engines. The first four-engine bomber of this war was the Stirling, which No 7 Squadron began flying in August 1940. Next came the Halifax in March 1941, followed by the Lancaster, which flew its first operation in March 1942. By the time the USA took up Japan's challenge, US Army Air Corps squadrons had been flying the Boeing B-17 for two and a half years and the Consolidated B-24 Liberator for six months.

The Allies' other four-engine aircraft was the Shorts Sunderland flying boat, which had been in service with RAF Coastal Command since May 1938. The Luftwaffe called it "The Porcupine," because it was armed with ten machine guns that gave it all-round defensive fire.

The Luftwaffe also had a four-engine maritime reconnaissance aircraft, the Focke-Wulf Fw 200 Condor, developed from a pre-war airliner that had made record flights to the USA and Japan. The military variant had nine guns and was a menace not only

Right: The Messerschmitt Bf 110 proved vulnerable as a long-range strategic fighter, but came into its own as a radar-equipped nightfighter in 1941. These are Bf 110F-1s of SKG 210, powered by Daimler-Benz DB 601Fs.

to surface shipping and submarines but also to aircraft.

Surprisingly, Italy, despite its successes in the early Schneider Trophy contests, produced no outstandingly successful fighters. The Savoia-Marchetti SM79 Sparviero (Sparrowhawk) was one of the war's fastest bombers, but its bomb load was not impressive.

NIGHT FIGHTERS
The Bristol Beaufighter, one of the most versatile aircraft of the war, was the first night fighter with a high enough performance to take advantage of AI and was the most heavily armed aircraft in the world at the time. Soon, it was delighting RAF Coastal Command as a formidable anti-shipping strike and torpedo airplane with a new type of radar in the nose: ASV (anti-surface vessel), which could pick up motor torpedo boats and even a submarine's periscope if it flew at 450–500ft (140–150m).

Another versatile warplane and regarded as the world's most handsome aircraft, the de Havilland Mosquito was the best of all photographic reconnaissance aircraft, in addition to its use as a night fighter, intruder and

bomber. It also heralded a new method of bombing accurately at night. The RAF formed the Pathfinder Force on August 11, 1942, and by early 1943 it comprised five squadrons of Stirlings, Halifaxes, Lancasters and Mosquitoes. Arriving over the target before the main force, they dropped bright, colored indicators as aiming marks.

THE USA ENTERS THE WAR
When the USA was propelled into the conflict in December 1941 by Japan's attack on Pearl Harbor, the United States Army Air Force (USAAF) was flying excellent bombers: the twin-engine North American B-25 Mitchell and Douglas DB-7 Havoc (Boston in RAF service), soon followed by the Martin B-26 Marauder. The four-engine Boeing B-17 Flying Fortress and the Consolidated B-24 Liberator were also very effective bombers whose names became legendary.

In Europe, operating by day, the Americans suffered very heavy losses because their own Lockheed P-38 Lightning fighters, and the RAF's Spitfires, even with long-range tanks, lacked the endurance to escort them all the way to their targets in Germany. This changed when the Repub-

Above: The 885hp Rolls-Royce Peregrine engines of the Westland Whirlwind single-seat long-range fighter proved troublesome, but it had four 20mm guns in the nose and served usefully as a fighter-bomber from September 1942.

lic P-47 Thunderbolt and North American P-51 Mustang were able to accompany them.

The campaigns in the Far East and Pacific pitted the Allied air forces against fighters and bombers based mostly on aircraft carriers. The Japanese Mitsubishi A6M, code-named "Zeke," was the first carrier-borne fighter with a better performance than land-based ones. Other good fighters were the Nakajima Ki-43 "Oscar" and the Nakajima Ki-84 "Frank," regarded as Japan's best.

In Europe, from the Normandy landings on June 6, 1944, to Germany's surrender on May 7, 1945, Allied specialist ground-attack fighters became the main air weapon. The star ground-attack type was the sturdy Hawker Typhoon. This, the RAF's first fighter to fly at over 400mph (644kph), was intended as a response to the Focke-Wulf Fw 190; but, above 15,000ft (4,572m) where the Fw 190 operated, the Typhoon became too slow.

The Hawker Tempest was a development of the Typhoon with elliptical, thin-section wings. Delivery to the first of only seven squadrons began in April 1944. With a top speed of 440mph (708kph), it was the only piston-engined airplane fast enough to catch the V1 flying bombs.

The Messerschmitt Me 262A-1a

Right: Japanese carrier crew cheer off a Mitsubishi A6M Zero-Sen "Zeke" apparently headed for the US Navy base at Pearl Harbor, December 7, 1941.

Above: Less well-known than the B-17, the B-24 Liberator was a better-performing, more versatile and more useful military aircraft. US industry built some 19,203.

Schwalbe (Swallow) fighter was the first turbojet-powered aircraft to go into action, towards the end of July 1944. The first Me 262 squadron was formed two months later. The bomber variant, Messerschmitt Me 262A-2 Sturmvogel (Stormbird), followed. Their respective maximum speeds were 540mph (869kph) and 470mph (756kph). The Me 163 Komet was the first rocket-propelled aircraft to see action.

The *Luftwaffe* Versus the RAF

The Battle of Britain epitomises the contrasting tactics of the RAF and *Luftwaffe*. To begin with, the British were too nonchalant to call on their 1914–18 allies to join them in enforcing the terms of the Armistice, which forbade Germany to have an air force; and they tolerated politicians who were rabidly pro-disarmament. In contrast, the diligent Germans had set about resuscitating their air force

Below: The Spitfire's elegant lines earned it a special place in British affections, although it proved a difficult aircraft to manufacture, especially the wing leading edges.

Above: A Heinkel He 111 forced down into a field in southern England. The "bumper" device, an attempt to cope with balloon barrage cables, reduced speed and bombload.

soon after their defeat, with the co-operation of their former enemy, the USSR, which provided them with a training school.

The *Luftwaffe* hugely outnumbered the RAF and, by sending fighters and bombers to fight on the anti-communist side in the Spanish Civil War, gained valuable experience of battle tactics. Foremost was the discovery that a fighter formation of pairs in echelon, with one pilot covering the other, and multiples of such pairs, was more efficient than the RAF's threes in "V" formation. After the battle, the RAF adopted this formation, usually in twos, forming a "finger four."

Britain's unique possession of radar stations along her coasts gave the RAF a tactical advantage in early warning of the enemy's approach.

Fighter Command's few fighters were able to take off and start climbing to meet the enemy sooner than the German planners expected, although there was not always time to do this.

The other great tactical superiority was the control organization which divided the country into Groups: so if No 11 Group, based in south-east England, could not scramble (the code for takeoff) in time, No 12 Group, its neighbor further north, could. This did not always happen, but the sheer fighting spirit of the

defending pilots made up for that. The Hurricane and Spitfire could both turn inside the Bf 109 – a huge bonus. Another advantage was the fact that both the latter and the German bombers broke when attacked head-on, a favorite RAF tactic.

Below: Ground crew readying a Spitfire Mk VC for a mission over Malta, where the pilots, and the people of the island, had a torrid time at the hands of the *Luftwaffe*.

Messerschmitt Bf 109, Legendary Fighter

> '*I flew only the 109.
> It was very maneuverable,
> and it was easy to handle.
> It speeded up very fast, if
> you dive a little. And in the
> acrobatics maneuver, you
> could spin with the 109,
> and go very easy out of
> the spin. The only problems
> occurred during take-off.
> We lost a lot of pilots in
> take-offs. If you were
> in the air, though,
> it was very nice to fly.*'
>
> ERICH HARTMANN

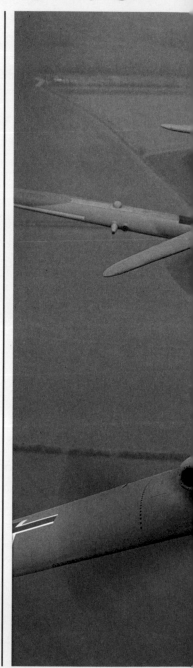

In 1935 the Messerschmitt Bf 109 was the shape of the future. It was a small cantilever monoplane fighter with fully retractable main landing gear and an enclosed cockpit. Some of these things had been featured on earlier aircraft, but not all together – the only exception being the inferior Polikarpov I-16.

The prototype made its first flight from the company airfield between Augsberg and Haunstten on May 28, 1935, piloted by Hans-Dietrich Knoetzsch. Ironically it was powered by a Rolls-Royce Kestrel engine, since its intended power-plant, the Junkers Jumo 210, was not ready. In timing it was ahead of the British Hawker Hurricane and Supermarine Spitfire.

The first variant to enter service was the Bf 109B, which also served with the *Legion Kondor* in Spain from April 1937. The C and D sub-types followed rapidly, also powered by the Jumo. The D saw action in the Polish campaign of 1939, but its shortcomings were exposed on

Right: A Messerschmitt Bf 109 tries every maneuver to escape the attentions of a Supermarine Spitfire in a mock battle for the camera. These old adversaries have been refurbished for postwar displays.

November 6, 1939, when about two dozen Bf 109Ds tangled with nine *Armée de l'Air* Curtiss Hawk 75s of GC II/4, losing eight for one French fighter.

The solution was already to hand in the shape of the much more powerful and more heavily armed Bf 109E, with a Daimler-Benz DB 601A engine. This, coupled with fuel injection, improved performance enormously, and the E, in various subtypes, was the main German fighter in the Battle of Britain. While speed for speed it could not turn as tightly as its British opponents, in other respects it was superior to them. With its pilots employing dive and zoom tactics, the Bf 109 did rather better than hold its own.

As the Second World War progressed, so the Bf 109 was steadily upgraded. The Bf 109E was succeeded by F, G and finally K models. Ever more powerful engines were fitted, and heavier armament, although with the increased weight handling gradually worsened. It was used for a multitude of roles: interceptor, ground-attack, high-altitude reconnaissance and bomber destroyer. Although in many ways outclassed by the later Focke-Wulf Fw 190, the Bf 109 was numerically the pre-eminent German fighter in all the major European theaters of war: Russia, Malta, the Western Desert, Italy – all knew the angular shape and the staccato Thor's Anvil song of the Bf 109.

More Bf 109s of various subtypes were built between 1939 and the end of the war in Europe than any other fighter in history. The total, at roughly 35,000 (records are incomplete), exceeds those of its nearest rivals, the Spitfire/Seafire (22,284) and the Fw 190 (20,001) by a considerable margin.

Almost all the *Luftwaffe* top scorers gained the majority of their victories while flying the Bf 109. Both Erich Hartmann, the greatest ace of all, with 352 victories, and Hans-Joachim Marseille, the top scorer in the Western theater, with 158 victories, flew nothing else.

Above: The Bf 109 (this is a refurbished G) became the main German fighter of the war. It was progressively up-gunned and up-engined, creating extra weight that adversely affected its ha... new... be... lan... Thi... op... an...

qualities, which had
n particularly
sses in takeoff and
cidents were high.
, it was a worthy
to Britain's Spitfires
anes, and virtually

all the high-scoring *Luftwaffe*
aces flew it at one time or
another. Ranking ace Erich
Hartmann (352 victories on
the Eastern Front) flew
nothing else.

The Spitfire

SPITFIRE MK IA

Supermarine chief designer Reginald Mitchell had learned much about high speed flight from his series of successful racing floatplanes, but his first attempt at producing a fighter, the Type 224, which first flew in February 1934, was slow and climbed poorly. His next attempt was the Type 300, work on which began in the summer of 1934. A development contract for a prototype was issued on December 1 of that year.

The engine selected was the new Rolls-Royce PV X11, which promised about 1,000hp when fully developed. Later named Merlin, this was a major factor in the success of what became the Spitfire. Even more important was the wing design. The elliptical planform chosen had the lowest lift/drag ratio of any shape, and for its day was astonishingly thin, with a thickness/chord ratio of 13 percent at the root and 6 percent at the tip. This gave the Spitfire a higher critical Mach number than any other

Right: The Spitfire prototype, K5054, seen during prewar trials. The Spitfire was the first all-metal, stressed-skin aircraft to go into production in Britain.

Below: Spitfires of 610 Squadron in the "search and cruise" formation. They still fly in threes, but the distances between the "vics" have been considerably increased as a result of battle experience.

wartime fighter, even the jets of 1944/45. The other effect of the thin wing was that when the specification was changed from four guns to eight, keeping the ammunition feeds out of each other's way meant that the guns had to be widely spaced, and the outboard guns needed just a hint of a bulge to accommodate them.

The Spitfire was tightly packaged, and this led to its greatest failing. The main gear legs were located in the wing roots, with the wheels retracting outboard into the wings. This resulted in a narrow track undercarriage, which was less than ideal for operating from rough strips, or in a cross-wind.

The prototype first flew at Eastleigh, Hampshire, on March 6, 1936, and, with few modifications, was ordered into production in November 1936. The first series aircraft flew on May 14, 1938. Tragically, Reginald Mitchell did not live to see it. Deliveries commenced in August of that year, to Nos 19 and 66 Squadrons at Duxford.

On October 16, 1939, Spitfires intercepted Ju 88s attacking naval units in the Firth of Forth, shooting down two and damaging a third, but not until May 21, 1940, did they encounter the Bf 109E over Dunkirk. Heavy fighting here was followed by the Battle of Britain, which lasted through the summer of 1940. Designed as an air defense fighter, the maneuverability of the Spitfire stood it in good stead against the '109s, which often had a positional advantage.

Further development had already started. The Mark II, which entered service in August 1940, mounted the Merlin XII, rated at 1,175hp. However, most of the performance improvements were swallowed up by the weight of extra armor protection for the pilot, the coolant header tank, and the upper fuel tank. Almost one fifth of these were Mk IIBs, with two 20mm Hispano drum-fed cannon each with 120 rounds, displacing the four inner machine guns.

In January 1941, the Bf 109F entered service. To counter it, the Spitfire V was rushed into service.

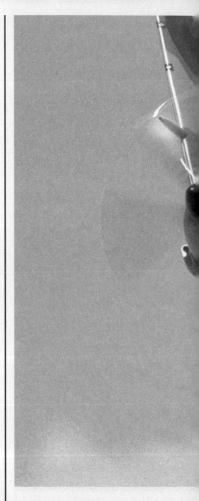

Bypassing the III and IV, which never entered production, the Mk V had the more powerful Merlin 45 in a strengthened Mk I airframe, and a larger radiator. The most numerous Spitfire variant, the Mk V was produced in many subtypes.

Development continued with the Spitfire VIII, arguably the most advanced of the Merlin-engined fighters. Entering service in August 1943, it was used in Italy, briefly in Russia, and in the Far East, but never in the West.

Once again the Spitfire had been overtaken by events. The Focke-Wulf

90A which entered service late
41, outclassed the Spitfire V in
partments except for turn
s. As the Mk VIII could not be
ble in time, Merlin 60 series
es were fitted to a VC airframe.
his hybrid produced the Spitfire
e second most numerous sub-
built. Entering service with No
quadron in July 1942, it quickly
d a match for the Fw 190A.
nally it was virtually identical to
Mk V, which made life very diffi-
or the *Jagdflieger*, because until
at was joined they could not be
which they were taking on.

**Above: First flown in 1936, the
Spitfire entered large-scale
production just in time for the war.
Its ability to hold tight turns was
outstanding, and it was
progressively improved right until
the end of the war, such that it
became widely regarded as the
greatest fighter of the conflict. It
served in every theater, was
tropicalized for desert and jungle,
and navalized for carrier
operations as the Seafire.**

The Spitfire IX was built in F, HF and LF subtypes, and remained in service until the end of the war.

The next few Merlin Spitfires were photo-reconnaissance types, and the only other major variant was the Mk XVI. This varied primarily in having a Packard-built Merlin, which was not interchangeable with the Rolls-Royce article.

The Spitfire was adapted for carrier operations with the addition of a tallhook, lifting points, and the ASI calibrated in knots rather than mph, to become the Seafire. The first was the Seafire IB, a converted VB, which entered service in June 1942. It was followed by the IIC, then the low altitude LF IIC, powered by a Merlin 32 with a four-bladed propeller. Late

model IICs were fitted with spools for catapult launching.

The final Merlin-engined Seafire was the Mk III, which was the first to have wing-folding. However, the narrow-track main gear was far too ladylike for the rough and tumble of carrier operations, while endurance was too short. As a carrier fighter, the Seafire was not a success.

SPITFIRE MK XIVE

Even before the war, Rolls-Royce were working on a larger successor to the Merlin, with a cubic capacity thirty-six percent greater. A requirement was that its size should be held down so that it could replace the Merlin in existing aircraft with a minimum of structural alteration. The

flown on November 27, 1941, it did not enter production. In early 1942 it was redesignated Mk XX to avoid confusion with the PR IV.

The Mk XX became the prototype Spitfire XII, which first flew on August 24, 1942 and entered service in the following year. A dedicated low altitude fighter, it had clipped wings, a broad-chord rudder, and a retractable tailwheel. Used by only two squadrons, at its best fighting altitude of 12,000ft (3,657m) it was far superior to the contemporary Fw 190A.

The major Griffon-engined Spitfire variant to see action in the war was the Mk XIV. Like the very successful Mk IX, this was a lash-up, with the Spitfire VIII airframe strengthened and modified to take the Griffon 65 and its five-bladed propeller. The fin area was increased, and the final production machines had a cut-down rear fuselage with a tear-drop canopy. Initially the armament was two 20mm cannon and four .303in (7.7mm) machine guns, but later the light machine guns were replaced by two 0.501n (12.7mm) Brownings.

Although tremendously fast, and possessed of an outstanding rate of climb, the increased weight took its toll on handling, and it was not nearly as nice as the Merlin-engined Spitfires. Controls were always on the heavy side, although moving the ailerons inboard a tad improved lateral control.

Other Spitfires developed included: FR XIVE photo-reconnaissance variant; Mk 21; Mk 22; and finally Mk 24. Notable Griffon-engined Seafires included the Mk XV, XVII, and Seafire 47.

new engine duly emerged as the Griffon; barely 3in (76mm) longer than the Merlin, while its frontal area was only six percent greater. It was of course about 350lb (159kg) heavier, and oddly enough, it ran rather slower; maximum rating was achieved at 2,750rpm rather than the 3,000rpm of the Merlin.

The Spitfire IV was the first planned to have the Griffon engine. The engine mounting was modified, and the cowling redesigned. Fuel capacity was increased with integral wing tanks, the landing gear was strengthened, and the proposed armament was six 20mm Hispano cannon. Slotted flaps were considered, but the original plain type were found to be quite adequate. First

The Hurricane

In 1934, Hawker Aircraft were working on a project provisionally known as the Fury Monoplane. The engine selected was the Rolls-Royce PV-1 2, later to become the Merlin. The design was finalised and a mockup prepared, on the strength of which the British Air Ministry ordered a single "high speed monoplane." Piloted by Percy "George" Bulman, this, the prototype Hurricane, first flew from Brooklands on November 6, 1935.

A low wing monoplane, its construction was traditional Hawker, with metal tube framing, fabric-covered from aft of the cockpit. Initially the wings were also fabric-covered, but this was replaced by light alloy skinning at an early stage. The shape of the tail surfaces instantly identified the Hurricane as a Hawker product. The cockpit was enclosed, and set slightly high, giving the fighter its

Above: The Hurricane bore the brunt of the air fighting during the Battle of Britain, and went on to serve in a variety of roles. Here a Sea Hurricane IB keeps company with two Seafire IICs.

characteristic hump-backed look, although this was not as extreme as its Italian contemporaries. It also gave a slightly better view over the nose than the Spitfire. The inward-retracting main wheels were located beneath the wings, giving a fairly wide track, and armament consisted of eight wing-mounted machine guns.

In February 1936 the prototype was delivered for official trials. These proved satisfactory, and in a bold move Hawker Aircraft started to prepare for mass production three months before the first official order

Left: The Hurricane was outperformed by the Bf 109, so its primary task in the Battle of Britain was dealing with *Luftwaffe* bomber formations. Some 696 were lost, either permanently or temporarily, in the two-month battle.

Right: False legs dangling beside the cockpit, celebrated Squadron Leader Douglas Bader, CO of 242 Squadron, poses with his beloved Hurricane. He scored 23 victories during the war, but on August 9, 1941, after bringing down two Bf 109s, he collided with a third, baled out and was taken prisoner.

was issued, on June 3, 1937. The first production aircraft flew on October 12, and deliveries to No 111 Squadron commenced before the end of the year; a remarkable performance.

With war looming, production was accelerated, and by September 1939 some eighteen squadrons had been equipped. A year later this had risen to thirty-two squadrons. Hurricanes were sent to France on the outbreak of war, and the first air combat victory, over a Dornier Do 17, was claimed by "Boy" Mould of No 1 Squadron on October 30.

Although outperformed by the opposing Messerschmitt Bf 109E, the Hurricane I had many strengths. It had no vices; in fact German ace Werner Mölders, who flew a captured Hurricane in the summer of 1940, commented that it was "very good-natured!" Although somewhat slow in roll acceleration, once the angle of bank was established speed for speed it out-turned the higher-wing-loaded German fighter with ease. The wide track undercarriage made operations from semi-prepared airstrips, which were the norm in France, quite easy, while the sturdy construction made it able to absorb a great deal of battle damage. It was a stable gun platform, and its thick wings were less prone to flexing when the guns were fired in maneuvering flight than were those of the Spitfire, reducing shot dispersion. Finally, the view "out of the window" was much better than that of German opponent, which was obstructed by heavy framing.

The *Blitzkrieg* opened on May 10, 1940. No effective early warning was available, and most engagements were coincidental. The Hurricane pilots largely held their own against

superior numbers in the air, but lost heavily due to the situation on the ground. Forced to continually retire by advancing German armor in France and Belgium, many damaged Hurricanes were abandoned or destroyed.

The Battle of Britain, which officially commenced in July 1940, saw a complete change of circumstance. Flying from bases which could not be over-run by ground forces, and with a well-honed early warning, detection, and control system in the air, the twenty-eight Hurricane squadrons that took a substantial part in the fighting acquitted themselves well, destroying a total of 638 German aircraft.

Two things were badly needed, however: greater performance and more hitting power. The first point

was addressed by the Hurricane IIA powered by the Merlin XX, rated at 1,460hp, which entered service from September 1940. This was followed by the Hurricane IIB with twelve wing-mounted Brownings, and the IIC with four 20mm Hispano-Suiza wing-mounted cannon. But in 1941, improved versions of the Bf 109 were in service, and towards the end of that year the Hurricane switched mainly to ground attack, although it continued as a fighter in the Middle and Far East, and in Russia.

Hurricanes also served as "cats eye" night fighters from the fall of 1940, fitted with shields to mask the glare from the exhausts which would otherwise have interfered with the pilots' night vision. But with the radar-equipped Beaufighter entering service, this was no more than a temporary measure.

Fitted with a tailhook, and with local strengthening, the Sea Hurricane was embarked aboard HMS *Furious* in July 1941. Superior to the Fulmar, its greatest failing was the lack of wing folding, which although proposed was never implemented. The last was delivered in August 1943, and by the end of that year it had largely been replaced by the Seafire and Hellcat.

Finally, mention must be made of the Hurricat. These were one-shot aircraft, catapulted from a ramp on a merchant ship to drive away shadowers, after which the pilot was forced, if he could not reach land, to ditch. Escort carriers soon made this hazardous procedure unnecessary.

The Mighty Eighth

Maggie's Drawers, Bomboogie and the punning Ascend Charlie (referring to a tail gunner) were typical names that were cheerfully emblazoned on the noses of United States Army Air Force (USAAF) bombers of the 8th Air Force stationed in England; they reflect the wisecracking and jaunty bravery of their crews. The 8th comprised fighters as well. The P-38 Lightnings, like the Hurricanes and Spitfires, lacked the range to escort bombers to the most distant targets in Germany.

The P-51 Mustang, which had a range of 1,050 miles (1,689km), was the response to a request for a new fighter made by the RAF in April 1940. The Mks I and II with Rolls-Royce engines entered RAF service in July 1942, the USAAF's in Decem-

Below: Bristling with .50 caliber machine guns, Eighth Air Force B-17 Flying Fortresses head for Germany in a raid on industrial installations as fighter escorts sweep above the bomber formation, leaving bright vapor trails.

Right: Keeping it company as it spirals to the ground, a wing has been chopped off a B-17 by Me 262 fighter cannon fire, April 10, 1945. Nevertheless, this bomber raid managed to destroy 285 enemy planes on the ground and 21 more in the air.

ber. The III (USAAF P-51B and C) and IV (P-51D) appeared in 1944.

In May 1938 the USA's Chiefs of Staff had decreed that land based aircraft should be limited to an off-shore radius of 100 miles (161km). It was President Roosevelt who told Congress in January 1939: "Our air forces are so utterly inadequate that they should be immediately strengthened."

On the outbreak of war in Europe it was agreed between Britain and the USA that if the latter entered the conflict her heavy bombers would operate with the RAF from English bases in strategic bombing. RAF day bombers took such heavy casualties that, from late 1940, most bombing was done by night.

The prototype Boeing B-17, the first new USAF bomber, made its maiden flight on July 28, 1935, and the Y1B-17 in January 1937. Delivery of the B-17B began in June 1939. Twenty B17-7s were given to the RAF in return for combat information. Reports told that the Browning guns froze, the Norden bombsight had defects and enemy fighters attacked from a blind area astern. Corrective action was duly taken. The four-engine Consolidated B-24 Liberator was delivered to American squadrons in March 1942.

The USAAF's introduction to combat came on July 4, 1942, when six crews borrowed Douglas Boston III bombers from the RAF for a raid on Holland. Two of them were shot down. In August 1942 it was agreed that the 8th AF and the RAF would co-ordinate a day and night offensive. On August 17 General Ira C. Eaker, Commander of the 8th, led twelve B-17Es, escorted by Spitfires, against the Rouen–Sotteville marshaling yards without casualties.

The following day 326th Bom-

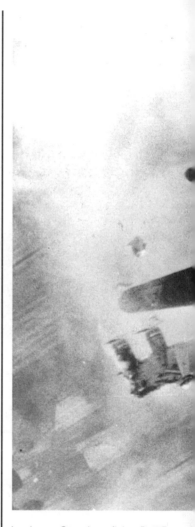

bardment Squadron, flying B-17Fs arrived to join the 92nd Bomb Group. Three heavy Bomb Groups were now in place, and there was one squadron of Boston IIIs. A fourth Bomb Group joined them from November 1942 to May 1943. In November 1942 two Groups went to North Africa.

There were two Fighter Groups with P-38s and two with Spitfire Vs. A raid on an engineering factory in Belgium and railway works at Lille, escorted by RAF and USAAF fighters, showed the B-24s' defects: of twenty-four, ten returned prematurely with various faults. Only three aircraft were lost, but thirty-six B-17s and ten B-24s were damaged.

By March 1943 the 8th's average bombing accuracy had risen from 15 percent to 75 percent. On July 24, some 324 B-17s crossed the North Sea. One target was a nitrate factory at Heroya; others were the harbors at Bergen and Trondheim and a nearby aluminum and magnesium plant.

In one week that month the *Luftwaffe* lost forty fighters, the 8th lost 128 B-17s.

On August 17, 1943, an attack on the ballbearing works at Schweinfurt was met by 200 enemy fighters from bases in Germany, France and Belgium. A total of thirty-six B-17s and 374 lives were lost. After this General Arnold ordered that the P-38s' and P-51s' priority would be to give cover. The tables were turned on the *Luftwaffe's* fighters, but ahead lay many more devastating raids and battles.

The Flying Fortress

> *'The Fortress inspired a tremendous confidence. It was the only propeller driven aircraft I have flown that was completely viceless; there were no undesirable flight characteristics. The directional stability was excellent and, properly trimmed, the B-17 could be taken off, landed and banked without change of trim.'*
>
> Lt. James W. Johnson, USAAF

With its combination of sleek lines and an inspirational name, the Boeing B-17 Flying Fortress caught the imagination as few other aircraft have, before or since. A four-engined long-range strategic bomber, the B-17 was originally designed to be able to reinforce Alaska, Hawaii or Panama from the continental USA.

Its first flight was made from Seattle on July 28, 1935, with test pilot Leslie Tower at the controls.

There is an old saying that if an aircraft looks right, it almost certainly will be right, and so it proved from the outset. Service evaluation of pre-production aircraft took place in 1937, and the first production aircraft was delivered on June 27, 1939.

Ironically, the combat debut of the B-17 came in RAF service, when three aircraft of 90 Squadron attacked Wilhelmshaven on July 8, 1941. This operation was rather ineffective, as were succeeding raids

Above: B-17s in "combat box"
formation and with P-51 Mustang
fighter escorts head out for a
daylight raid on German
installations. It took several hours
for the formation to build up to its
full size before leaving the skies
over England.

made at very high altitude, and the
experiment was not pursued.

Meanwhile, the Japanese attack
on Pearl Harbor on December 6, 1941,
brought the USA into the war. B-17Ds
were already in the Pacific, and were
immediately caught up in the fighting.
But it was in Western Europe that the
Fortress was to earn undying fame.
The USAAF's policy was of accurate
bombing in daylight. It was some time

Left: This is the last flyable Flying
Fortress in existence today that
flew combat missions in the
Second World War, B-17G "Shoo
Shoo Baby" lovingly restored by
the US Air Force 512th Military
Airlift Wing in Delaware.

before long-range escort fighters became available, and large numbers of heavily armed bombers flew in close formation for mutual protection. On shallow penetrations losses were acceptable, but for raids deep into Germany the cost was too high. On the other hand, the Fortress gained an excellent reputation for surviving battle damage. Later variants of the B-17 had heavier armament, and the massed defensive guns of the B-17 formations exacted a heavy toll of *Luftwaffe* fighters.

If the Fortress had one outstanding virtue, it was that it was easy to fly. This was a tremendous advantage because, in the Second World War, pilots were being turned out on production lines. Although they were well trained, they were young and lacked experience.

The other American four-engined bomber was the Consolidated B-24 Liberator. Designed several years later, it was in many ways a more effective bomber. It was faster and carried a heavier bomb load, but its

high wing loading gave rise to some tricky handling characteristics. The slower B-17 was less fatiguing to fly, it was easier to hold in a tight defensive formation, and it could be flown in formation at greater altitudes.

A total of 12,723 B-17s were built between 1939 and 1945, with production tailing off from April 1944 in favor of the B-29. By comparison, 18,188 Liberators were built during this period, nearly half this as many again, but despite this the Fortress has the more enduring reputation.

The combat swansong of the B-17 came in 1948, when Israeli aircraft bombed targets in Egypt.

Below: Head-on attacks by *Luftwaffe* fighters led to increased frontal armament. This B-17G, the definitive and best version, has twin .50 caliber Browning machine guns in the remotely controlled chin turret, as well as two cheek-mounted Brownings. There were further machine guns in dorsal, ball and tail turrets.

A Thousand Bombers Over Cologne

> *Against this pale, duck-egg blue and greyish mauve were silhouetted a number of small black shapes: all of them bombers, and all of them moving the same way. One hundred and thirty-four miles ahead, and directly in their path, stretched a crimson-red glow; Cologne was on fire. Already, only twenty-three minutes after the attack had started, Cologne was ablaze from end to end, and the main force of the attack was still to come.*

GROUP CAPTAIN LEONARD CHESHIRE, VC, DSO

The 1,000-bomber raid on Cologne at the end of May 1942 was a turning point in the air war. Daylight raids were too costly, and the RAF bombing offensive had long since switched to the cover of night for strategic operations.

At this stage of the war, RAF Bomber Command was the only force able to carry the fight to the heart of the German homeland, but results were poor. Only one crew in every five managed to place their bombs within five miles (8km) of the target; and only one in ten did so in the Ruhr, where haze made target location even more difficult.

In 1942 bombers were urgently needed to reinforce Coastal Command against the U-boat menace, and also to interdict Rommel's supply lines to the desert. With operations over Germany demonstrably ineffective, the whole future of Bomber Command was in doubt. Then, on February 22, Air Marshal Harris assumed command.

What was needed was a success, something to show that the bombers could achieve worthwhile results. A really big raid was the answer. The *Luftwaffe* had put 500 sorties over London on a single night during the Blitz; double this number, a nice round figure of 1,000, would be the answer.

Three main problems had first to be solved. Scraping together 1,000

Right: The mighty Avro Lancaster was the spearhead of RAF Bomber Command's night offensive against the Third Reich. Docile to fly, it carried the heaviest bomb loads of any aircraft during the entire war – 14,000lb (6,350kg). Controversy still rages over the "1000 raids" over Germany.

bombers was a mammoth task, and was achieved only by using aircraft and crews from training units. This was a tremendous risk, as it jeopardized the whole future of the force if things went wrong.

Concentration of force was next. On previous raids bombers had roamed the sky haphazardly, each aircraft responsible for finding and bombing its own target. This was not good enough; Harris wanted to put the entire force over the target in the space of one hour, a bomber every 3.5 seconds. This was too great a collision risk, and the time was extended to 90 minutes. Using three aiming points also helped to space the bombers more widely. Good timing was essential; seven different types of bomber, each with its own cruising speed and altitude,

were to be used. Finally, the target had to be easy to find, even in less-than-perfect conditions. Cologne, marked by the river Rhine, was eventually chosen.

On the night of May 30 no fewer than 1,046 bombers set out over the North Sea. Bringing up the rear were sixty-seven of the new and fast Lancasters. All converged on a point off the Dutch coast, from where they headed directly for the target. The German night fighter defenses were swamped by the concentrated bomber stream; for each bomber intercepted dozens passed through unscathed.

In all, forty-eight bombers were lost that night; an acceptable level of attrition. Cologne was devastated. This was the beginning of the road back for Bomber Command.

Naval Air Power 1941-1945

The first carrier-based fighters in action in the Second World War were British. For most of the inter-war years, the airplanes were controlled by the RAF; not until May 1939 did they revert to the Fleet Air Arm. As a result, carrier fighters were acquired on the basis of how safe they were to fly from ships, rather than how good they were for their tasks. Consequently they were much inferior to their land-based counterparts.

At the outbreak of war, the primary FAA fighter was the Sea Gladiator biplane. The first monoplane fighter was the Blackburn Skua, a two-seater which doubled as a dive-bomber. Slow, and with a pathetic rate of climb, the Skua was armed with four wing-mounted .303in (7.7mm) Browning machine guns, and a rear Lewis gun operated by the second crew member.

Most Skua operations took place off the coast of Norway in 1939/40. While it proved effective in driving off reconnaissance airplanes and shadowers, poor performance and lack of hitting power prevented many victories being scored. Top-scoring Skua pilot William Lucy shared in the destruction of seven twin-engined bombers before being killed by return fire from Heinkel He 111s on May 14, 1940.

The Fleet Air Arm for long insisted that its fighters needed a navigator for long overwater patrols. This built-in "headwind" was perpetuated in the Fairey Fulmar, which entered service in June 1940. Based on the Battle light bomber, its performance was better than that of the Skua, although still very much inferior to contemporary land-based fighters. But armed with eight wing-mounted .303in(7.7mm) Browning machine guns, it at least packed a hefty punch.

The Fulmar saw most action against Italy's Regia Aeronautica while escorting convoys through the Mediterranean to Malta, and were moderately successful against Italian torpedo-bombers. Top scorers were Stan Orr and Bill Barnes of 806 Squadron, and Rupert Tillard of 808 Squadron, with six each. All victims were multi-engined types except one Fiat CR.42 shot down by Orr.

The inadequacies of the Fulmar led to the navalization of the Hurricane and Spitfire, but these lacked the endurance to be fully effective as a fleet fighter, while the latter was in any case too delicate for deck-landing. American carrier fighters, such as the Wildcat (known to the British as the Martlet), then later the Hellcat and Corsair, were acquired by the Fleet Air Arm.

The final venture into the field of single-engined two-seaters was the Fairey Firefly. Powered by a Rolls-Royce Griffon engine, and armed with four 20mm Hispano cannon, it was far better than the Fulmar, but for interception and air combat, it was mediocre, and achieved little.

Above: British Fleet Air Arm Fairey Swordfish torpedo-bomber of 820 Squadron over the carrier HMS *Ark Royal* early in the war.

Below: The agility of the A6M2 Zero carrier fighter became legendary, while ventral drop tanks significantly increased its range.

War in the Far East

When the Japanese offensive burst like a tidal wave across the Far East and the Pacific, the capability of her fighters came as a nasty shock to the Allies. It should not have done; the Japanese had been in action against China, and to a lesser degree the Soviet Union, during the 1930s, while Claire Chennault, the commander of the American Volunteer Group in China, had already encountered them and devised suitable tactics against them.

Japanese fighter doctrine was to defeat the enemy in the air wherever they could be found, and to this end dogfighting was the means employed. For this, maneuverability was the primary requirement. Japanese aero-engines were no great shakes, and to compensate for lack of power airframes were built as

Above: In China, pilots of General Claire Chennault's American Volunteer Group, the "Flying Tigers," scramble to their Curtiss P-40 fighters to intercept marauding Japanese bombers.

light as possible, thus increasing power loading and minimising wing loading. This was not done at the expense of structural strength – the Zero and Oscar could pull as much "g" as their western opponents – but such essentials as armor protection, self-sealing for fuel tanks, and even radios, were omitted. Consequently they were very vulnerable to hits; the clever bit was in scoring hits on such agile machines while flying a less maneuverable fighter.

The other Japanese advantage lay in experience. Fighting over China had been hard, and in some ways

Left: The Curtiss P-40 was the most numerous USAAF fighter type in the early years of the Pacific war, and although largely supplanted by the P-38, remained in service until the end. The final variant, seen here at a Burma airfield, was the P-40N Warhawk.

encounters with the Russian I-153s, and particularly with the heavily armed and armored, but still very agile I-16s over Nomonghan, had been even harder. When in December 1941 they entered the Second World War, Japan possessed a cadre of very experienced and battle-hardened fighter pilots.

At the end of 1941, the RAF in the Far East, as it had been in Egypt, was equipped with second-rate fighters, of which the Hurricane was the best. The others were Curtiss Mohawks (Hawk 75s as used by the French in 1939) and Brewster Buffaloes. The latter was a real clunker; slow, with a poor rate of climb, sluggish in pitch and roll, and with an engine which showed a decided tendency to overheat. Not one of these airplanes could take on a Zero or a Ki-43 Hayabusa in a turning fight with any hope of winning, although, amazingly, Australian Alf Clare and New Zealander Geoffrey Fisken both claimed six victories against the Japanese while flying Buffaloes! Fisken went on to score a further five with the Kittyhawk.

Above: The wartime censor has obliterated the RAF code letters on this Brewster F2A Buffalo squadron flying in "vics" of three formation over Malaya in 1941, in company with a Blenheim IV. The Buffalo was totally outclassed by the rival Japanese A6M Zero, although the RAF did its best to increase performance by replacing the 0.50 caliber guns by .303 caliber, reducing ammunition to 350 rounds and fuel to a mere 84 gallons. The F2A-1 Buffalo was the US Navy's first monoplane fighter, and 54 were ordered in 1938, although only 11 reached the carrier USS *Saratoga*; the remainder went to Finland where, from February 1940 until the end of the war, they did extremely well. The US Navy later bought 43 more powerful and more heavily armed F2A-2 (Model 339), and then 108 F2A-3 with armor and self-sealing tanks. In 1939 bulk orders were placed by Belgium, the Netherlands, although these were not delivered, and Britain, whose RAF operated 170 delivered in 1941 to Singapore.

Air War in the Pacific

The vast wastes of the Pacific, studded on its westernmost part by innumerable islands, posed unique problems in power projection, and made the aircraft carrier indispensable. The first blow was struck at Oahu in December 1941, when Japanese airplanes from six carriers made a surprise attack on the US Navy base at Pearl Harbor. A few Curtiss P-40s of the USAAF managed to get airborne, but were overwhelmed by sheer numbers. By great good fortune, all three USN carriers in the Pacific were away at the time.

For the next few months, Japanese forces swarmed in all directions – out across the Pacific islands; down the East Indies to New Guinea; across Malaya and Singapore – while in April 1942, a strong carrier force mounted a raid against Ceylon. Opposing Allied fighters, including the Dutch, were decimated. The inexperienced Allied pilots persisted in trying to dogfight with agile Zeros and Hayabusas, often flown by veterans of China.

The Zero in particular posed problems. Its inherent long range was increased by flying at minimum engine revolutions and hanging in the air just above the stall. This gave it an endurance of eight hours, enabling it to operate over distances previously considered impossible, and appear where it was least expected. Before long, the only effectives in the area were a handful of USAAF fighter squadrons, equipped with P-40 Tomahawks and P-39 Airacobras, the Royal Australian Air Force, mainly with Tomahawks, and the US Navy and Marine Corps with Grumman F4F Wildcats, carrier- and land-based.

The Wildcat, which bore the brunt of the Japanese onslaught for the next two years, was an extremely rugged fighter, which was just as well; it was rather slower, was out-climbed, and easily out-turned by the Zero. However, it had a few advantages. The pilot sat up high, with a

good view over the nose, which aided shooting at high deflection angles. Whereas in a high speed dive the ailerons of the Zero stiffened, becoming almost immoveable above 290mph (467kph), the Wildcat retained its effectiveness in the rolling plane. Consequently, once a Zero was committed to following it in a steep diving turn, the Wildcat could evade by reversing the turn, leaving the Japanese fighter unable to follow.

Tactically, the experienced Imperial Japanese Navy was far ahead of the Americans, but in part this was offset by American technical superiority. The American carriers had both

Above: A6M2 Zero fighters warm up on the deck of the carrier *Hiryu*, one of six carriers that took part in the raid on Pearl Harbor.

radar and a fighter control system based on the British model of 1940. They also had an IFF and homing system, to enable their fighters to return to the carriers over the trackless wastes of the ocean, even though the carriers had changed their position by several tens of miles since takeoff.

Whereas land-based fighters tended to fly at high cruising speeds, carrier fighters worked on the assumption that while the enemy might rate 50 percent, the sea rated 100 percent. Unless operational con-

siderations dictated otherwise, they flew at economical cruising speed, optimizing their endurance on the principle that at the end of the mission they would most probably have to search for the carrier, then await their turn to land. The disadvantage of this was that the low cruising speed made them more vulnerable to the surprise bounce.

A historic engagement took place in May 1942. This was the Battle of the Coral Sea, the first encounter between two fleets whose surface units never once sighted each other.

An amphibious Japanese force sailed to capture Port Moresby, on the south coast of New Guinea, and the fleet carriers *Shokaku* and *Zuikaku* were detached to support the light carrier *Shoho*, which was already in the area. They were opposed by the *Yorktown* and *Lexington*.

The battle was a comedy of errors. *Shoho* was sunk before noon on May 7; at the same time an American destroyer and oiler had been misidentified as a cruiser and a carrier, both of which were sunk by airplanes from the Japanese fleet carriers.

Low cloud and rain made visibility poor; the returning Japanese strike was engaged by a patrol of

Wildcats, became confused, and two groups actually tried to line up and land on *Yorktown*. Unfortunately the Americans, understandably nervous about allowing Japanese bombers anywhere near them, did not allow them to do so!

On the following morning the opposing carrier forces located each other, and launched air strikes. Fighter defense on both sides was faulty. *Shokaku* was hit by two bombs and badly damaged. Both American carriers were hit. *Lexington* was lost some hours later due to faulty damage control, while *Yorktown* was damaged by a single bomb.

The Coral Sea battle can be accounted an honorable draw. It was

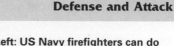

Left: US Navy firefighters can do nothing but watch as the battleship USS *Virginia* sinks following the surprise Japanese aerial bombardment of Pearl Harbor, December 7, 1941.

their opponents. The answer was the head-on attack, in which each fighter had an identical shot, and in which, if each pilot aimed accurately, the advantage went to the most surviv-able airplane. He came up with the Beam Defense Maneuver. A section of four fighters flew in two pairs abreast, with spacings related to minimum radius of turn at the current speed. Attacked from astern, one pair turned hard towards the other. On seeing this, the other pair turned hard towards the attacked section, passing below them. If the attacker had followed his prey around, he would end in a head-on pass with the other section, with the disadvantage of having to drop his nose, thereby risking a head-on collision, in order to shoot back.

MIDWAY, THE TURNING POINT

Midway Island was well-named; 1,300 miles (2,092km) northwest of Oahu, it was strategically placed on the direct route to Japan. Admiral Yamamoto conceived a plan to occu-py it in June 1942, as the first step in launching an assault on the Hawaiian Islands. Unfortunately for him, the Americans had broken the Japanese codes, and knew precisely what he intended.

Direct support of the Midway invasion fleet was provided by four Japanese carriers: *Akagi*, *Kaga*, *Soryu* and *Hiryu*, the fighter comple-ment of which was 103 A6M2 Zeros. Opposing them were three American carriers: *Hornet*, *Enterprise*, and the hastily repaired *Yorktown*. The garri-son of Midway itself included twen-ty-one Buffaloes and seven Wildcats of the US Marines.

The Japanese opened the ball on June 4 with a strike against Midway. Directed by radar, the defenders intercepted, but were badly cut up

also a learning time for the American Wildcat pilots. Shaken by being out-maneuvered by the Japanese air-planes, not only the Zeros but the dive- and torpedo-bombers also, they endeavored to find tactical answers to redress the balance.

The US Navy pilots had learned a great deal from RAF pilots sent to the USA to exchange ideas. They had already adopted the pair as the basic fighter element and, unlike virtually every other air arm in the world, had developed attacks which involved deflection shooting.

Jimmy Thach, commanding the Wildcats of VF-3, considered tactics which made the most of the relative survivability of their fighters vis-a-vis

205

by the Zeros. Japanese losses totaled nine, but only five American fighters survived the initial attack in operable condition.

The riposte, from carrier- and Midway-based torpedo- and dive-bombers, was uncoordinated, and the first attackers were cut to pieces for no result. Every aircraft of VT-8 was lost, mostly to Zeros, but the succession of attacks had drawn the defending Zeros down to low level. When Dauntless dive-bombers arrived over the Japanese fleet, they were unopposed, and in short order disposed of *Akagi*, *Kaga*, and *Soryu*.

Hiryu, the sole survivor, struck back. Her bombers penetrated the defensive fighter screen, albeit with heavy losses, seriously damaging

Above: The F4F-4 Wildcat made its combat debut at the Battle of Midway in June 1942, and for the first nine months of the war held the ring for the US Navy against the much more maneuverable Zero.

Yorktown, which finally sank on June 7. *Enterprise* launched a counter-strike, and this scored four bomb hits on *Hiryu*, setting it ablaze. By morning of June 5, all four Japanese fleet carriers had sunk. Airplane losses during

the battle, mainly due to fighters, were horrendous. Eighty-five American machines and the entire Japanese complement were destroyed, with the loss of many experienced and irreplaceable pilots. From this

Above: Ensign Ardon R. Ives, the pilot of a Grumman F6F Hellcat, scrambles to safety as his airplane erupts in flames after a barrier crash on landing aboard the carrier USS *Lexington*.

defeat the Imperial Japanese Navy air arm never recovered. Thach's Beam Defense Maneuver was first employed during this battle, which proved a turning point in the Pacific War. Thach himself became an ace at Midway; his total for the war was seven, and he became an admiral.

GUADALCANAL

Two months after Midway, the USN took the offensive for the first time, when the Marines invaded Guadalcanal. Three carriers, *Enterprise*, *Saratoga* and *Wasp*, covered the landings with ninety-nine Wildcats. The first Japanese counter-attack, of twenty-seven twin-engined bombers escorted by eighteen Zeros of the Tainan Air Group, which included Japanese aces Saburo Sakai and Hiroyoshi Nishizawa, was met in force, but nine Wildcats were shot down and several others badly damaged by the escorts, for four bombers and a Zero.

Desultory fighting ensued, with an average of slightly fewer than twenty fighter sorties per day. Over the next seven months, American fighter losses amounted to 79; 45 per 1,000 sorties, while the equivalent Japanese figures were 136; 73 per 1,000 sorties. By February 7 1943, Guadalcanal was firmly in American hands. Top-scoring Wildcat ace was US Marine Joe Foss, commonly known as "Swivel-Neck Joe", with twenty-six victories, thus equaling Eddie Rickenbacker's score in the Great War.

Foss was closely followed by John L Smith with 19 victories; Marion Carl with 15 1/2, Robert Galer with 14; Eugene Trowbridge (13); Ken Frazier (12 1/2); and Harold (Indian Joe) Bauer, who was killed on November 14, 1943, his score 10.

Many top-scoring aces of the crack Tainan Kokutai of the Imperial Japanese Navy were lost during the Guadalcanal fighting. Notably these were Saburo Sakai (61 victories),

Above: Douglas Dauntless dive-bombers over Midway Island. In the battle of Midway, Japanese fighters were drawn down to low level by waves of American torpedo bombers, leaving the Dauntless with an unopposed run.

who was withdrawn wounded, having lost an eye; Toshio Ohta (34); Junichi Sasai (27); Kazushi Uto (19); Toraichi Takatsuka (16); Shigetaka Ohmori (13); and Keisaku Yoshimura and Motosuna Yoshida (12 each), who were all killed. Ranking Japanese ace Hiroyoshi Nishizawa died shortly after, shot down as a passenger in a

transport aircraft. The hastily recruited replacements were of such poor quality that the unit, like many others, became a shadow of its former self.

PACIFIC STRATEGY

While the USN and USMC played a tremendous part in the Pacific War, they were not alone. The RAAF and

Right: Lieutenant-Colonel Jimmy Doolittle's B-25B Mitchell bombers crammed aboard the carrier *Hornet* on their way to the morale-boosting raid on the Japanese homeland, April 1942. While no great damage was caused, the Japanese army and navy suffered loss of face.

RNZAF fought alongside them, albeit in small numbers, while the USAAF was present in strength.

The conduct of the Pacific War bred two schools of thought. The US Navy favored an island-hopping campaign via the Gilberts, bypassing the Marshalls to Eniwetok; then bypassing the Japanese base at Truk to advance upon the Japanese home islands. By contrast, the USAAF, tied to fixed land bases, preferred an advance from New Guinea to the Philippines, then on to Japan. In the event both were adopted.

While apparently wasteful of resources, this had one tremendous advantage. The Japanese, already badly overstretched, never knew where the next thrust was coming from, and consequently remained weak everywhere. All they could do was to react when the next blow fell, using their depleted forces as a fire brigade and rushing them from place to place.

The Americans made no attempt to drive back the Japanese in a linear manner. Instead, they frequently bypassed Japanese garrisons, cutting them off from supplies and reinforcements, to wither on the vine, having first neutralized their offensive capability, usually via air strikes. In this manner several Japanese enclaves were left on New Guinea, which is a huge island, while among others the Marshall Islands were bypassed in a leap to Eniwetok, as was the large naval base at Truk.

Some idea of American numerical superiority combined with changing technical superiority can be given by the statistics. The campaign for Eastern New Guinea between February 1 and August 31, 1942, saw 1,900 Allied fighter sorties flown, against about 1,000 Japanese. Allied fighter losses amounted to 177; Japanese fighter losses totaled just 41; an adverse ratio of 4.32:1. The campaign for New Guinea and New Britain, between September 15, 1942, and June 30, 1943, yielded 8,600 Allied fighter sorties against about 4,000 by the Japanese, with losses of 114 and 380, respectively; a positive ratio of 13.33. The fighting over Rabaul which followed between October 1, 1943, and February 17, 1944, was marked by 5,345 Allied fighter sorties against about 2,400 Japanese; losses were 112 Allied fighters against 330 Japanese; a positive ratio of 1:2.95.

In all cases, the Allies flew roughly two fighter sorties to each Japanese one, whereas the

victory/loss ratio switched from extremely adverse to very positive. This actually reflects three factors. Firstly, the introduction of American fighters which were superior to their Japanese counterparts. Secondly, the effect of superior training and teamwork, which allowed the numerical superiority to afford more coincidental support. Thirdly, the Japanese fighter arm, both army and navy, had lost many experienced pilots by the end of 1943. This even allowed Wildcats, which flew from the smaller escort carriers for the remainder of the war, to hold their own.

THE USAAF IN THE PACIFIC

At the outbreak of the war against Japan, the two main USAAF fighter types were the Curtiss P-40, which we examined earlier, and the Bell P-39 Airacobra.

The Airacobra was unconventional in that its engine, the Allison V-1710, was mounted amidships, behind the pilot, and drove the propeller by means of a long and weighty transmission shaft. This arrangement promised several advantages. The cockpit could be located forward, improving the view over the nose. Placing the engine on the center of gravity should have improved maneuverability, while this configuration allowed for a nose-wheel undercarriage, with superior ground handling and view on takeoff.

Alas, the Airacobra proved a turkey. The unorthodox engine loca-

Above: US Navy Seabees watch as a B-24 Liberator takes off from the hurriedly built airfield at Eniwetok, Marshall Islands. The B-24's range enabled it to reach targets far beyond the reach of the B-17.

tion resulted in extreme weight penalties; in an already underpowered fighter this proved disastrous, and it was easily outfought by the Zero and Hayabusa. The unreliability of the Allison was compounded by poor access for routine maintenance; the result was chronic unserviceability.

By far the most successful USAAF fighter in China and the Pacific was Lockheed's P-38 Lightning, which largely supplanted the P-40 Warhawk from mid-1943. Its exceptional range made it ideal for the long-distance missions which were standard in the Pacific, while its speed and altitude performance gave it a distinct edge over most Japanese fighters that it encountered. Its high wing loading meant that it was unable to

turn with them but, by staying high and choosing their moment, Lightning pilots were able to succeed against their better-turning adversaries by using dive and zoom tactics.

Both top-scoring American pilots of the war, Dick Bong (40) and Tommy McGuire (38), achieved most of their victories with the Lightning. Bong survived the war only to die shortly after in a takeoff accident with the P-80 Shooting Star jet. McGuire died in action while trying to save a fellow pilot under attack; he attempted a too-tight turn just above the treetops but stalled and went in.

OFFENSIVE IN THE PACIFIC

The Grumman Aircraft Corporation has traditionally been known as "The

Ironworks," its airplanes being so rugged that rumor had it that they were carved out of the solid. Even before America's entry into the war, it was obvious that the performance of the Wildcat was inferior to that of land-based fighters in Europe. Chance Vought's Corsair was undergoing trials as a potential Wildcat replacement, but in a "belt and braces" decision, the US Navy went to Grumman for an upgraded Wildcat.

The result, first flown on June 26, 1942, was the F6F Hellcat. Powered by a Wright Double Wasp 18-cylinder radial engine, the Hellcat retained the simple lines of its predecessor, and although considerably

Below: The P-40 Warhawk performed well for USAAF (as here) and other Allied air forces in the Pacific. Part of the ubiquitous Curtiss Hawk family, it was tough, nimble and particularly useful in close support of armies.

Above: The Nakajima Ki-27, codenamed Nate, was actually obsolete by the time of Pearl Harbor, but it still eqipped all but two Japanese army fighter units. It was short-ranged, but its agility still made it a formidable opponent.

larger and heavier was much faster, climbed better, and out-turned it with ease. From its combat debut in August 1943, the Hellcat comfortably out-performed the Zero, and gave the US Navy a measure of air superiority over the next two years. British Corsair pilot Norman Hanson tried the Hellcat for a local flight on one occasion. He commented afterwards: "In landing particularly I found it a lot safer and easier to handle largely, I think, because of its superior visibility and better stall characteristics."

Even before the requirement that led to the Hellcat, another fighter powered by the Double Wasp was under development for the USN. This was the Chance Vought F4U Corsair. To make the most of the available

Right: The AGM5 Model 52 Zero-Sen was faster than previous versions, max speed 351mph (565kph), and had heavier-gauge duralumin skinning for more protection. This captured example is flown by a US Navy pilot.

power, a huge four-bladed propeller was needed. This caused problems with ground clearance, to solve which an inverted gull-wing configuration was adopted. The resultant bird became known as "The bent-wing bastard from Stratford, Illinois."

One of the fastest fighters of the war, the Corsair was less than ideal for carrier operations. It had the endurance; it had the speed; it had the hitting power; but forward view from the cockpit, so important in a carrier-based airplane, was appalling, while for deck landing it had a built-in bounce which compromised safety. British Fleet Air Arm pilot Norman Hanson's reaction on first seeing it was to go and make his will!

The Corsair was originally judged unsuitable for carrier operations, and issued instead to the Marines. Combat debut was made on February 13, 1943, over Guadalcanal, and within six months all USMC squadrons had re-equipped with the Corsair, the blinding performance of which com-

pletely outclassed its opponents. While much more heavily wing-loaded than the Zero, it could generally stay with it for the first 90 degrees of turn, and this was usually enough. Not for nothing did it earn the name of "The Whistling Death!" from the Japanese.

It was in fact left to the Royal Navy to operate the Corsair from carriers, which they did from April 1944; nine months earlier than the US Navy. It was certainly a fact that more Corsairs were lost as a result of landing accidents than ever fell to Japanese fighters. But FAA Corsairs had the wings clipped to fit below decks, and surprisingly this cured the floating that occurred over the deck due to ground effect. Another innovation was a small spoiler under the starboard wing, which ensured that at the stall that wing always dropped first. But when, at the end of 1944, the British Pacific Fleet, with Corsairs, Hellcats, Fireflies and Seafires, joined the Americans in the assault

Above: Operating out of Henderson Field on Guadalcanal, B-17 Flying Fortresses hit the island of Gizo in New George Sound, known as "the Slot," October 5, 1942. While the US Navy carrier fighters generally grabbed the headlines, the land-based bombers made an enormous contribution as the US fought back against the Japanese.

on Japan, opportunities for air combat were few, and there were virtually no aces in their ranks.

Meanwhile Marine Corps Corsairs operated the type with great success from island bases. The top-scoring Marine pilot of the war was Gregory Boyington, with twenty-eight victories. The antithesis of the clean-cut, milk-drinking and early-to-bed all-American boy, Boyington was a hard-living, whiskey-drinking hell-raiser. Having prejudiced his career by a tangled private life, he joined the Flying Tigers, the American Volunteer Group in south-east Asia.

Flying P-40s from Rangoon in Burma, he downed six Japanese aircraft in four weeks, before returning to the USA. On his return to the USA, he rejoined the Marines, and in September 1943 was in command of VMF-214, the Black Sheep squadron.

Tactical finesse was no part of Boyington's makeup; on his first mission, on September 16, the Black Sheep blundered into about forty Zeros, and an unholy dogfight resulted. When Boyington returned, he claimed five Zeros. One of the fightingest men ever to strap an airplane on his back, he sought every opportunity to bring the Japanese to battle, and by Christmas of that year had reached the American record of twenty-six victories, held jointly by Eddie Rickenbacker in the Great War, and Marine pilot Joe Foss. On January 3, 1944, Boyington got two more, but was himself shot down while attempting to protect his stricken wingman. He survived a low-level bale-out by a miracle, to end the war in a Japanese prison camp.

THE MARIANAS TURKEY SHOOT

By the middle of 1944, the Japanese were being driven back on all fronts. Overmatched, the Japanese carriers had avoided battle for the past year, but now it had become do or die. When in June 1944 the American Pacific fleet sallied forth against the Marianas, bypassing Truk and the Caroline Islands, the Japanese were forced to act.

Below: The first American fighter to exceed 400mph (644kph), the F-4U Corsair owed its success to its overwhelming performance. Ace Greg Boyington scored most of his "kills" with it.

The American Task Force contained seven fleet carriers and eight light carriers, with two groups of escort carriers to provide close air support. Total fighter strength was 470 F6F-3 Hellcats. Against this armada, the Japanese could bring nine carriers, reinforced by many more land-based aircraft.

The Japanese plan was to catch the American Task Force between the anvil of land-based air power and the hammer of carrier aircraft. As the poet said, the best laid plans.... Poor intelligence, operational inadequacies, and a determined foe added up to utter disaster for the Japanese.

On June 11 over 200 Hellcats carried out a sweep over Japanese airfields in the Marianas. On the following day, heavy raids were launched against Saipan, Tinian and Guam. That evening, part of the force raced north to attack Iwo Jima and Chichi Jima. Its task complete, it rejoined two days later. By now the anvil had been irreparably shattered.

This left only the hammer. Belatedly, the Japanese fleet sailed on June 13, and was immediately reported by US submarines. Unaware that the anvil no longer existed, Admiral Ozawa divided his force into two parts. The first was bait to draw the American carriers within range of the second, killer group.

The carrier battle commenced on June 19, when the first Japanese strike was launched. The force was detected by radar at the extreme range of 150 miles (241km), and defending Hellcats were scrambled

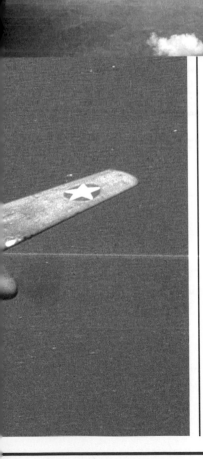

Above: Its exceptional range helped make the P-38 Lightning the most successful US Army Air Force fighter of the war.

to meet them. An unexpected bonus was that the Japanese paused to orbit 75 miles (120km) away while the strike leader briefed his inexperienced crews by radio. This hiatus enabled the American fighters to intercept far out from the Task Force, with all the advantages of height and position. The ensuing engagement was more a massacre than a battle.

Wave after wave of Japanese aircraft set out for the American carrier force, but were met by wave after wave of defending Hellcats, which wrought tremendous destruction.

Left: The USAAF's Allison-engined P-51 Mustang, also known as the A-36 in its close-support incarnation, gave first class service against the Japanese in Burma and China, where it did not need high-altitude capability.

Above: Already fatally damaged, a Japanese torpedo bomber explodes in mid-air after a direct strike by a 5 inch shell from USS *Yorktown* which the Japanese pilot is trying to hit in a *kamikaze* attack, April 12, 1943.

Japanese losses during the day amounted to 218, and only a few attackers broke through the defenses, causing minimal damage.

American submarines now played their part. They torpedoed and.sank the carriers *Taiho* and *Shokaku*. On the following day the American carriers went over to the offensive, sinking *Hiyo* and damaging *Zuikaku* and *Chiyoda*. US Navy losses to all causes amounted to 130 airplanes and 76 aircrewmen. Total Japanese losses, including land-based airplanes, were 476, including about 445 aircrewmen. The Imperial Japanese Navy never recovered from this setback. The last great carrier battle of the war, it had been a great American victory, thanks mainly to the prowess of the Hellcat pilots.

Aloft during the Marianas battle was top-scoring US Navy pilot David McCampbell. An "old man" of thirty-four at the time, he was Carrier Air Group Commander aboard the USS *Essex*, and his first victory was scored over Saipan on June 11. Then on June 19 he led a flight of fourteen Hellcats to intercept a Japanese raid near Guam, claiming five Yokosuka D4Y dive-bombers during the one sortie. Later that day, over Guam, he claimed two more. But at the end of that trip he was outmaneuvered by a Zero flown by one of the few remaining Japanese honchos, and forced to disengage with a high-speed dive. Other Hellcats intervened, and brushed the Zero off his tail.

McCampbell's biggest day came on October 23, 1944, when he and his wingman Roy Rushing encountered about forty Japanese Zeros escorting a bomber raid. While others tackled the bombers, McCampbell and Rushing set about the fighters. The latter were not very aggressive and appeared to be totally inexperienced, and allowed the two Hellcats to attack as and when they chose. At the end of the engagement McCampbell claimed nine and Rushing five. McCampbell survived the war with a score of thirty-four victories.

THE ASSAULT ON JAPAN
Gradually the Japanese had abandoned their doctrine of fielding light and maneuverable, but extremely

vulnerable, fighters, in exchange for more heavily armed and protected airplanes. Of these, the Ki-61 Hien was unusual in that it was powered by a liquid-cooled V-12 engine. The Ki-43 Shoki was relatively highly wing loaded, while the performances of the J2M3 Raiden and the Ki-84 Hayate were good by any standards. The best Japanese Navy fighter of the war was however the N1K2 Shiden, which in the hands of an experienced pilot had the mastery over the Hellcat. But with all these, the story was too little, too late.

B-29 heavy bombers commenced raiding the Japanese home islands from the Marianas on November 24, 1944. Lack of effective early warning and airborne radar meant that defending Japanese fighters were hard-pressed to intercept. Aircraft factories and airfields were high on the list of targets, and Japanese fighter production fell alarmingly.

Daylight bombing began in March 1945, once fighter escort became available. This was provided by Mustangs based on Iwo Jima, flying the longest (eight hour) escort missions on record. Mustangs over Tokyo signaled the beginning of the end for the Japanese. In July 1945, the US Navy joined the assault on Japan, with fourteen or more aircraft carriers at a time, supplemented by the British Pacific Fleet, and able to put more than 1,000 airplanes into the air at one time.

Heavily outnumbered, the Japanese defenders fought back with the strength of desperation, but unavailingly. The final British air combat of the war took place on August 12, when ten Seafires accounted for eight Zeros, losing one of their own number. The final victory of the war fell to a USN Corsair, which shot down a C6N Saiun, only minutes before the end of hostilities.

Below: The *Yorktown's* gunners in action again as a Nakajima B6N2 bursts into flames, torpedo still in place, during an attack on the carrier near Truk, in the Caroline Islands, April 29, 1944.

Mitsubishi A6M2 Model 21 Zero

The first American pilots to encounter the legendary Zero were impressed by its outstanding maneuverability, which at normal combat speeds far outclassed that of their own fighters. Only later did they realize that the Japanese pilots paid a high price for this. While the Zero had been stressed for the usual combat maneuvers, it had been lightened by leaving off everything regarded as non-essential. This included armor protection, self-sealing fuel tanks, and even the radio. As a direct result the Zero was very vulnerable, and could sustain little battle damage. Another failing was that as speed increased, rate of roll became progressively slower, making it difficult to change direction quickly. The Zero was progressively upgraded throughout the war but, failing to keep pace with American fighter developments, was shot from the skies.

Dimensions: Span 39ft 4½in (12m); length 29ft 8½in (9.06m; height 10ft (5.05m); wing area 242sq ft (22.48sq m).
Power: One Nakajima NK1C Sakae 14-cylinder air-cooled radial engine rated at 950hp.
Weights: Empty 3,704lb (1,680kg); loaded 6,164lb (2,796kg).
Performance: Maximum speed 331mph (533kph); ceiling 32,810ft (10,000m); climb 7min 27sec to 19,685ft (6,000m); range 1,161 miles (1,870km).
Armament: Two wing-mounted 20mm Type 99 cannon with 60rpg; two nose-mounted 7.7mm Type 97 machine guns with 500rpg.

Below: While agile and fast, able to outrun Allied fighters, the Zero's lack of armor and self-sealing tanks made it vulnerable if hit.

Chance Vought F4U-4 Corsair

The first American fighter able to exceed 400mph (644kph), the Corsair owed its success to its overwhelming performance. It was designed as the smallest possible airframe wrapped around the largest possible engine, although this involved a very poor view from the cockpit. Intended as a carrier fighter, it had tricky handling coupled with bad bounce while deck-landing, ensuring that it made its combat debut with the US marine Corps, operating from land bases. The cockpit was later raised and the bounce cured; once this was done the Corsair became a very successful naval fighter, in service with many nations, which did not cease production until 1952, long after all its contemporaries.

Dimensions: Span 41ft (12.50m); length 33ft 8in (10.26m); height 14ft 9in (4.50m); wing area 314sq ft (29.17sq m).
Power: One Pratt & Whitney R-2800-18W 18-cylinder air-cooled radial engine rated at 2,100hp.
Weights: Empty 9,205lb (4,175kg); loaded 14,670lb (6,654kg).
Performance: Maximum speed 446mph (718kph); ceiling 41,500ft (12,649m); climb 7min 42sec to 20,000ft (6,096m); range 1,005 miles (1,617km).
Armament: Six wing-mounted .50in (12.7mm) Browning machine guns with 2,350 rounds total.

Above: A Vought F4U Corsair fighter-bomber of the US Navy displays the distinctive cranked wing that allowed a short undercarriage while providing sufficient ground clearance for the large three-bladed propeller of its Pratt & Whitney R-2800 Wasp radial engine.

Left: An F4U fires off eight 5-inch rockets, reckoned to be equivalent to a broadside from a destroyer, at Japanese targets on Okinawa, June 1945. The photo was taken by David Duncan, US Marine Corps photographer, in a P-38 on the Corsair's tail, the first such photo. The blast blew the P-38 upon its right wing, and then down, so that it almost crashed into the target area. The photo plane was only about 40 to 50 feet off the tail of the Corsair, and both aircraft were flying around 30 knots.

Grumman F6F-3 Hellcat

The most important ship-board fighter of the war, the Hellcat made its combat debut on August 31, 1943. It was faster than the Japanese Zero, although it culd not climb at such a steep angle, and was exceptionally well-protected against enemy fire. With 456lb (207kg) of armor plating, bullet-proof glass, duralumin deflector plates and self-sealing for the fuel tanks, it could absorb an enormous amount of battle damage and still function. Flown by former Wildcat pilots who had learned the hard way to offset the superior maneuverability of the Zero through teamwork and tactics, it immediately established an ascendancy over the Japanese fighter that it never lost throughout the war.

Below: Hellcats made their combat debut over Marcus Island on August 31, 1943, and scored more victories in the Pacific than any other fighter.

Above: An F6F-3 Hellcat of VF-12 prepares for carrier launch in 1944. Top-scoring Hellcat pilot was US Navy ace David McCampbell with 34 victories, nine of them on a single mission over Leyte Gulf, October 23, 1944.

Dimensions: Span 42ft 10in (13.06m); length 33ft 7in (10.23m)); height 11ft 3in (3.43m); wing area 334sq ft (31.03sq m).
Power: One Pratt & Whitney R-2800 Double Wasp 19-cylinder air-cooled radial engine rated at 2,000hp.
Weights: Empty 9,042lb (4,101kg); loaded 12,186lb (5,528kg).
Performance: Maximum speed 376mph (605kph); ceiling 37,500ft (11,430m); climb 14 min to 25,000ft (7,620m); range 1,085 miles (1,746km).
Armament: Six wing-mounted .50in (12.7mm) Colt-Browning machine guns with 400rpg.

Kawanishi N1K2-J Shiden-Kai

With the entry into service of the Hellcat and Corsair, Japan urgently needed a high-performance interceptor. New fighters were under development, but this took time. Readily available was the Kyofu, a floatplane fighter with mid-wing configuration and, like the American Mustang, a low-drag laminar-flow aerofoil. This was rapidly developed into the Shiden. Man euverability was increased using a unique combat flap system which changed angle automatically to provide extra lift during high-g maneuvers. While it was as fast as the Hellcat, and climbed and turned much better, the Shiden was tricky to fly, and only an experienced pilot could get the best out of it.

Dimensions: Span 39ft 3¼in (18.98m); length 30ft 9in (9.35m); height 13ft (3.96m); wing area 253sq ft (23.50sq m).
Power: One Nakajima NK9H Homare 21 18-cylinder air-cooled radial engine rated at 1,990lb.
Weights: Empty 5,858lb (2,675kg); loaded 9,039lb (4,100kg).
Performance: Maximum speed 370mph (595kph); ceiling 35,300ft (10,760m); climb 7min 22 sec to 19,685ft (6,000m); range 1,069 miles (1,720km).
Armament: Four wing-mounted 20mm Type 99 cannon.

Fairey Firefly

The first two-seat monoplane fighter to enter service with the British Fleet Air Arm was the Fairey Fulmar, in June 1940. Essentially it was a scaled-down version of the Battle light bomber, while navalization made it slightly heavier. Slow, and with a derisory rate of climb, it was not very effective even against unescorted bombers. Something better was needed, and that was the Firefly, a name revived from a less than successful series of fighters in the 1920s. The prototype was first flown in December 1941, but service entry was delayed until mid-1943. The pilot sat over the leading edge with the observer behind the wing. The main wartime version was the Firefly F 1, which carried a hefty punch in the form of four fixed 20mm Hispano cannon in the wings. Handling at the low end of the speed range was good; it was 38mph (61kph) faster than the Fulmar at sea level, and considerably better than this at altitude; it outclimbed the Fulmar comfortably, and had a ceiling some 25 percent higher. But by the time the Firefly F 1 entered service it was outmatched by almost every aircraft it was likely to encounter in air combat. The FAA had by this time started to equip with American Hellcats and Corsairs, and the Fireflies were used primarily for defense suppression and anti-shipping strikes. Only in the Far East did the type see any real air combat, and No 1770 Squadron registered nine victories against the Japanese.

Dimensions: Span 44ft 6in (13.56m); length 37ft 7in (11.46m); height 13ft 7in (4.14m); wing area 342sq ft (31.77sq m).
Power: One 1,990hp Rolls-Royce Griffon XII V-12 liquid-cooled engine.
Weights: Empty 8,925lb (4,048kg); normal takeoff 12,131lb (5,503kg).
Performance: Maximum speed 319mph (513kph); ceiling 28,000ft (8,534m); climb 5min 45sec to 10,000ft (3,048m); range 1,364 miles (2,195km).
Armament: Four wing-mounted 20mm Hispano cannon with 160 rounds per gun; eight air-to-surface rocket projectiles or two 1,000lb (454kg) bombs.

Above: The N1K2-J Shiden-Kai evolved from the complex, N1K1-J landplane version of the Kyofu floatplane, but with low wing, new tail, simpler airframe and 23,000 fewer parts; it could be built in half the man-hours. Both N1K1-J and N1K2-J were used as *kamikazes* at Okinawa.

Above: Deck parties aboard a fleet carrier (probably HMS *Illustrious*) fold the wings of a Firefly F 1 after an attack on Japanese installations. The folding elliptical wings had trailing edges with Youngman flaps for use at low speeds. Some aircraft were fitted with underwing rocket rails.

Boeing B-29 Superfortress

Development and mass production of the B-29, the Boeing Model 345, was one of the biggest tasks in the history of aviation. It began with a March 1938 study for a new bomber with pressurized cabin and tricycle landing gear. This evolved into the 345 and in August 1940 money was voted for two proto-types. In January 1942 the US Army Air Force ordered fourteen YB-29s and 500 production aircraft. By February, while Boeing engineers worked night and day on the huge technical problems, a production organization was set up involving Boeing, Bell, North American and Fisher (General Motors). Martin came in later and, by VJ-day more than 3,000 Superforts had been delivered. This was a fantastic achievement because each repre-sented five or six times the technical effort of any earlier bomber.

In engine power, gross weight, wing loading, pressurization, arma-ment, airborne systems and even basic structure the B-29 set a wholly new standard. First combat mission was flown by the 58th Bomb Wing on June 5, 1944, and by 1945 twenty groups from the Marianas were sending 500 B-29s at a time to flat-ten and burn Japan's cities. (Three air-craft made emergency landings in Soviet territory, and Tupolev's design bureau put the design into production as the Tu-4 bomber and Tu-70 trans-port.) The -29C had all guns except those in the tail removed, increasing speed and altitude. After the war there were nineteen variants of B-29, not including the Washington B.1 supplied to help the RAF in 1950-58.

Above: Note the twin 0.50 gun turrets above and below the cockpit of this crew-decorated unpainted B-29. Prior to the nuclear attacks on Hiroshima and Nagasaki, the bomber concentrated on conventional raids against targets in Japan. US authorities reckoned that continuing these, together with an Allied invasion of Japan, would have claimed many, many more casualties.

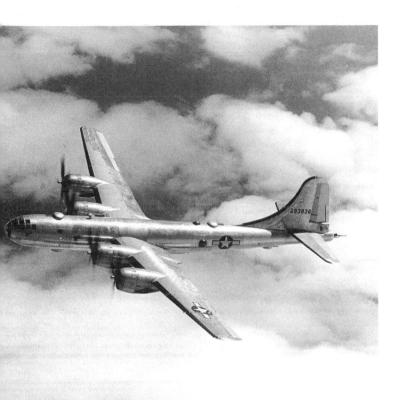

Above: Boeing's B-29 Superfortress heavy bomber achieved dubious fame as the deliverer of the two atomic bombs on Hiroshima and Nagasaki. First flown in 1942, it was powered by four 2,200hp Wright R-3350 air-cooled radial engines.

Dimensions: Span 141ft 3in (43.05m); length 99ft (30.2m); height 27ft 9in (8.46m).
Power: Four 2,200hp Wright R-3350-23 Duplex Cyclone 18-cylinder radials each with two exhaust-driven turbochargers.
Weights: Empty 74,500lb (33,795kg); loaded 135,000lb (61,240kg).
Performance: Maximum speed 357mph (575kph) at 30,000ft (9,144m); cruising speed 290mph (467kph); climb to 25,000ft (7,620m) in 43min; service ceiling 36,000ft (10,973m); range with 10,000lb (4,540kg) bombs 3,250miles (5,230km).
Armament: Four GE twin-0.50in turrets above and below, sighted from nose or three waist sighting stations; Bell tail turret, with own gunner, with one 20mm cannon and twin 0.50in; internal bomb load up to 20,000lb (9,072kg). Carried first two nuclear bombs. With modification, carried two 22,000lb British bombs externally under inner wings.

Hiroshima

> '*A column of smoke rising fast. It has a fiery red core. A bubbling mass, purple-gray in color, with that red core. It's all turbulent. Fires are springing up everywhere, like flames shooting out of a huge bed of coals.... Here it comes, the mushroom shape.... It's coming this way. It's like a mass of bubbling molasses. The mushroom is spreading out. It's maybe a mile or two wide and half a mile high. It's growing up and up and up.... The base of the mushroom looks like a heavy undercast that is shot through with flames.*'
>
> TECH. SGT. GEORGE CARON

At 02.42 on the morning of August 6, 1945, the huge Boeing B-29 Superfortress was cleared for takeoff from the island of Tinian in the Marianas. At the controls was Col. Paul Warfield Tibbets, a man carefully selected and trained to carry out the most destructive bombing mission ever. In the bomb bay was Little Boy, the first atomic bomb.

Little Boy, a Uranium 235-based weapon, was the culmination of the Manhattan Project, a nuclear research program lasting many years and costing many billions of dollars. Along with Fat Man, its plutonium-based companion, later to be dropped on Nagasaki, it was to be used to bring the war in the Pacific to a quick end.

The flight engineer opened the throttles, and slowly the B-29 started to move down the runway. For those in the know, this was a fraught time. A crash on take-off could possibly cause premature detonation, which would wipe out the whole of Tinian.

The B-29 was overloaded, and Tibbets held it on the ground until the

Above: A Little Boy nuclear weapon of the type that was launched from B-29 *Enola Gay* and detonated over Hiroshima. It was 10ft long and 28in in diameter, weighed about 9,000lb, and had a yield equivalent to approximately 20,000 tons of high explosive.

Above: Three days after Hiroshima, the mushroom cloud of a Fat Man nuclear bomb, released from B-29 *Bock's Car*, rises above Nagasaki. The Japanese surrendered eleven days later.

very last moment before easing back on the yoke. Slowly the huge bomber, named *Enola Gay* after Tibbets' mother, left the runway and climbed away into the darkness. On board, the navigator, radar operator and radioman were busy checking the course. Nothing could be left to chance. Ahead lay the target, Hiroshima.

Enola Gay arrived over Iwo Jima as dawn broke, and the pilot set course for Shikoku, climbing to bombing altitude of 30,600ft (9,325m) as it neared the Japanese coast. Ahead, a weather reconnaissance B-29 had reached Hiroshima and reported conditions satisfactory. The die was cast.

At 08.14, Tibbets gave the command, "On glasses," and the crew donned heavy Polaroid goggles to protect their eyes from the flash. Bombardier Maj. Thomas Ferebee lined up the aiming point, the Aloi bridge in the middle of the city, and at 08.15.17 Little Boy fell clear.

Tibbets instantly swung *Enola Gay* into a hard, diving right-hand

turn through 155 degrees, away from the detonation. They had less than a minute to make good their escape from the blast. No-one knew whether this would be enough; they could only hope.

At precisely 08.16 the bomb detonated with a force equal to 20,000 tons of TNT, and a glare far brighter than the sun. Tibbets could "... taste the brilliance; it tasted like lead." On the ground a firestorm raged, and radiation, the quiet, insidious killer, passed unnoticed through walls and bodies. Some 71,379 people died, 68,000 were

injured, and 49,000 buildings were destroyed.

Above, the mile-wide mushroom cloud rose to 60,000ft (18km), marking the place where a city called Hiroshima had been. The nuclear age was born, and the world would never be the same again.

Above: The damage wrought by one nuclear bomb on Hiroshima was horrifying – the most significant single raid in aviation history – although greater damage, and many more deaths, had already resulted from conventional raids on Tokyo.

The Jet Era Begins

The early jet aircraft were either experimental or, in keeping with the mood of the times, fighters. The first was of the former kind, the German Heinkel He 178, which made a short hop on August 24, 1939, and a circuit of the airfield three days later. On November 1 it was demonstrated to General Udet, head of the *Luftwaffe* Technical Department, and General Milch, head of the Air Ministry, but neither showed interest. It was in the Berlin Air Museum when an air raid in 1943 destroyed it. The next was the Heinkel He 280 fighter, the world's

first combat jet aircraft and first twin-engine jet, which made its maiden powered flight on April 2, 1941.

Britain's first jet aircraft, the experimental Gloster E28/39, made its maiden flight on May 15, 1941, powered by an 860lb (390kg) thrust Whittle W1 turbojet. The first and only Allied jet fighter to go into action in the Second World War was the Gloster Meteor F1. Its design, to Air Ministry specification F9/40, had begun in 1940. The twin-engine configuration was forced on the designers because the jet engines of the

Below: The Gloster-Whittle E28/39 takes off from Farnborough during its test program under the power of its 1,760lb (798kg) thrust Power Jets W2/500 turbojet. It originally had an 860lb (390kg) thrust Power Jets W1 (inset).

Right: The USA's first jet fighter design was the XFJ-1, later the FJ-1 Fury, produced for the US Navy. Powered by a 3,820lb (1,733kg) thrust General Electric J35-GE-2 engine, the XFJ-1 made its maiden flight on November 27, 1946.

Above: Italy's Caproni-Campini N-1, first flown on 28 August 1940, was not a true jet aircraft. A 900hp Isotta-Fraschini 12-cylinder piston engine drove a compressor with three stages of variable-pitch blading to blow air out of its tail nozzle. Its performance was inferior to that of a similarly powered propeller-driven two-seater.

day lacked the thrust to give a single-engine type the required performance. The first Meteor to be completed had two Rover-built W2B turbojets: these failed to develop more than 1,000lb (454kg) of thrust each, so the airplane was limited to taxying trials. The first Meteor to fly was the

Above: The first British jet fighter to enter service, and by a narrow margin only the second in the world to do so, was the Meteor, of which the last and best was the F 8 shown here. In 1952 this variant flew against the Russian-built MiG-15, which outclassed it.

Above: The Vampire F.3 was the first British single-engined jet fighter. Deliveries of the first Vampires began in April 1945, too late for the type to take part in World War Two.

fifth prototype, with two 1,500lb (680kg) thrust Halford H1 turbojets.

Twenty Mk 1 Meteors were built, of which sixteen were received by the RAF. Delivery to 616 Squadron began on July 12, 1944, and its first success was the destruction of a V1 flying bomb fifteen days later by toppling it with a wingtip when the guns jammed.

In the USA, the Bell P-59 Airacomet was the world's first jet to undergo service trials, which began in 1944. Its General Electric turbojet engine was based on the Whittle engine. In all, sixty-six P-59s were built but, not being combat worthy, were used only as trainers.

The Messerschmitt Me 262 made its first flight on March 25, 1942, an abortive event because the engine flamed out and the pilot barely completed a circuit. After further vicissitudes, the first production Me 262A-1as were delivered to the test unit in April 1944. In July they shot down two P-38 Lightnings and a Mosquito. The first regular Me 262A-1a squadron was formed in November 1944. Me 262s shot down 427 Allied aeroplanes, among them 300 four-engine bombers. In October the Me 262A-2a was declared operational.

THE COLD WAR

The return to what was euphemistically called peacetime did not lessen the recently warring nations' interest in the development of military aircraft. There was growing tension between the Soviet Bloc and the Western Allies. The Soviet blockade of Berlin that began on June 25, 1948, enabled Britain and the USA to demonstrate their readiness to defy their potential enemy. RAF and civilian Dakotas and Yorks and the USAF's C-54 Skymasters began to fly in the food and fuel

Above: Typical of the early Russian jets was the Yakovlev Yak-23, initially powered by a 3,500lb (1,588kg) thrust Rolls-Royce Derwent engine given to the USSR, and later by a copy, the RD-500. First flown on June 17, 1947, the Yak-23 served with several Eastern Bloc air forces.

necessary to feed the city's inhabitants. It was a total success and the disgruntled Soviets reopened the supply routes on May 11, 1949. Britain and the USA remained on the brink of an armed confrontation with the USSR that cast a shadow over the next four decades.

The greatest attention was being paid to rapid evolution of the jet engine. The early turbojet engines were of two types, axial flow and centrifugal flow. In the first of these, which Germany pioneered, air sucked into the engine is compressed longitudinally as it flows through a series of axial compressors before entering the combustion chamber. In the second type, which Britain was the first to build, the air is compressed radially by a centrifugal compressor, then turned again through a right angle before entering the combustion chambers arranged around the back of the engine casing. Before long the British engineers perceived that their method produced a much bulkier

engine, so resorted to axial flow.

The next step was the addition of re-heat, or afterburning, to give increased thrust. This is done by mixing additional fuel with the exhaust gases in a jet pipe extension to the gas turbine engine. In order to ignite the fuel and gases in the reheat process, extremely high temperatures are necessary. One system, which is known as the "hot shot unit," acts as a miniature rocket motor to produce a stream of already heated fuel to be fed into the jet pipe.

The attention of designers was focused not only on the engine: to give maximum aerodynamic efficiency attention to the aircraft's shape was equally essential. At very high speed, the air meeting the wings and fuselage was compressed around the leading edges and other areas, which caused turbulence, buffeting and drag. German scientists' solution to the problem was to sweep the wings back, out of the line of the shock wave.

In Britain, the Meteor was followed by another fighter, the de Havilland Vampire, first known by the grotesque name Spider Crab. There were night and day variants of both aircraft types.

During the war, Britain and the USA had been under pressure to manufacture large numbers of aircraft, with no time to spare on development. In Germany, on the contrary, scientists working in government and university research institutes were allowed time to experiment, building and testing in wind tunnels or flight. At the war's end the relevant designs were seized by the Allies, but the USA and USSR made more dynamic use of them than did Britain. During the next five years France and Sweden also made remarkable progress. The former introduced the Dassault MD-450 Ouragan, and the latter the Saab J29A Tunnan.

Below: The USA's first jet aeroplane, the Bell P-59 Airacomet, made its maiden flight on October 1, 1942. The unreliable 1,300lb (500kg) thrust General Electric I-A turbojets were succeeded by 1,650lb (748kg) thrust I-16s (later J31). This is a YP-59A on Service trials.

The greatest achievement of the late 1940s was supersonic flight. On October 14, 1947, Captain Charles "Chuck" Yeager of the renamed United States Air Force (USAF), flying a rocket-powered Bell X-1, exceeded the speed of sound.

WAR IN KOREA

In the first week of the Korean War in June 1950, four Lockheed F-80Cs fought eight Lavochkin La-11 piston-engined fighters and shot down four. Close-support aircraft were the most urgently needed, and the P-51 Mustang had to be resorted to. The USAF were flying the Lockheed F-80 Shooting Star, Republic F-84 Thunderjet and North American F-86 Sabre, while the US Navy flew the Grumman F-9F Panther and McDonnell F-2H Banshee. Boeing B-29s based in Japan were able to carry out strategic bombing.

China, almost as formidable a country as the USSR, sprang a surprise on South Korea's allies by coming briskly to support North Korea with vast numbers of ground troops and swept-wing MiG-15 fighters supplied by the USSR. On November 7, 1950, the first combat ever between two jet fighters brought victory to an F-80C, which shot down a MiG-15.

PASSENGER AIRPLANES

Between 1939 and 1945 hundreds of thousands of military personnel became used to trooping all over the world by air instead of by sea, and returned to civilian life with no qualms about safe air travel. They were to pass this confidence on to their families and friends. In the 1960s fear of flying was still a strong deterrent, however. To reassure the public, airline advertisements depicted rock-jawed aircraft captains and pretty stewardesses.

When not fighting one another with weapons, nations are in commercial competition that is no less fierce. The end of world war was the starting pistol for a scramble after rich prizes in the aviation world: not only among aircraft manufacturers but also air carriers. The major airlines were solidly established before the war: British Overseas Airways Corporation

Above: The Gloster Meteor F4 entered service with first-line fighter squadrons in 1948, and also equipped the RAF High-Speed Flight, being used to set two world air speed records of 606 and 616mph (975 and 991kph) in 1945 and 1946. The powerplant was two 3,500lb (1,588kg) thrust Rolls-Royce Derwent 5 turbojets.

Above: An intimate look inside the flight deck of a Lockheed Constellation 749 airliner, with the pilot on the left, copilot on the right and the engineer nearest the camera, facing the banks of instruments for the four 2,200hp Wright Cyclones.

(BOAC), Pan American, Air France, Lufthansa, Alitalia, Swiss Air, Sabena, and KLM among them. Now there was a new category of operators, the charter firms, which offered cheaper fares than the airline companies. As standards of living rose in developed countries, people who had never been able to afford foreign travel were beginning to take for granted holidays abroad. This did not mean a sudden boom in the sale of new aeroplanes, for many small companies made do by buying secondhand from the major ones.

Manufacturers turned their attention to the requirements of those operating on short-haul routes with a small number of passengers or light cargo.

The first big airliner to make an impact was the Lockheed Constellation. It had first flown in 1943 and began life in military livery as the C-69. In 1946 it entered service with Pan American Airways.

Britain's first postwar airliner was the Vickers Viking, with room for thirty-six passengers. Several Vikings were still at work for airlines and charter firms in the early 1960s. Other aircraft competing for sales to airlines were the French Breguet 761 Provence (Deux-Ponts) and the

Above: Chance Vought's XF6U-1 Pirate, first flown on October 2, 1946, had a 3,000lb (1,360kg) thrust Westinghouse J34-WE-22. The US Navy took delivery of three prototypes and 30 production F6U-1s, but cancelled an order for a further 35.

Languedoc. Despite its small population, Sweden too was more than keeping pace; its Saab Scandia 36-seater was built both there and also in the Netherlands in small numbers.

Some of the early postwar passenger airplanes appear to have fulfilled eccentric fantasies. One of these, designed originally for the military, was the Hughes Hercules flying boat, intended to carry 700 passengers. On November 2, 1947, Howard Hughes himself flew it on its only flight, which was about a mile long – a poor return for the $25 million it had cost.

Of similar capricious concept was the Bristol Brabazon. This originated in 1943 when a committee sponsored by the British government authorised the Bristol Airplane Company to design and build an aircraft of large capacity that would be able to fly the Atlantic nonstop. Construction began in 1945 and the first aircraft was completed five years later. A special hangar had been built to accommodate it. The wingspan was 230ft (70m) and length 177ft (54m). Eight Bristol Centaurus engines coupled in pairs drove contra-rotating propellers. The Brabazon accumulated only 400 flying hours before being scrapped because it was so expensive.

A disappointment in 1952 was the Saunders-Roe Princess flying boat. In 1943 the company began designing it to meet BOAC's requirement for a long-range aircraft to operate on the Southampton-New York route. The Princess had a maximum cruising speed of 360mph (579kph). She could carry a crew of six and 105 passengers. The maiden flight on August 22, 1952, was at least five years too late, for by then BOAC, like all the other international carriers, was seeking faster and even bigger landplanes.

SCHEDULED SERVICES

The year 1952, however, also saw compensating triumph. On May 2, BOAC introduced the world's first scheduled jet passenger service with the 36-passenger DH Comet 1, which had a maximum cruising speed of 480mph (772kph). Many other airlines wanted to add Comets to their fleets, until, on May 2, 1953, one crashed on takeoff at Calcutta and everyone aboard was killed. On January 12, 1954, another Comet dived into the sea near Italy and again there were no survivors. On April 8, 1954, yet another broke up in the air with total fatalities.

All Comets were grounded. From studying pieces of wreckage it was decided that metal fatigue around a window had been caused by the constant increase and decrease of pressure in the cabin.

Some redesign of the fuselage was done and heavier gauge metal was used. The Comet 4, with seats for eighty-one passengers, first flew in 1958 and the type proved a success. BOAC ordered nineteen and on October 4, 1958, one of these flew the first ever North Atlantic jet service: London to New York in 10hr 22min.

The second European turbojet airliner to enter service was the Sud-Aviation Caravelle, which first flew on May 22, 1955, and had its two turbojets mounted on each side of the rear fuselage.

Five years after the pure-jet Comet began operating in the BOAC livery, the company introduced the 90-seat Bristol Britannia, which had four Bristol Proteus turboprop engines. It made its debut on the London-Johannesburg route on December 19, 1957, and was the first turboprop airliner to cross the North Atlantic. British European Airways (BEA) also flew another turboprop, the 139-seat Vickers-Armstrongs Vanguard, which had four Rolls-Royce Tyne engines.

The only USA-built turboprop, the Lockheed Electra, began service in January 1959 with American Airlines. Its four engines were Alison 501s. In October 1955 Pan American Airways ordered twenty of Boeing's 707-120 four-engined jet airliners. The first of the type made its maiden flight on December 20, 1957. In the following year, on October 26, Pan American operated the first 707 route, from New York to Paris, across the North Atlantic.

Below: SAAB's rotund J29A fighter, nicknamed the Tunnan (flying barrel), first flew on September 1, 1948, and deliveries to the Swedish Air Force began in May 1951. Its 5,000lb (2,268kg) thrust de Havilland Ghost turbojet gave it a top speed of 643mph (1,035kph). The type was also operated by the Austrian Air Force.

Germany's Military Jets

> *' For the first time I was flying by jet propulsion. No engine vibrations. No torque and no lashing sound of the propeller. Accompanied by a whistling sound, my jet shot through the air. Later when asked what it felt like, I said, 'It felt as though angels were pushing.'*

GENERALLEUTNANT ADOLF GALLAND

The Heinkel He 178 was a small and fairly basic aircraft. What made it exceptional was that it was powered by a gas turbine, or jet engine. Work on this type of propulsion was in hand in other countries, but Germany had reached the starting line first. Now, at 06.00 on Sunday, August 27, 1935, Flugkapitan Erich Warsitz opened the throttle and sent the strange-looking propellerless machine trundling down the runway at Marienehe. Gradually it gained speed, and after a rather long run, lifted into the air.

The landing gear was locked down, and no attempt was made to explore the flight envelope. It was enough to prove the new propulsion system. Warsitz turned back towards the airfield, but mist was rolling in, and he had to fly several circuits before it was clear enough to land. This first flight by jet propulsion lasted fifteen minutes.

Ernst Heinkel's next jet was the He 280, the world's first jet fighter. Piloted by Fritz Schaefer, this duly flew on March 30, 1940. Although it showed considerable promise, offi-

Below: The Bachem Ba 349 Natter (Viper) semi-expendable, vertically launched piloted missile was intended as a fast-climbing interceptor. It had a Walter 109-509A-2 rocket motor in the rear fuselage and four external Schmidding booster rockets to assist launch, and its nose was loaded with 24 Föhn 73mm unguided rockets.

Above and below: The Arado 234 Blitz was the world's first jet bomber. Seen in these two shots is one of the early prototypes, which took off on a three-wheeled trolley and landed on a central skid. Junkers 004B-0 turbojets of 1,848lb (838kg) thrust provided the power.

cial reactions were cool, and no orders were placed.

Rival Willi Messerschmitt had better luck with his Me 262, which made its first turbojet-only flight on July 18, 1942. This was ordered into service, and thirteen evaluation models were delivered in March and April 1944. The Me 262 had an outstanding performance for its day, with a top speed of 540mph (869kph) and the ability to reach 30,000ft (9,144m) in seven minutes. It became operational with *Kommando Nowotny* in September 1944.

Above: Surrendered by a defecting company test pilot on its maiden flight in 1945, this Messerschmitt Me 262A-1a single-seat interceptor had two 1,980lb-thrust Jumo 004B turbojets which gave it a top speed of 540mph (869kph) at 19,685ft (6,000m).

It has often been suggested that large numbers of Me 262s could have turned the tide of the war in Europe in 1944/45. This seems unlikely. While the performance of the Me 262 was exceptional, it was bedeviled throughout its service career by unreliable engines. The fact was that German propulsion technology had outrun metallurgical capability.

Quite apart from unreliable engines, the Me 262 had several operational shortcomings. Acceleration was poor, endurance was short, and if it could be caught low and slow on its landing approach, or shortly after take-off, it was vulnerable. This weakness was exploited by Allied fighter pilots, who loitered by the approaches to known Me 262 airfields.

The only other German jet to become operational was the Arado Ar 234 Blitz light bomber, first flown on June 15, 1943. As a bomber it was not terribly effective, but at operational speeds and altitudes it was virtually uninterceptable, and it carried out some very valuable high-level reconnaissance missions.

The only Allied jet aircraft to enter service during the war was the Gloster Meteor I, which made its first war sortie on August 4, 1944. Me 262s and Meteors were fated never to meet in the air.

ove: The Heinkel He 280, the world's first twin-engine jet aircraft, comes in
and at the end of its first powered flight, on April 2, 1941. Its two 1,290lb
5kg) thrust HeS 8A engines were uncowled at the time.

249

Above: Another bomber interceptor was the Messerschmitt Me 163
Komet, which had a Walter 109-509A-2 rocket motor. This Me 163B-1a,
seen at Bad Zwischenahn in 1943, had a maximum speed of 596mph
(959kph) at 9,840ft (3,000m) and a powered endurance of eight minutes,

if the throttle was used sparingly. However, the aircraft could be held on the ground until the USAAF heavy bombers were almost in sight and, when launched, could reach their altitude in about two minutes. Its speed enabled it to penetrate the escort fighter screens with ease.

Mach 1

> ' Leveling off at 42,000 feet, I had thirty percent of my fuel, so I turned on rocket chamber three and immediately reached .96 Mach. I noticed that the faster I got, the smoother the ride. Suddenly the Mach needle began to fluctuate. It went up to .965 Mach – then tipped right off the scale.... We were flying supersonic. And it was smooth as a baby's bottom; Grandma could be sitting up there sipping lemonade. '
>
> GEN. CHARLES "CHUCK" YEAGER

The Bell Experimental Sonic (XS)-1 was developed by the US National Advisory Committee for Aeronautics (NACA, later NASA) for research into transonic and supersonic flight. In 1944, when the program was launched, the newly emerging jet engine was opening up previously unexplored areas of high-speed flight, and severe buffet and control problems were being encountered. Three XS-1s were ordered, to investigate these phenomena.

The XS-1 was modeled on the shape of the 0.50 caliber bullet, which was known to have excellent aerodynamic qualities, and given unswept but very thin wing and tail surfaces. It was powered by a four-chamber liquid-fuel rocket engine, which not only gave greater thrust than any jet of the period, but did not depend on external air for functioning.

Rocket motors use fuel at a prodigious rate, and to extend its endurance the XS-1 was air-launched at 25,000ft (7,620m) or more from a specially equipped Boeing B-29. The initial test flights were made by Bell test pilot Chalmers Goodlin, who explored the envelope up to Mach 0.80. At this point the Air Force took over, and the task fell to Mustang ace Chuck Yeager.

Right: Captain Charles Elwood "Chuck" Yeager squeezed into the cockpit of the XS-1 in which he achieved the world's first supersonic flight in a manned aircraft, producing the first sonic boom.

Familiarization flights, with no fuel aboard, began in August 1947. The fourth.flight, on August 29, was 'hot." The assault on the so-called

Right: The compact cockpit of the Bell X-1A test aircraft.

sound barrier had begun. Failure at this point could have ruined the entire program, so it was taken in easy stages, starting at Mach 0.82.

The XS-1 was unlike all other airplanes. The pilot sat semi-reclining, with his knees high. The view from the cockpit was poor, since the "canopy" consisted simply of transparent panels which followed the shape of the fuselage. An emergency bale-out would probably result in the pilot hitting the sharp, knife-edged wing or tail surfaces. Behind the cockpit were fuel tanks containing alcohol and liquid oxygen, the chill from which reached through to the pilot. There was no heater and no defroster.

Gradually, speeds were increased. Buffeting was encountered at Mach 0.86, and control was sluggish. Then, at Mach 0.94 on the seventh powered flight, the elevators ceased to function. This was overcome by using a trim switch to alter the angle of the stabilizers.

Above: Developed from the X-1, the X-1A married the earlier aircraft's wings, tailplane and powerplant to a completely new fuselage with increased fuel capacity. Yeager took this aircraft beyond Mach 2.

On the ninth powered flight Mach 0.97 was the target speed. As the laden B-29 clawed for altitude, Yeager climbed down the ladder from the bomber into the XS-1's cramped cockpit, wherein was a length of broom handle. Yeager had broken two ribs two days before, and the broom was to be used as a lever to close the cockpit door.

Dropped at 20,000ft (6,100m), the XS-1 fell clear. Yeager fired the rockets and climbed like a bird. The actual speed achieved was Mach 1.07 at 43,000ft (13,105m). Man was supersonic!

Swept Wings

> '*I've been followed by a MiG from 27,000ft (8,229m)
> to 5,000ft (1,524m), pulling maximum 'g' at high speed.
> So violent were the turns that both my oxygen mask and flying
> helmet slipped. In following me down the MiG was, however,
> unable to hit me as he could not get enough deflection –
> although he appeared to use all his ammunition in trying to do so.*'
>
> SQN. LDR. W. "PADDY" HARBISON, RAF, CFE

Below: With the end of the war in Europe, German research on swept wings became available, leading to the design of the F-86 Sabre, first flown on October 1, 1947. Wing sweep was 35 degrees. This is an F-86E, the first Sabre to have an all-moving tailplane.

The advent of the jet engine made transonic speeds possible, but these were accompanied by a large drag rise. However, it was found that this could be delayed by sweeping the wings at an angle of 35 degrees or more. This effectively reduced the velocity of the airflow and with it the drag, by a factor of the cosine of the sweep angle. This knowledge was put to good use in the design of two of the greatest fighters of the early 1950s, the F-86 Sabre and the MiG-15.

The Sabre first flew on October 1, 1947, and the MiG-15 three months later, on December 30. They were both swept-wing, single-engined, single-seaters. The Russian jet was the smaller of the two; it was also considerably lighter. Whereas the Sabre was a very sophisticated fighter for its day, the MiG-15 was basic. The American fighter was armed with six 0.50 caliber machine guns, whereas the MiG carried two 23mm and one 37mm cannon. Their engines were of comparable power, the F-86 having a General Electric J47, and the MiG an RD 45 based on the British Rolls-Royce Nene.

The Russian fighter possessed far superior high-altitude and climb

Above: All Japanese Self-Defense Force Sabres were F-86Fs, first flown on March 19, 1952, and the best type to see service in the Korean War, where Sabres claimed a victory/loss ratio of 7.5:1.

performance, but the American aircraft had incomparably better handling qualities. It could also exceed Mach 1 in a dive, which it did for the first time on April 26, 1948, whereas the MiG-15 was firmly subsonic. Both were for years the mainstays of their respective countries' air defenses, and were widely exported.

The war in Korea saw them clash. The first engagement came on December 17, 1950, exactly forty-eight years after the Wright brothers' historic flight, when Lt. Col. Bruce Hinton of the 336th

Fighter Sqn shot down a MiG-15. It was the first of many.

The period for which full data is available runs from July 1951 to the end of the war, in July 1953. During this period, F-86s accounted for 757 MiGs while suffering 103 losses, a ratio of slightly less than 7.5:1, achieved while operating at an average force advantage, measured in sorties flown, of just under 2:1. This was a remarkable achievement, in view of the fact that altitude had traditionally been held to be the greatest advantage in air combat, and the

MiG-15 had by far the better altitude performance of the two, with the added advantage of ground radar coverage of much of the area.

Why, then, did the Sabre emerge the victor by such a clear margin? Basically because it was the better fighter of the two. It combined superb handling qualities with a radar ranging gunsight which, although often temperamental, gave very accurate aiming. Its ability to remain under full control at very high Mach numbers was not matched by its Russian opponent. These factors allowed the USA to establish a qualitative superiority over Soviet products, a technical lead which was never lost during the decades of the Cold War.

Below: A 35 degree wing sweep was chosen for the MiG-15, and two fences per side were installed to reduce the effects of spanwise airflow. Two degrees of anhedral were used to aid stability, and the wing was set in the mid position. The Mig-15 had a much better climb rate and a higher ceiling than the American Sabre it met over Korea. These are Polish MiG-15bis variants.

The First Turboprops

> ' *Your seat pushes you firmly in the back. Even then there is none of the shuddering brazen bellow of the high-powered piston engine.... Combined with a seemingly uncanny lack of vibration, this gives the impression almost of sailing through space, the engines with their glinting propeller discs utterly remote from the quiet security of this cabin.* '
>
> DEREK HARVEY

The quoted passage was the impression of a passenger taking his first ride in a Vickers-Armstrongs Viscount airliner powered by four Rolls-Royce Dart turboprops.

While air travel has always been fast and convenient, in the early years it was uncomfortable and fatiguing to a degree that would be unbelievable to modern travelers accustomed to jets. The only form of power available was the piston engine, which, in spite of the best attempts at soundproofing, was noisy enough to make conversation difficult, and which also set up a continuous vibration throughout the airframe which could be distinctly felt by the passengers.

Reciprocating engines vibrated because they had a lot of parts going up and down. During the Second World War the jet engine was developed. Instead of pistons and conrods going up and down, motive power was provided by a turbine which went round and round, with a noticeable absence of vibration.

The jet engine is at its most efficient at high altitudes and speeds,

making it ideal for long-range flight. For medium-range work it was less than optimum. A compromise solution was to couple a propeller to the turbine shaft through a gearbox, to produce a turboprop engine.

The Viscount was designed for medium range and economic cruising speed, and the choice of a turboprop seems now to have been obvious. It was, however, the first civilian airliner to be so powered.

The first flight took place at Wisley on July 16, 1948, with veteran test pilot "Mutt" Summers at the controls. Not only was the flight uneventful, but the subsequent flying program was almost entirely trouble-free. The Viscount's first appearance at the Farnborough Air Show the next year was notable for its quietness. Certificated on July 28, 1950, it flew its first scheduled passenger service the following day.

The original V.630 Viscount design seated no more than forty passengers, and greater capacity was needed. To provide this, the fuselage was stretched to form the V.700 series, seating up to fifty-three. This variant was immediately ordered by British European Airways, and other orders followed.

So popular was the type in service, not only for its quietness and comfort but for its large oval windows, that the trickle swelled to a flood. Remarkably, it was even bought by American airlines, who could find nothing homegrown to match it.

The Viscount was also used to set class records, London-Cologne, etc. The V.700 prototype also took part in the London to New Zealand Air Race of 1953, becoming the first transport aircraft to finish.

The final Viscount series was the V.800, a slightly stretched aircraft seating up to seventy. The Viscount, of which 444 were built, was the first of a new generation.

Left: A fine in-flight study of a BEA Viscount V701. Large windows and a spacious cabin made the Viscount popular with passengers. This version had 1,540shp Rolls-Royce Dart R.Da.3 engines, which gave it a cruising speed of 316mph (508kph).

Jet Airliner

> ' *Millions wonder what it is like to travel in the Comet at 500 miles an hour eight miles above the earth. Paradoxically there is a sensation of being poised motionless in space. Because of the great height the scene below scarcely appears to move; because of the stability of the atmosphere the aircraft remains rock-steady.... One arrives over distant landmarks in an incredibly short time but without the sense of having traveled. Speed does not enter into the picture. One doubts one's wristwatch.*'
>
> C. MARTIN SHARP

The above description will be entirely familiar to anyone used to modern jet travel, but when these words were written, in 1949, they were new and fresh, a paean of joy celebrating the opening of a whole new era. The era of jet travel.

The first jet airliner, de Havilland's Comet 1, was rolled out in April 1949. Resplendent in shiny aluminum, it was a sleek cigar shape into which the windows of the crew cabin were smoothly faired. Four de Havilland Ghost turbojets were buried in the wing roots, adding to the impression of speed and grace.

The first flight took place on July 27. At the controls was former night fighter ace John Cunningham, by then de Havilland's chief test pilot. His first reaction was one of surprise at the acceleration, which was exceptional for such a large machine. Handling qualities were good, and a

year of intensive flight-testing followed, during which many international point-to-point speed records were set.

So impressive were these that orders started to come in, not only from the British Overseas Airways Corporation, but also from Canada and France. Then, on May 2, 1952, the first scheduled Comet service left Heathrow with a full complement of 36 passengers. After stops at Rome, Beirut, Khartoum, Entebbe, and Livingstone, Comet G-ALYP 'Yoke Peter' arrived at Johannesburg two minutes ahead of schedule after 23 1/2 hours and 6,774 statute miles (10,900km).

The initial success of the Comet 1 sparked more interest, and orders now came from Japan and South America. By this time the Comet 2, powered by Rolls-Royce engines and with 44 seats and longer range, was under development, and a stretched version, the Comet 3, with 78 seats, was projected. With no immediate competitors in sight, the Comet looked like being a runaway success.

But all was not roses. The record was marred by two takeoff accidents, one at Ciampino, Rome, and another at Karachi, in Pakistan. While the verdict on both was pilot error, a new high-lift wing section was proposed. Then, exactly a year after the inauguration of the London to Johannesburg service, disaster struck.

Comet 'Yoke Victor,' en route from Calcutta to Delhi, broke up in mid-air. Close investigation revealed no weaknesses, and the cause remained a mystery. Then, on January 15, 1954, 'Yoke Peter' broke up near Elba. Again the cause was a mystery, but when on April 8 'Yoke Yoke' fell into the Bay of Naples the fleet was grounded.

The truth was that the Comet had been too far ahead of its time, and had fallen victim to the then little known phenomenon of metal fatigue. It had pioneered the way, and had paid a high price, although the knowledge gained was to benefit every airliner that followed it. The final variant, the Comet 4, gave years of troublefree service.

Left: Following a series of accidents caused by metal fatigue around the square window apertures, all Comets were grounded. By the time the fault was overcome the Comet's market had been taken by Boeing's 707.

Defending the Peace

It is a paradox that, in order to conduct a peaceful life, a nation must be so well prepared for war that potential adversaries will not dare to challenge it. The end of the Second World War was the beginning of an era in which the USSR regarded the USA, Britain and soon the other NATO nations with deep suspicion. Possessed of the world's largest strategic bomber force, and the most destructive weapons ever invented, the USA felt totally secure. But the nuclear age had dawned, and the deadly threat of wind-blown nuclear contamination had not been fully appreciated.

The 1950s saw a resurgence of making ready to attack as well as defend if the USSR's threatening posture developed into global war. By the middle of the decade the USA had about 300 nuclear weapons, and approximately 840 bombers capable of delivering them. Western intelligence estimated that at this time the USSR had about 24 nuclear weapons and 200 suitable bombers. A nuclear war appeared to be a distinct possibility.

The tension was enhanced by the jet age. The piston-engined Boeing B-29 Superfortress or its Russian counterpart, the Tupolev Tu-4, could carry nuclear weapons at 300mph (483kph) at 30,000ft (9,144m). The new breed of jet bomber, exemplified by the Boeing B-52 Stratofortress, first flown in April 1952, had eight engines, allowing it to carry a huge nuclear weapons load from one continent to another at speeds up to 660mph (1,062kph) at 40,000ft (12,192m). When the Boeing engineers designed the B-52 in the late 1940s they could have had no idea that the giant bomber, following a massive structural rebuild program and other technical equipment upgrades, would still be in service over 55 years later, into the next millennium.

AUTOMATED INTERCEPTION

The next move was to supersonic bombers, capable of Mach 2 and above, such as the Convair B-58 Hus-

tler and the North American XB-70 Valkyrie (which never entered service), which would make fighter interception problematical. Given the destructive capability of nuclear-armed bombers, not one could be allowed to slip through defenses. High speeds, coupled with the restricted maneuverability at high altitudes, reduced the value of the traditional interception from astern, so more effective interception procedures, and weapons, would have to be devised. The necessity of maneuvering for position could be avoided by a collision course attack from the front quarter. The interceptor could be vectored towards its target, lock its radar on the target, and arm the weapon system. Its computer would then launch the weapons automatically when the target came within range.

Above: Not only was the North American F-100 Super Sabre the first of the USAF's "Century Series" fighters, but it was also the world's first operational fighter capable of supersonic speed in level flight. Wingspan 38ft 9⅓in (11.82m), length 47ft 42⁄3in (14.44m), height 16ft 22⁄3in (4.94m), weight 21,847lb (9,910kg), engine one 16,905lb (7,675kg) thrust Pratt & Whitney J-57 turbojet with afterburner, maximum speed 891mph (1,434kph), range 1,150 miles (1,840km), crew 1.

Guns would be totally inadequate for this task. They were first replaced by batteries of unguided rockets, then later by homing missiles. Automated interception reached its zenith with the Convair F-106 Delta Dart, which had a fire control system and autopilot tied to ground control via a data link. The interception could thus be guided from the ground, with the pilot reduced to the status of system manager. The Soviet equivalent was the MiG-25 Foxbat, of similar concept but with even higher performance.

From 1958, long-range, high-altitude, surface-to-air missiles (SAMs) entered service, with an anticipated kill probability of around 90 percent. Against this, the high-speed, high-altitude bomber did not look such a good option. The response was to switch to low-level, subsonic penetration, under the defender's radar.

Such factors also affected the development of another important military aircraft at the time: strategic reconnaissance. The most significant of such aircraft was the Lockheed

Above: When Boeing's designers first flew the B-52 strategic bomber in 1952, they couldn't have guessed that some would still be operational over fifty years later. Here a Stratofortress drops a string of 51 750lb general-purpose bombs against Viet Cong targets in Vietnam.

U-2, the first aircraft to be designed specifically for obtaining reconnaissance photographs by illegal overflights – in other words, by boldly flying across hostile territory without permission in order to locate and photograph military or strategically interesting installations. The U-2 was followed by a second-generation reconnaissance aircraft, the Lockheed SR-71 Blackbird, able to fly not only as high (above 85,000ft/25,908m)

Right: The North American XB-70 Valkyrie number 1 takes off for one of its research flights undertaken by NASA/USAF. It was planned as a Mach 3 bomber, but a crash, escalating costs and a preference for strategic missiles ended the program in 1968.

but almost five times faster (2,100mph/3,380kph). Despite such valuable and (in the case of the U-2) ongoing service, because of the huge cost of such aircraft, and the fact that they would be vulnerable during the penetration of defended airspace, it is generally accepted that strategic reconnaissance is best left to space-orbiting satellites.

With such threat and counter-threat developments, huge sums of money were being spent by the USSR and the NATO allies on increasing the performance of airplanes and their weapon capabilities. For the Western nations it was as much to obtain commercial advantage as in anticipation of a war against the Communist bloc. Manufacturers also pursued the sale not only of military aircraft but also of civil variants and aero engines. For the airlines, passenger fares were the motivation as well as, perhaps more than, safety. For the USSR, which would impose its aircraft and powerplants on the Communist bloc countries, the prime purpose of development was to be one step ahead of NATO and the USA in the event of another war.

OVERTAKING SOUND

When "Chuck" Yeager became the first person to exceed the speed of sound on October 14, 1947, he heralded in a raft of speed record-breaking feats, including another of his own on December 12, 1953, when in the Bell X-1A he set a new record of

Mach 2.42. At very high speed, heat generated by the friction between the aircraft's skin and molecules of air becomes a great danger, because it not only degrades the strength of the structure but can cause the fuel to boil. Bell built an experimental aircraft, the X-2, with swept-back wings to minimise these problems. This was to be air-launched from a modified Boeing B-52 Superfortress and, in 1956, attained a speed of 2,094mph (3,369kph), Mach 3.2.

In France, the Sud-Ouest SO 9000 Trident, which had two wingtip-mounted turbojet engines and a booster rocket in the fuselage, reached Mach 1.6 in 1953. On August 3, 1954, another French aircraft, the delta-winged SFECMAS (Nord) Ger-

faut (Gyrfalcon), became the first European aircraft to exceed Mach 1 in level flight without the assistance of a rocket or afterburner. Three years later, the mixed turbojet/ramjet-powered Nord 1500 Griffon (Griffin) reached Mach 1.85.

In 1957 the next US project was decided upon. The end product, to be built by North American Aviation and designated the X-15, would be capable of flying at almost Mach 7 – 4,500mph (7,240kph) – and to an altitude of over 250,000ft (76,200m).

The Soviets were ahead of the West in some respects, having studied German aerodynamic research into the benefits of sweep-back as a way of delaying the drag created by compressibility. Their engine technol-

Above: The MiG-25 was the fastest fighter to enter service, with a max speed of 1,864mph (3,000kph). A stripped version, the YE-266, set 16 world records, including an absolute altitude of 118,867ft (36,240m).

ogy was derived from the Jumo 004B axial-flow turbojet. They also employed many German engineers who had worked on jet aircraft development in the Second World War.

The Mikoyan-Gurevich MiG-15, which had first flown on December 30, 1947, with a 5,000lb (2,268kg) thrust Kimov RD-45F turbojet engine, attained a maximum speed of 665mph (1,070kph). It owed little to original Russian inspiration, for it was the product of wartime German research in aerodynamics and British Rolls-Royce jet-engine technology. The USSR repaid the British Govern-

ment's trust by copying the Nene engine without having a license production agreement. The first Russian fighter to break the sound barrier in level flight was the twin-engine MiG-19, which entered service in 1955.

When Britain's first jet bomber, the English Electric Canberra, entered squadron service in May 1951, few were aware that the first jet bomber to have flown in combat was the German Arado Ar 234B Blitz, a twin-jet single-seater, which began flights over Britain in September 1944. In the last winter of the war, Ar 234s operated over the Normandy battlefields.

Remarkably, an ejector seat was fitted; and, even more unusually, although it was a single-seater, it was equipped with an automatic pilot.

On February 22, 1957, the RAF's latest bomber, the first in the world with a delta-wing planform, the Avro Vulcan B1, entered squadron service. It was powered by four 17,000lb (7,711kg) thrust Bristol Siddeley Olympus 201 engines and had a maximum speed of 620mph (998kph).

While preparations for future wars were in hand, the USSR introduced a jet airliner. It was a development of the Tupolev Tu-16 ("Badger") medium bomber, and the timing of its first appearance was well judged: the Comet was grounded as a result of three fatal mid-air accidents. The Tupolev Tu-104, which had two 21,385lb (9,700kg) Mikulin turbojets,

Right: The F-4G Advanced Wild Weasel dedicated EW and anti-SAM aircraft was the final US Air Force variant of the long-serving Phantom, whose military career included conflict in South Vietnam and (for Israel) the Middle East.

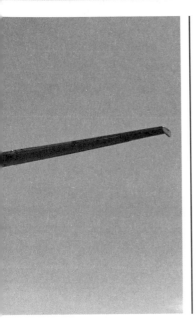

Left: The high-flying U-2 spyplane, the cause of some Cold War heat when one piloted by Francis Gary Powers was shot down over the USSR on May 1, 1960. Versions of the U-2 have been in service since 1957 and some still fly today.

first flew on June 17, 1955, and had a maximum cruising speed of 560mph (901kph). It could carry fifty passengers and transformed the USSR's medium-range services, but proved uneconomical. Later it was replaced by the 70-seat Tu-104A and then the Tu-104B, which carried 100 passengers. From 1956 to 1958 the Tu-104 was the world's only operational jet airliner.

THE VIETNAM WAR

The Vietnam War, never formally declared, was a civil war between South Vietnam and the Viet Cong (Communist guerrillas) operating from

the north, ultimately aided by and allied with the North Vietnamese Army (NVA). It was a war in which the USA became increasingly heavily embroiled for more than ten years. It spilled over into Vietnam's neighboring states, and involved, to varying degrees, many other nations, if not directly in the hostilities then in the supply of weapons systems and training.

In 1961 US Army helicopter squadrons were sent to help the South Vietnamese Air Force. Four years later the Viet Cong began to receive help from the NVA. In February 1965 the American base at Pleiku, where fighter-bomber and medium bomber squadrons had been based since the previous year, was attacked. The USAF therefore considered itself free to retaliate.

The war dragged on, and while the USSR provided the North Vietnamese and the Viet Cong with surface-to-air guided missiles, the range and number of fighters, fighter-bombers, heavy bombers, transports and electronic/recce aircraft committed by the US Air Force, Navy and Marine Corps grew. Apart from having long-range bombers (B-52s), other fixed-wing US aircraft that were used on operations were the Republic F-105 Thunderchief, the Douglas A-1 Skyraider, the McDonnell F-4 Phantom, the Douglas A-4 Skyhawk, the Grumman A-6 Intruder, which could hit targets by night or in bad weather, and the Vought A-7 Corsair II. Transport aircraft in the campaign were the Lockheed C-141 Star-Lifter and the Lockheed C-130 Hercules. The nature of the terrain and the US forces' strategy and tactics called for heavy involvement by attack and transport helicopters.

By contrast, the North Vietnamese Air Force (NVAF) was com-

paratively small, operating Soviet-built MiG-17s and MiG-21s. In the last two years of the war the NVAF operated the Shenyang J-6, a Chinese-produced version of the MiG-19. The NVAF was trained by Soviet instructors, and its aircraft operated under Soviet-style close ground control. Too weak even to think of inflicting a decisive defeat on the US air forces, it settled for a policy of air deniability, remaining in being as an effective force and thus making the US waste a lot of resources in providing fighter escort and electronic countermeasures for their strikes. Nevertheless, in December 1972, when the USAF made an all-out attack, and the North Vietnamese failed to shoot down a US aircraft, SAMs accounted for the loss of seventeen B-52 Stratofortresses.

In April 1973 the US forces were evacuated, and the North Vietnamese marched into Saigon two years later.

Right: The Lockheed C-130 Hercules has been serving military and civil operators in a variety of roles (from transport through electronic warfare to gunship) for about fifty years. Here a USAF Military Airlift Command delivers a light tank by low-altitude extraction in 1976.

FREIGHTERS

Meanwhile, the competition among manufacturers of transport aircraft, for both civil and military use, was growing, and the active life of the aircraft born out of this became stretched. The market for short- and medium-haul types was as important as for long-haul aircraft, and the demand for freighters grew and continues to do so.

Airframes had to be built that were more versatile. The adaptation of airliners as military versions continues: the Boeing 707 was adapted to carry radar and other equipment that provided an airborne warning and control system (E-3 Sentry AWACS). The Boeing 747 has been fitted out as an advanced airborne command post (E-4B)

On the other side of the Atlantic, the 1970s saw the emergence of credible competition to the might of the US airline industry. The Airbus Industrie consortium brought together France, Britain, Germany and Spain to produce a wide-bodied airliner, the Airbus A300 (first flown on October 28, 1978). It was followed by the A310 (1982), intended to compete with the USA's 737, and then the A320 (1987) and the similar but shorter A319 and the stretched version, the A321. The ultra-long-range A340 four-engined airliner entered service in 1996.

Antonov builds the An-226 Mriya, the world's largest aeroplane, in the Ukraine. It has six turbofans and can carry 60-70 passengers, with freight.

Seldom are civil aircraft built with components totally indigenous to one country. For example, in Sweden, the Saab 2000 short-haul regional transport, which seats 50-58 passengers, has twin Allison turboprops from the USA. International cooperation, and competition, are the order of the day.

B-52 – The Big Stick

> '*I felt a drop in the seat of my pants, as though the nose had fallen. It was the pilot pushing down to avoid the missile. I turned and looked at the instruments. The altimeter was shooting through 700ft (213m), and we were doing about 440kt (815kph), heading down fast. At 500ft (152m) I grabbed the yoke and started pulling. The plane being heavy with fuel, it was just not responding. I was sure we were going to hit. The plane eventually dished out at 60ft (18m) above the ground.*'
>
> CAPT. CARL GRAMLICK, USAF

The Boeing B-52 Stratofortress is, as a design, older than its oldest crewman, and probably older than many of its crewmen's fathers. It was conceived in the early days of the Cold War, when strategic bombing was a fashionable concept and an all-out war between the Soviet Union and the West seemed not only possible, but probable. For many years strategic bombers have been one leg of the US nuclear triad, the others being land-based intercontinental ballistic missiles (ICBMs), and ballistic missiles carried by sub-marines. Strategic bombing has been one part of the ultimate deterrent; the "Big Stick."

The B-52 was initially planned as a straight-winged bomber powered by six turboprop engines. While a jet bomber would have been more survivable on account of its greater speed, the early jet engines were too prodigal of fuel to meet the stringent range requirement of 10,000 miles (16,000km).

The change to jets came about because of the increasing importance placed on flight refueling at

Above: A B-52G approaches a KC-135 tanker during refueling, as seen from the boom operator. This variant switched to conventional duties from the 1980s following strategic arms reduction talks with the Soviets.

Above: The cockpit of a B-52H, with throttles and other controls for eight engines. There is a crew of five: commander, co-pilot, radar navigator, navigator, and electronic warfare officer. Range with refueling is limited only by crew fatigue; unrefueled range is 8,800 miles (14,080km). It is believed that the B-52 could be upgraded to serve until 2045, achieving an unrivaled 100 years in operational service.

that time. The design was revised, and emerged with eight turbojets slung below a shoulder-set wing swept to an angle of 35 degrees. The detonation in 1949 of the first Soviet nuclear weapon hurried the program along, and the preproduction YB-52 first flew on April 15, 1952.

Externally it resembled the smaller B-47 Stratojet, which at one point was the most numerous aircraft in US Strategic Air Command (SAC), but in fact it was considerably different. Few changes were made during the development period, although the tandem cockpit initially adopted gave way to a roomy airliner-style "office."

The first production B-52 left the ground on August 5, 1954, and the type started reaching the Bombardment Wings in June 1955. Production continued for ten years, a total of 744 machines in eight major types being built.

The B-52 had been designed to operate high in the stratosphere, but the increasing effectiveness of Soviet air defenses forced a change to low level. A structural rework was needed to cope with the harsh low-level environment. This was underlined in 1964, when a B-52H lost most of its vertical stabilizer in flight owing to a wind gust of incredible severity, although it returned safely to base.

Left: Aircrews "scramble" toward a line-up of B-52Gs during exercises in 1979. This was during a period when the United States felt its aircraft and airfields were vulnerable to surprise missile or bomber attack.

For many years the B-52 flew in the manned penetrator role, using Quail decoys and Hound Dog missiles, before it was supplanted by the B-1B Lancer. It then became a stand-off missile launcher. In the more conventional bombing role it has given sterling service in every conflict in which it has participated – Vietnam, Gulf War of 1991, the Balkans in the late 1990s, in operations against the Taliban and Osama bin Laden's al-Qa'ida terrorists in Afghanistan in 2002, and the war against Saddam Hussein's Iraq in 2003.

The Stratofortress has been the backbone of the manned strategic bomber force for the United States for almost fifty years and is capable of dropping or launching the widest array of weapons in the US inventory. This includes cluster bombs, precision guided missiles, and joint direct attack munitions. Updated with modern technology, the B-52 will continue to be capable of delivering the full component of joint developed weapons and will continue into the middle of the 21st century as a vital component of the US defense system. Current engineering analyses show the B-52's life span to extend beyond the year 2045, suggesting that it could well be possible for this mighty bomber to achieve an unrivaled record of one hundred years in operational service.

Vertical Takeoff and Landing (VTOL)

Frank Whittle's invention, the world's first turbojet engine, first run on April 12, 1937, set off a revolution in aircraft design, though full development of the engine did not occur until the war ended. As autogyros and helicopters were past the initial stages of development before the war, engineers throughout the aviation industry must surely have been thinking already of a means of obtaining vertical takeoff and landing (VTOL) with this new type of engine, which could develop a thrust of higher value than its own weight.

By 1953 the Rolls-Royce Nene engine had developed a thrust of 4,000lb (1,814kg), which was approximately twice its weight, and could therefore easily lift the structure on which it would be mounted. The first feasibility trial was made with two Nene engines, the tailpipes modified so that the efflux blew vertically down, mounted horizontally on a four-legged framework. To study the attitude control system when hovering, air was bled through four nozzles from the engines' compressors: one nozzle blew forward, one astern, one on each side downward. When publicly demonstrated at Farnborough, England, this rig became known as the "Flying Bedstead."

Rolls-Royce now concentrated on designing engines with very high power-to-weight ratios. That of the first, the RB108, was 8:1. Short Brothers & Harland used it for their SC-1, the first-ever fixed-wing VTOL aircraft. It made its first vertical takeoff in 1958, and first transition from hover to wing-borne flight in 1960. The four lift engines could be swiveled aft slightly to add to the thrust of the forward-propulsion unit. They could also be swiveled forward to help as brakes.

Meanwhile, Bristol Siddeley (later Rolls-Royce) had developed a vectored thrust turbofan engine, the BS53 Pegasus. Hawker Siddeley Aircraft were approached to design an airframe to suit the engine. The

result was the P1127, later named Kestrel, and evaluated as a prototype strike and reconnaissance fighter by a tripartite squadron assembled from British, US and German aircrew. In 1964 it flew at supersonic speed in a shallow dive. Not judged adequate for squadron service, it was developed into the Harrier.

In France Marcel Dassault began flight trials in 1962 using a Bristol Siddeley Orpheus to adapt a Mirage fighter to VTOL. This version, the Balzac V-001 with eight Rolls-Royce

Above: Seen here during an air show at Domodedovo, Moscow, in 1967, Yakovlev's experimental Yak-36 made its first free hovering flight in September 1964. The long nose boom housed a reaction control nozzle; there were others in the wingtips and tail.

RB162 jets and a SNECMA TF306 with afterburner, was abandoned after many accidents.

In Germany a research group of Bolkow, Heinkel and Messerschmitt in collaboration with Vereinigte Flugtechnische Werke (VFW) was formed in 1960. Using two banks of four Rolls-Royce RB162s and two Bristol Siddeley Pegasus 5s, flight trials of a prototype high-wing monoplane transport, the Dornier Do 31E, with an intended cruising speed of 466mph (750kph), started in 1967 but came to an end in 1971. There was no further development. Bolkow, Heinkel and Messerschmitt also formed a research group in 1960

to develop the VJ-101C small high-wing monoplane, using six Rolls-Royce RB108 lift jets. Flight trials began in 1963, and stopped in 1964. Also in Germany VFW-Fokker flew the VAK-191 in November 1970, but this was not a success.

In the USA, Lockheed built and flew the XV-4A Humming Bird VTOL fighter prototype with two Pratt & Whitney JT12A-3 turbojets. The intended maximum speed of 520mph (837kph) was not reached, so work on the aircraft ceased.

Above: Dornier's Do31E was the first and, until the Bell Boeing V-22 Osprey, the only VTOL jet transport. It proved highly successful, if excessively noisy, and established several world records in its class. It spanned 59ft 3in (18m) and had a cruising speed of 400mph (644kph) at 19,685ft (6,000m).

Above: Early attempts to produce VTOL aircraft are typified by the Convair XFY-1 "Pogo" of 1954, powered by a specially developed 5,850shp Allison YT40-A-14 turboprop. Successful transitions were made, but the return to earth in a "backwards" descent was a delicate manoeuvre.

Between 1950 and 1970 Ryan Aeronautical, Boeing Vertol and Canadair experimented with various concepts including tilting propellers.

The world's first VTOL strike and reconnaissance fighter, the brilliant and long-lived Hawker Siddeley Harrier, developed from the Kestrel, entered squadron service with the RAF in June 1969. Vertical lift is achieved by four rotatable nozzles, two on each side, which point down for lift and are then gradually rotated rearward to give forward propulsion.

Following a keenly fought competition, in October 2000 the Lockheed Martin F-35, with a lift-fan, was chosen over the vectored-thrust Boeing YF-32 as the Joint Strike Fighter (JSF) for service with the USAF

(1,763 to replace the F-16 and A-10 as a strike aircraft), the US Navy (450), the US marine Corps (480) to replace the current AV-8B and F/A-18A/C/D, while the British RAF and Royal Navy will purchase about 150 to replace the RN Sea Harrier F/A2s and RAF Harrier GR7/GR9s.

There are to be four versions of the JSF, all with the same fuselage, identical wing-sweep, canopy, radar, and avionics, as well as a common engine, the Pratt & Whitney F119, a derivative of that being used in the USAF's F-22 Raptor. Simplest version of all will be the USAF's F-35s, which will not have a hovering capability, nor will it operate from aircraft carriers, which means it will not require the strengthened airframe and

Below: The pioneer free-flying jet VTOL device was the first Rolls-Royce TMR (thrust-measuring rig), popularly called The Flying Bedstead, seen in 1953. The two Nene engines supplied air for four reaction control nozzles.

Above: The Balzac V 001 was constructed from the Mirage III prototype by Dassault and Sud Aviation to prove three-axis electronic auto-stabilization, jet reaction controls for the hover, and many other systems in its research program for the Mirage IIIV VTOL experimental fighter. The Balzac flew on October 12, 1962, but the program was cancelled following the crash of the second Mirage IIIV prototype on November 28, 1966.

undercarriage associated with carrier operations. The Marines' version will have short takeoff/vertical landing (STOVL) capability, plus full controllability in all axes while hovering.

No successful civilian use for VTOL has yet been achieved.

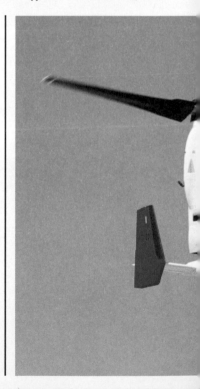

Above right: The Sea Harrier FRS.2 (subsequently redesignated F/A 2) in a carrier ski-jump takeoff. This version first flew in 1989. The origins of the Sea Harrier date back to October 21, 1960, when the Hawker P.1127 made its first hovering flight. This evolved through the Kestrel to the Harrier close support aircraft. Both Harrier and Sea Harrier types, as well as US Marine Corps AV-8 variants, have seen action since the Falklands War of 1982.

Right: First flight of the Bell Boeing V-22 Osprey occurred in March 1989. It is a tilt-rotor transport combining vertical lift with fast forward speed. Some 446 are on order for the US Marines, Air Force and Navy (including Special Operations Forces).

Fastest and Highest

> '*As I blasted towards the heavens, I alternated between side-arm control and center stick, pumping in tentative control motions to feel her out. Even then the X-15 remained firm and stable. I stared in fascination at the Machmeter, which climbed quickly from Mach 1.5 to Mach 1.8, and then effortlessly to my top speed for this flight, Mach 2.3....*'
>
> SCOTT CROSSFIELD

Since the first powered flight, the quest had been for ever-greater speeds and altitudes. It reached its apogee with the North American X-15 hypersonic research aircraft. Like the Bell XS-1, the X-15 was air-launched from a modified bomber, now a B-52.

Intended to explore a speed/altitude range of Mach 5+/50 miles (80km), the X-15 was powered by a rocket motor giving 57,000lb (25,855kg) of static thrust on a mix of liquid oxygen and anhydrous ammonia. Special chrome-nickel

alloys were used to offset extremes of aerodynamic heating; and three control systems were provided: a conventional center-stick for landing; a side-stick (anticipating the General Dynamics F-16 by more than a decade) for launch, acceleration, and climb-out; and a reaction system using hydrogen peroxide thrusters for control at very high altitude.

The first flight, on June 8, 1959, was unpowered. Dropped from 40,000ft (12,191m), the X-15 handled well until the final approach, when the nose suddenly pitched up. Test pilot Scott Crossfield tried to catch it, but got out of phase with the system, which was too sensitive. The result was a porpoising motion. However, he succeeded in making a good if fairly heavy landing at the bottom of an oscillation.

The first "hot" flight took place on September 17. It reached Mach 2.3 in a shallow climb to 50,000ft (15,240m), albeit with an engine less powerful than that intended. Crossfield commented, "It was immedi-

Below: The pilot of a North American X-15 rocket-powered research aircraft prepares to be launched from beneath the wing of the parent Boeing B-52 bomber that carried his machine aloft.

Above: On 10 March 1956 test pilot Peter Twiss set a new world absolute air speed record of 1,131.76mph (1,821kph) in the elegant Fairey Delta 2, powered by a Rolls-Royce Avon turbojet.

ately apparent that we had built a beautiful airplane. Its nose held straight and firm without the yaw and pitch common to most high-performance airplanes."

Inevitably problems arose, but these were gradually overcome, and the definitive XLR99 motor was fitted to the No 2 aircraft. On the first flight with the new powerplant, on November 15, 1960, Crossfield reached Mach 2.97 at 81,200ft (24,749m). Shortly after this the North American flight program was concluded, and the X-15s were turned over to the National Aeronautics and Space Administration (NASA), the USAF and USN.

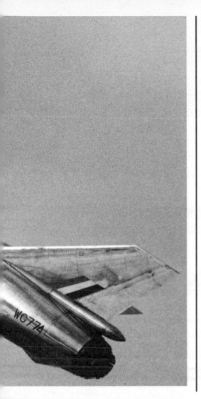

Over the next few years a dazzling series of flights took place, as the X-15s explored the flight envelope. NASA test pilot Joe Walker reached 246,700ft (75,190m) on April 30, 1962, then on August 22, 1963, took the third X-15 up to 354,200ft (107,955m), slightly more than 67 miles – an altitude never since exceeded by a winged aircraft. Space begins 50 miles (80km) above the Earth's surface.

Nor was speed neglected. Air Force pilot Bob White reached Mach 4.43 on March 7, 1961, exceeded Mach 5 on June 23, and then, on November 9, flying at 101,600ft (30,966m), attained Mach 6.04.

Meanwhile, the No 2 aircraft had been rebuilt as the X-15A-2, and in this machine Major William Knight reached Mach 6.72 on October 3, 1967. After 199 flights, the program ended on October 24, 1968.

Below: The X-15A-2's speed of Mach 6.72 was the highest recorded speed yet achieved by man in an airplane capable of being controlled in normal flight.

Swing Wings

> '*I'm not sure if anyone really knows what the F-111's top speed is. On my first flight in the F-111 we reached Mach 2 while climbing out from takeoff, still relatively heavy, and had to reduce speed only to keep from running out of the supersonic corridor. A nice turn was made at 1.8, and the aircraft performed exceedingly well (turns, rolls, etc) while supersonic. It is designed to provide a stable bombing platform while supersonic on the deck, and it does this very well.*'
>
> MAJOR PETER DUNN, USAF

Aircraft design consists of a series of compromises. A short-span, highly swept wing is optimum for high-speed flight, especially in the bumpy air encountered at low level, whereas a long-span, straight wing allows economical cruising, higher ceiling, and most importantly, slower takeoff and landing speeds, reducing the runway length required.

What was obviously needed was a method of varying the wing sweep in flight. Like all aviation ideas, this dated back many years. The first variable-sweep aircraft to fly was the Westland Pterodactyl IV, in March 1931. It was a modest beginning, as the variation in sweep was a mere 4.75 degrees, and was intended only to trim the aircraft for different loads.

Next in the field were the Germans, but the Second World War ended before any flight trials could be made. The aircraft in question, the Messerschmitt P.1101, was shipped to the USA after the war, where it became the basis for the first true variable-sweep aircraft, the Bell X-5. It was in this aircraft, on June 27, 1951, that Bell test pilot Skip Ziegler first changed the sweep of the

wings from 20deg to 50deg in flight.

Next came the Grumman XF10F-1 Jaguar, in which Corky Meyer

Right: An F-111 with wings swept almost fully forward. The original requirement was for an aircraft optimized for very low penetration, including a final "dash" at Mach 1.2, and also capable of the high-level Mach 2.5 interceptor role.

experienced some moments most kindly described as "interesting." The main problem was that the wing had to move through its full range of sweep without significantly moving the aerodynamic center. This could be done, but the mechanism was heavy and mechanically complex.

The idea lapsed, to be revived when NASA discovered that having a separate pivot point for each wing, mounted outboard and slightly aft of the normal location, would produce acceptable characteristics. Coincident with this came the USAF Specific Operational Requirement (SOR) 183 for a multi-role tactical fighter,

the performance and handling demands of which could best be met by variable sweep.

The contract was eventually won by General Dynamics with what became the F-111, which first flew on December 21, 1964. With this, swing-wing aircraft could truly be said to have come of age.

This was far from the end of the story. The F-111 was unable to fulfill the fighter role, and was plagued by technical problems. But at minimum sweep it could get off the ground in a reasonable distance with a heavy load of ordnance, cruise economically for long distances, and then, with

wings swept back, give a stable ride at supersonic speeds in the dense air close to the ground. The addition of terrain-following radar coupled to the autopilot allowed this to be done in total darkness or bad weather.

After an inauspicious combat debut in Vietnam, the F-111 clearly demonstrated its unsurpassed capabilities later in that war. Although the design was elderly by the time of the Gulf War in 1991, the type remained extremely effective.

Several other swing-wing types have been successfully developed and deployed, among them France's

Mirage G and G.8, Russia's MiG-23/27 fighter-attack aircraft, Sukhoi Su-24 fighter-bomber, and Tu-160 strategic bomber, the US Navy's F-14 Tomcat carrier-based interceptor fighter, the USAF's B-1B strategic bomber, and the RAF's Tornado fighter/strike aircraft.

Above: The US Navy's F-14 Tomcat is the most potent swing-wing fighter ever built. Computerized wing sweep automatically gives the optimum setting for every combination of speed/altitude, and it is fully maneuverable at all settings.

The Ultimate Spyplane

> ' ... we were in a continuous shroud of high thick cirrus which extended to the mid-sixties (thousands of feet). We were moving at Mach 2.6 when we blasted from the cloud tops. It was like being shot from a rocket as we bolted from the high tropopause into the clear stratosphere. We did another fast circuit of North Vietnam... then descended back into Thailand where the other storms bad been. '
>
> MAJOR DON WALBRECHT, USAF

It was as a reconnaissance vehicle that the aircraft first proved its worth in war. Survival lay in great speed, great altitude, or a combination of both. The SR-71 Blackbird, a product of Lockheed's famed "Skunk Works," was the greatest of this breed. In a service career spanning a quarter of a century it proved totally uninterceptable.

The predecessor of the SR-71, the Lockheed U-2 (of which the U-2S version is still operational), flew at moderate speeds and used very high altitudes to evade interception. That this was not enough was demonstrated on May 1, 1960, when a U-2 was brought down inside the Soviet Union by a surface-to-air missile (SAM).

Greater altitudes were an obvious need, but overwhelming speed was the real solution. Not only would this make interception by a manned fighter tremendously difficult, but it would crimp in the engagement envelope of even the most capable SAM. The difference between the 450kt (834kph) of the U-2 and the Mach 3 of the SR-71 reduced the time available for missile engagement by 75 percent and demanded four times greater accuracy from the weapon's guidance system.

First flown on December 22, 1964, the two-seat SR-71 was developed from the A-12 single-seat reconnaissance aircraft built to meet a CIA requirement. Optimized for sustained cruise at Mach 3 at 80,000ft (24,383m), it was built mainly of titanium to withstand the kinetic heating of prolonged supersonic flight. A tailless delta wing carried two huge J58 turbo-ramjets located outboard. This layout had the advantage of keeping boundary layer air away from the sensitive intakes, but at the cost of poor asymmetric handling qualities in the event of power loss on one side. Other fea-

tures were inward-canted twin fins and a pronounced chine along each side of the nose, both contributing to a reduced radar cross-section.

The SR-71 entered service in January 1966. In all, thirty-two were delivered, including two SR-71B trainers, distinguishable by their raised rear cockpits.

For many years Blackbirds flew reconnaissance missions, operating mainly out of Beale AFB in California, Mildenhall in Suffolk, England, and Kadena on Okinawa. North Vietnam was frequently visited, and overflights of Egypt and other Middle Eastern countries were made during and after

Above: Despite being the first Western aircraft to incorporate features that significantly reduced radar cross-section (RCS), including "Iron Ball" paint, the SR-71 also offered Mach 3 performance and an undeniable beauty.

the October War of 1973. The aircraft used a special high-density fuel, JP-7, and thus needed dedicated tanker support for longer missions, which could last up to ten hours.

The SR-71 is credited with having had the ability to scan more than 100,000sq miles (259,000sq km) of the Earth's surface every hour. It was

able therefore to probe the Soviet air defenses from international airspace. Lt. Viktor Belenko, a MiG-25 pilot based at Chuguyevka in the Far East, reported many unsuccessful attempts to intercept SR-71s.

By the late 1980s the USAF was operating only nine SR-71s and decided that the cost of operating such a small fleet was not viable, so the fleet was retired in 1990.

Most of the aircraft were sent to or made available to museums, but on the instructions of Congress five SR-71As and one trainer were set aside for possible future use. By 1994, realizing that there was a continuing shortfall in US reconnaissance capability, Congress ordered reactivation of two SR-71s. USAF reactivated two, making them fully operational, but did not use them

for any significant missions. Two years later the aircraft were temporarily grounded since funds for their operation were not authorized. Although Congress authorized the funds, in 1997 then-President Clinton used his veto powers to delete the budgeted funds, and on October 30, 1998, the SR-71 was officially retired, after a 32-year military career.

Above: The Lockheed SR-71 Blackbird made extensive use of RAM – radar-absorbent materials – in all the sharp horizontal edges that might be seen by an enemy radar, including the chines, elevons and wing leading edges. Most of the sensor payload was packed into the chines which were carefully blended with the fuselage, measures again aimed at reducing RCS.

Attack Helicopters

> ' I tried to slow down the attacking force in the field
> with rockets and 20mm cannon fire. I had never seen
> several hundred men in the open before, so I was in
> hog heaven.... I slowed to about 40kt (74kph)
> and opened up with the twenty. I was having
> a great time, the 20mm was tearing them to shreds,
> and I continued my run all the way to about
> 30ft (9m) and then broke to the left over the river. '
>
> CAPTAIN TERRYL MORRIS

In its early days the army helicopter was regarded very much as a utility machine that could be adapted for various missions by a simple change of equipment. While the flexibility bestowed by this arrangement was in many ways a tremendous advan- tage, the use of rotary-winged aircraft in the battle zone inevitably suggested that an offensive capability was possible.

A few helicopters were fitted with *ad hoc* weapons in Korea, and by the French in Indo-China, but it

Above: An AH-1S HueyCobra fires a pair of 2.75in (70mm) rockets.

Left: US Army HueyCobras deployed to Panama during hostilities there in 1989-1990.

was not until the French-Algerian War of 1954-1962 that helicopters equipped for the fire-support mission emerged.

The next war of note was the "in-country war" in Vietnam, where helicopters were used on a vast scale in air cavalry operations. While transport machines routinely carried door gunners, these were insufficient to suppress ground fire, and other helicopters of the same type were armed and flown as gunships. This, however, was only a temporary solution; what was really needed was a helicopter dedicated to the task.

This duly emerged as the Bell AH-1 HueyCobra, the first flight of which took place on September 7, 1965, when tested as the Model 209. The proven dynamics of the UH-1 were married to a new narrow body which reduced presented area and drag, and gave its two-man crew a much better all-round view. They sat in tandem, with the pilot behind the gunner. Stub wings were introduced to provide attachment points for a heavy load of weapons, and they also unloaded the rotor in fast forward flight, increasing agility. A degree of armor protection was provided to reduce vulnerability.

Armament initially comprised a 7.62mm Minigun in a traversing chin turret, pods of unguided rockets, and grenade launchers, although the gun was quickly replaced by a far more effective 20mm cannon.

The HueyCobra reached Vietnam in mid-1968, and quickly proved its worth. Later variants had flat-plate canopy transparencies to reduce sun glint, more power, and a much wider variety of weaponry which included anti-tank missiles, enabling it to be used in the anti-armor role. As the SuperCobra and SeaCobra, it is used by the USMC, Israel and Iran, while armed with Sidewinder or Stinger air-to-air missiles it can be used in the anti-helicopter role.

The HueyCobra is important because it pioneered the attack helicopter concept and proved it in action. The layout has become standardized: a two-man crew with the gunner in front of the pilot, angular flat transparencies, stub wings to carry ordnance loads, and armor for protection.

There are other, newer attack helicopters in service, of which the AH-64 Apache is probably the best known, but variants of the Cobra are still around in large numbers, and gave sterling service in the Gulf War 1991 and subsequently in Afghanistan and the war against Saddam Hussein's Iraq in 2003.

Below: The US Marine Corps' two-bladed AH-1W SuperCobras are in line for a remanufacture to AH-1Z standard, with four blades and significantly enhanced performance.

Widebody Transports

> *'Pilot Jack Waddell eased throttles forward; Co-Pilot Brien Wygle called out speeds as a gentle giant of the air began to move; Flight Engineer Jess Wallick kept eyes glued to gauges. The Boeing Model 747 Superjet gathered speed. The nose lifted. After 4,300ft – less than half the 9,000ft runway – main gear of the plane left the concrete. At 11.34 a.m., with a speed of 164 miles an hour, quietly and almost serenely, the age of spacious jets began.'*
>
> BOEING MAGAZINE

The Boeing 747, familiarly known as the "Jumbo Jet," set a new trend in air travel as the first of the widebody airliners. This came about less by intent than by a series of happy coincidences.

In the mid-1960s Boeing was a hive of activity, turning out airliners

and commercial transports by the score. Four-jet 707s and 717s, and tri-jet 727s, were all in production, and the short-range twin-jet 737 was coming along nicely. The company had lost the USAF C-5 Galaxy military transport contract to Lockheed, but was working on an SST (supersonic transport) which it confidently expected would sweep the board in the future.

At the time container ships were proving a huge success. Boeing felt that there was a niche in the market for a long-range freighter which would add the advantage of speed to the convenience of container handling. Drawing on their experience

Below: The "dumpy" 747SP (Special Performance) was built at the behest of Pan American World Airways to provide non-stop range between New York and Tokyo. Only 45 were built, as the improvements of the larger models soon provided similar performance. Syrianair was one of the few airlines to purchase it. Others still operating the type include Iran Air, Saudi Arabian Airlines, Corsair and South African

with the C-5 project, the company produced a design wide enough to permit two 8ft (2.44m) wide containers side by side, and it was this, rather than any other factor, which resulted in the first widebody jet.

Further research showed that the projected growth in passenger traffic would require greater capacity. One advantage of a really large airplane was that costs per seat-mile or per ton-mile would be considerably reduced, whereas those of the SST (already the object of doubts about its viability) would be much higher.

Consequently, the Boeing 747 was designed to serve as a passenger transport with ten-abreast seating, as a freighter, or as a combination of the two. On April 13, 1966, long before the first flight, Pan American Airways signed a contract for two cargo aircraft and twenty-three airliners configured to carry 350 to 400 passengers.

On February 9, 1969, the flight test crew of Jack Waddell, Brien Wygle and Jess Wallick lifted the huge machine into the air for the first time at Paine Field. The 747 was

Above: Korean Air operates several 747 models, including this 747-300.

remarkably quiet by the standards of the day, while its enormous size belied its speed, making it seem to hang in the air. That first flight was uneventful, as was the succeeding test program, and the aircraft was awarded FAA certification at the end of that same year.

Shortly after, on January 22, 1970, Pam Am made the inaugural flight with the type from New York to Heathrow. Since then, well over 1,000 Boeing 747s have been com-pleted in many variants. Engines are provided by Rolls-Royce, Pratt & Whitney or General Electric accord-ing to operator's choice; passenger accommodation varies between 366 and 550, while maximum takeoff weight is 833,0001b (377,850kg).

Cruising at speeds in excess of 500kt (925kph) at altitudes of up to 45,000ft (13,715m), this superb machine will be with us for many years to come.

Concorde

> '*The sun is now climbing from the west. In winter it is possible to leave London after sunset, on the evening Concorde for New York, and watch the sun rise out of the west. Flying at Mach 2 at these latitudes will cause the sun to set in the west at three times its normal rate, casting, as it does so, a vast curved shadow of the earth, up and ahead of the aircraft.*'

FIRST OFFICER CHRISTOPHER ORLEBAR

The quoted commentary is fairly typical of that given to passengers on the London/New York Concorde service. Other comments have been that the cruising speed of Mach 2 covers a mile every 2.75 seconds, and that the cruising altitude is twice the height of Mount Everest, where the sky looks much darker, almost black, and on a clear

day the curvature of the Earth can just be made out.

Concorde, the result of Anglo-French collaboration, was the world's only supersonic airliner, operated only by British Airways and Air France. In service with the former it could typically carry 100 passengers from London Heathrow to New York J.F. Kennedy in less than three-and-a-half hours. This was rather faster than the change in time zones, with the amusing result that arrival time in New York was more than an hour earlier than the departure time in London.

In the 1950s aircraft performance increased faster than ever before. While this was mainly applicable to military aviation, the possibility of building a supersonic transport (SST) looked increasingly attractive.

The Anglo-French agreement which led to Concorde was signed in November 1962. Within a year the USA announced that it, too, would develop an SST, while the Soviet

Below: The British-assembled prototype made its first flight on April 9, 1969. In January 1976 Concorde began service with Air France and BA; the latter hoped to extend the airframe life until 2017, but dwindling passenger bookings forced them to announce Concorde's retirement in 2003.

Union also determined not to be left behind.

The American SST was intended to be larger and faster than its European rival and, therefore, would have been far more expensive. It eventually foundered on the twin rocks of technology and finance. The Russian Tupolev Tu-144, dubbed "Concordski" owing to its superficial resemblance to the Anglo-French aircraft, was of similar size to it, with a "paper performance" slightly better.

The Tu-144 was the first SST to fly, some two months ahead of Con-

corde, on December 3, 1968. On June 5, 1969, it went supersonic for the first time, and on May 26, 1970, it exceeded Mach 2. In both cases it was a few months ahead of Concorde.

A radically revised Tu-144 appeared at the Paris Air Show, Le Bourget, in 1973, but crashed during its display. The type was used by Aeroflot from December 1975 on the Moscow-Kazakshtan run, but was withdrawn from service in June 1978.

By contrast, Concorde first flew on March 2, 1969, piloted by Andre Turcat, began passenger services on

Above: An Air France Concorde is shown landing in New Zealand on one of the extensive program of charters.

January 21, 1976, and flew almost continually until fall 2003. (A tragic accident – the aircraft's first – of an Air France aircraft on July 25, 2000, led to the withdrawal of Concorde's certificate of airworthiness, which was restored about a year later after modifications, including to the fuel tanks, had been carried out.)

Concorde's would have been one of the greatest success stories in aviation history had it not been for one unforeseen factor. The impact of vociferous environmental groups made it increasingly difficult to obtain routes to the USA, and these routes were the ones that counted. The routes were finally granted, but too late to help sales. The result was that only twenty Concordes were built, of which sixteen were production models. In spring 2003 British Airways announced that its fleet would be retired later that year.

Advanced Technology

Until the dreadful and tragic airborne terrorist attacks in New York, Washington and Pennsylvania on September 11, 2001 (generally referred to now as "9/11"), the number of passengers traveling by air was generally increasing every year. From time to time, the rate of growth was arrested, as happened in 1986 because of tension and terrorism in the Middle East, in 1991 as a result of the Gulf War, and in 1997, when the financial crisis in Asia threatened the world's biggest growth market. But the overall trend was determinedly upward, with air freight increasing even more dramatically than passenger traffic.

According to the International Civil Aviation Organization (ICAO), some 1.6 billion passengers traveled on scheduled services in the year 2000. At the same time, the world's airlines carried 3.7 million tonnes of cargo. Some industry analysts still predict that these figures will spiral to around 5 billion passengers and 12 million tonnes respectively by 2020.

Based on these expectations, some aircraft manufacturers have predicted that over the next twenty years the world's airlines will need some 15,400 new aircraft. The vast majority, say experts, will be required to meet new demand, with a large number also required to replace older types nearing the end of their design lives.

"9/11" certainly adversely affected air travel figures, and this has been expected to be reflected in reduced orders for new aircraft.

The year 1970 was a figurative watershed in civil aviation. Until then, flying was a novelty for most people; thenceforward it increasingly became the norm, due largely to package holidays that encouraged people to go abroad and to do so cheaply. In the 1970s many aircraft that had been in service during the previous decade were still holding their market share in terms of passengers carried, but there was as great a need for small and medium-sized passenger airplanes as for the biggest.

Technological advances in aircraft production and maintenance as well as in airline services have facilitated greater capacity for the attractive short- and medium-haul commercial passenger and freight business, particularly city-center-to-city-center services, where environmental issues have had to be accommodated.

Progress in the performance of military aircraft during the last forty years or so has been no less impressive. One constant demand is that today's military aircraft have to be versatile. The days of specialized interception or ground-attack fighters and bombers are, generally speaking, at an end. The warplanes of the last two decades or so have had to be built such that versions can fire missiles that can be guided against targets in the air or on the surface. And modern military aircraft are exorbitantly expensive to build, such that the rate of new types entering service has dramatically fallen compared with previous decades. It is difficult to believe that the F-16 Fighting Falcon first flew in 1974, that the MiG-21 first took to the air almost twenty years before that (and a version is still being built in China today), and that the F-14 Tomcat and F-15 Eagle are both the result of designs tabled over thirty years ago.

Among the more interesting combat aircraft have been Russia's MiG family of fighters and fighter-bombers. The MiG-23/MiG-27 "Flogger" was the first to employ variable-geometry swing-wings (with three sweep angles), and it has a hinged ventral tailfin that can be folded sideways to avoid scraping it on the ground when taking off or landing. It enjoys a combination of good short-field performance with acceleration and high speed, but it turns relatively poorly, which is a disadvantage in air combat.

The MiG-29 "Fulcrum", first flown in October 1977, was designed as an agile air combat fighter to counter America's F-16 and F-18. One of its

Above: One of Russia's Sukhoi "Flanker" series, the Su-34 fighter-bomber, oozes with high-technology features, and some unusual ones for military aircraft too, like toilet and galley for the crew.

most remarkable features was its helmet-mounted sight, which allowed missiles to be launched at high (45-degree) off-boresight angles. The MiG-31 "Foxhound" is a two-seater interceptor. Developed from the MiG-25, it is specifically designed to counter cruise missiles. Operational from 1982, it has a multiple-target kill capability and its radar is claimed by the Russians to be able to detect stealth aircraft.

Above: The F.3 definitive version of the Tornado: two-seat, twin-engined, bisonic, variable-sweep, long-range interceptor capable of 1,452mph (2,336kph/Mach 2.20) at altitude.

Right: Based on a 1970s design, but continually developed to high-tech standards, a multi-role F/A-18C Hornet prepares for takeoff from the deck of USS Saratoga.

Another Russian family of fighter aircraft, designed by Sukhoi, include some extremely useful types. The Su-27 "Flanker" is huge, long-range, very capable and carries up to ten air-to-air missiles (AAMs). Developments of it, the Su-35 and Su-37 (fitted with thrust-vectoring engine nozzles), have displayed amazing maneuverability at recent air shows, making Western fighter designers stop and think.

Not that the West has been slow in introducing highly capable and often unusual warplanes. Sweden's Saab J37 Viggen, for example, first flown in 1967, is a canard aircraft and has interesting features that enable it to operate from short stretches of highway. Using reverse thrusters, its landing run needs only 1,700ft (518m). Various versions assume many roles: strike, reconnaissance, interception or training.

Like the MiG-23/MiG-27, the Grumman F-14 Tomcat is a variable-sweep aircraft, and is used mainly as a fleet air defense interceptor by the US Navy. Its radar can detect targets at over 230 miles (370km) and can track up to 24 targets and guide missiles at six targets simultaneously. It is also a formidable opponent in close combat, although combat successes have been meager, basically through lack of opportunity.

Another variable-sweep combat aircraft is the Panavia Tornado, produced during the 1970s by a European consortium of Britain, Germany and Italy. One version is optimised for the interdiction strike role, in which it is capable of blind, first-pass attack at over 920mph (1,480kph) at sea level, and another is an interceptor combining high speed with long endurance, capable of operating autonomously

far away from base in the teeth of electronic jamming. It represents not only a shift to all-round aircraft but also to joint design and manufacture.

AIR STRIKES

Both versions of the Tornado took part in the Gulf War of 1991, when a coalition of Western and Arab forces joined ranks to liberate Kuwait from an invasion by its neighbor, Iraq. Against an estimated 7,000 SAMs and 9,000-10,000 anti-aircraft guns, as well as the Iraqi Air Force, the coalition sent wave after wave of land- and carrier-based attack aircraft, which were escorted by fighters and assisted by dedicated radar jamming and SAM suppression warplanes. Within 72 hours the Iraqi defense system was rendered almost completely impotent.

Prominent among the carrier-based aircraft were Sea Harriers, a variant of the first short takeoff and vertical landing (STOVL) type to enter service with any air force in the world.

The first production Harrier made its maiden flight on August 31, 1967. Sea Harriers had their combat debut in 1982, when a British task force was sent by sea to the South Atlantic to recover the Falkland Islands from Argentine invaders.

The Harrier can perform unconventional maneuvers with thrust-vectoring, but this was never used. However, the ability of the Sea Harriers to land vertically allowed them to operate in weather conditions that grounded other carrier aircraft. Armed with the latest AIM-9L Sidewinder air-to-air missiles, the Sea Harrier performed superlatively in the Falklands, assisting in an overwhelming victory.

Other Western warplanes that participated in combat during the last twenty-five years include the ubiquitous McDonnell Douglas F-4 Phantom, the F-15 Eagle and F-18 Hornet from the same US company, and the Lockheed Martin (formerly General Dynamics) F-16 Fighting Falcon. The Phantom, originally a carrier-fighter

Above: Although it started life as an all-out air-superiority fighter, it wasn't long before air-to-surface weapons were introduced to the F-15 Eagle, here carrying no fewer than 24 bombs – not bad for a "fighter"!

Above: One of the test aircraft of the Eurofighter EF 2000 Typhoon program for a single-seat, twin-engined, canard-delta, bisonic air-defense and multi-role fighter. The "smiling" chin intake is stated to be a stealth measure; its lower lip is automatically maneuverable.

but later developed into a bomb hauler, defense suppression aircraft, and as a fighter, fought against a variety of MiGs in the Arab-Israeli Wars and also in the skies over Southeast Asia. More than 5,000 Phantoms were built. Ageing now, although still in service with several air forces, the Phantom was a fast two-seater (with a weapons systems operator in the back seat), could carry an enormous weapons load externally, and incorporated a weapons system that was better, because it was more flexible, than any other warplane of its era. Although the Phantom first flew in May 1958, the F-4G Wild Weasel version hunted for and killed SAM radars in the 1991 Gulf War.

Alongside it in that conflict flew the F-15 Eagle, whose combat debut came, however, while in service with the Israeli Air Force, against Syrian MiG-21s in June 1979. Later it was responsible for the first ever defeat of

a MiG 25 interceptor. The Eagle has proved a superlative air combat fighter that for years far outclassed anything in the Russian stable in both performance and maneuevrability.

Also engaged in both conflicts in the Middle East was the F-16, a small, single-engined, lightweight and much cheaper fighter of unparalleled agility, with computerized fly-by-wire avionics and capable of sustaining a 9g turn in close combat. As with other aircraft, versions of the F-16 have also carried out bombing raids, testament once again to the much-needed versatility of modern combat aircraft.

When the F-16 was first developed it was in competition for the role of new lightweight fighter. The loser was the Northrop F-17, a development of which was adopted by the US Navy as a multi-role fighter to supplement the Tomcat and replace the Phantom and the also-ageing A-4 Corsair in the attack role. Having been navalized by

McDonnell Douglas, it emerged eventually as the F/A-18 Hornet, which was more carrier-capable than the F-16, offered greater development potential and, for operations far out over the ocean, twin-engined safety. It was also the first of the advanced "glass-cockpit" fighters, in which the old-fashioned dial instruments were replaced by screens on which all relevant information could be called up at the touch of a button. As such, it set the trend for all future fighter cock pits. The F-18 went into combat in both Gulf wars Gulf, launched from US Navy carriers.

STEALTH TECHNOLOGY

The Gulf War also saw the operational value of stealth technology, which includes careful airframe shaping, internal carriage of all fuel and weapons, curved inlet ducts to shield the compressor face of the engine, the extensive use of radar-absorbent materials, minimum active radar emissions, and the reduction of the heat signature from the engines. The angular black Lockheed F-117 Nighthawk made its combat debut over Panama in 1989. In the Gulf just over a year later it made precision attacks against targets in and around Baghdad against modern air defense systems, ultimately flying a total of 1,271 missions. Practically the first the Iraqis knew of its presence was when the bombs hit the targets.

In 1999 twenty-four F-117As deployed to Italy in support of Operation Allied Force in the Balkans. Little information was released about their operations in that theater, but one

F-117A was shot down, with some reports suggesting it was a victim of a SAM strike.

Stealth will exert a decisive influence on future air warfare for those few nations able to afford it. First shown to the public on November 22, 1988, the Northrop Grumman B-2A Spirit stealth bomber was so hugely expensive that of an original total of 133 planned, just twenty-one were funded. It has a weird, all-wing shape, and its tiny radar signature and diffuse exhaust make it difficult to detect by conventional means, and almost impossible to intercept.

Stealth concepts are included in many other warplanes, including the Lockheed F-22 Raptor. Called the fighter of the future, it combines stealth with supercruise and thrust-vectoring, making it as good in beyond-visual-range combat as it is in

Right: The Northrop B-2A is the result of many year's research by that company into the feasibility of "flying wings." Built as a stealth bomber the advanced aerodymic airframe is constructed mainly of carbonfiber and other composite materials. It is powered by four General Electric F118-GE-1110 turbofans, carries a crew of two and is armed with conventional, laser-guided and nuclear weapons.

the close dogfight.

In Europe, the latest co-operative type, the Eurofighter, is being produced by Britain, Germany, Italy and Spain. It will reach Mach 2 and climb to 35,000ft (10,668m) in 2min 30sec. The Eurofighter project is the largest procurement program that Britain's Ministry of Defence has ever supported, it having invested £15 billion in the scheme and ordered 232 of these fighters.

BIGGER JUMBOS

Meanwhile, the world's biggest airliner, the 550-seat Boeing 777-300, which is more than 33ft (10m) longer than the 777-200, was rolled out in October 1997 and began a seven-month flight test program prior to series production and delivery. The 777 project is undoubtedly a product of the computer age. It was the first

jet airliner to be 100 percent digitally defined and pre-assembled using a powerful Dassault/IBM CATIA CAD/CAM (computer-aided design and computer-aided manufacturing) system and made extensive use of finite element analysis, so that virtually no paper drawings were made.

Currently in planning is yet a bigger passenger-carrying airliner, the Airbus A380 (formerly A3XX), available in different versions. One of these would carry up to a thousand passengers in high-density configuration. It would have ten-abreast layouts on the main deck, with eight-abreast on an upper deck, and passengers would be able to visit shops, bars, fitness centers and many other facilities during their journey. Customer deliveries of this four-engined transport could be as soon as 2006.

MILITARY TRANSPORT

Military transport aircraft are as important as passenger-carriers. The frequency of minor wars in the past four decades has necessitated the speedy movement of troops, usually from the USA or a former colonialist continental European country. In consequence, huge carriers of soldiers and cargo, including tanks, other vehicles and artillery, have been in demand.

NATO has had to be the world's police, able quickly to staunch the outbreaks of minor wars. During the 1991 Gulf War, for example, the Coalition effort was underpinned by the biggest strategic airlift in history.

The requirement is for airplanes big enough to carry up to 400 troops or a vast amount of cargo, or smaller numbers and quantities of both. Typical cargoes would comprise motor vehicles, tanks, artillery and even small helicopters. They must cruise at no less than Mach 0.75 and have a range of at least 2,500 miles (4,022km). Loading and unloading has to be quick. A high wing and low-slung fuselage are essential in order to give clearance for moving cargo in and out. Unlike civil aircraft, they need missile jammers and radar warning sensors.

SPEED AND MOBILITY

For the oncoming years the major NATO countries need a strategy that will focus on member nations' military strengths and enable them to be ready to move anywhere to meet any challenge. Speed of reaction and instant mobility are the touchstones. Taking Britain as an example, one possibility could be a carrier-based air group comprising Fleet Air Arm Sea Harriers and RAF Harrier 7s, escorted by nuclear-powered submarines armed with Tomahawk cruise missiles. Another expeditionary force could comprise troops and tanks backed

by air power and some form of anti-ballistic missile protection. For this, strategic lift aircraft such as the American McDonnell Douglas C-17 Globemaster II, able to carry heavy armored vehicles, would be necessary.

UNMANNED AIRCRAFT
In air combat, perhaps the future lies with the Unmanned Combat Air Vehicle (UCAV). This would have a new airbreathing engine, a third, steering, wing at the front to increase maneuverability, and reach a speed of Mach 15. Its acceleration would be 20g, which is twice that of any present aircraft, and it would be guided towards targets by the global satellite positioning system (GPS). It could enter service by 2005. A second, smaller version under development could be launched from current bombers, which would increase the UCAV's range.

Unmanned aerial vehicles (UAVs) have already seen combat, the US RQ-1 Predator and Global Hawk among them. They can be used for reconnaissance or as strike aircraft armed with missiles. Today, the US Deprtment of Defense is developing UAVs in three main categories: Tactical, with a range of less than 125 miles (200km); Endurance, with a range of over 125 miles; and Shipboard.

Below: The US Air Force's Lockheed C-5A military transport is currently being upgraded to serve until the middle of the 21st century. Like its sister transports, the C-141 and C-17, it can carry troops and tanks/helicopters, plus undertake clandestine missions with Special Operations Forces.

Super-agility

> *The angle is about ninety degrees and the MiG's silvery body is every fighter pilot's dream. The missile slides off the left wing.... Five seconds pass – they seem an eternity – until the missile explodes with a small plume of smoke. Contact. The MiG simply stands still in the air. Another second and his right wing is suddenly torn from place; the aircraft spins and catches fire.*
>
> MAJOR R., ISRAELI F-16 PILOT

In the late 1960s the main perceived threat to the free world was all-out war in Central Europe against the Soviet Union and her allies, against vastly superior numbers in the air. The seriousness of this was underlined in Vietnam, where the latest US fighters had been forced into close combat, a role for which they had never been designed, by light and agile Russian-built aircraft.

The latest US air superiority fighters were unaffordable in the numbers necessary. A Pentagon group that came to be known as the "Fighter Mafia" studied the problem and arrived at a solution. It was the "hi-lo mix," a core of very large and expensive fighters backed by many super-agile lightweights to add quantity to the existing quality.

The accent for the new light fighter was on close combat, with maneuverability, acceleration and endurance stressed, rather than maximum speed and ceiling, the previous goals of fighter design.

General Dynamics (now Lockheed Martin) at Fort Worth, Texas, set up a secure establishment to design the new fighter. In essence they took a large but proven engine and packaged a small airframe, stressed for

Right: The first F-16 to explore the strange world of decoupled flight movements was the YF-16/CCV (Control-Configured Vehicle) which during the 1970s was flight-tested to change its flight path without changing its attitude).

the then unusual figure of 9g, around it. To increase maneuverability it was designed to have "relaxed stability," and featured wing/body blending and strakes. To save weight, fly-by-wire was used instead of hydraulic control runs (also tested on the F-4 in 1972). Pilot control demands were fed into a computer which automatically translated them into the maximum that the aircraft could take for the speed/altitude combination at the time. Other new features were a steeply raked seat to increase g tolerance, and a side-stick controller. The canopy was a one-piece bubble, giving an all-round view. Variable-camber wings provided optimum lift in all flight regimes.

The first flight of the F-16 Fighting Falcon took place on January 20, 1974, with GD test pilot Phil Oestricher at the controls. Later that year it was evaluated against the

Northrop F-17, and a year after its first flight it was selected as the new USAF air combat fighter. Within a matter of months it had also been selected by four European air forces.

The F-16 set new standards of agility which became the yardstick by which other fighters were judged for the next two decades. It could sustain a 9g turn (albeit over a small portion of the performance envelope) while at the same time establishing a maneuverability plateau close to the limits that a pilot could take.

In the Beka'a action of 1982, to which the accompanying quotation

refers, F-16s accounted for forty-four Syrian MiGs for no losses. They also carried out the precision strike against the Osirak nuclear reactor in Iraq in 1981, shot down several Afghan intruders while in Pakistani service, and played a notable part in the Gulf War of 1991.

Above: The F-16 has been under continual development since 1974, with deliveries now well over 4,000 to several nations including (as shown here) Belgium, Denmark, the Netherlands, Norway, and of course the US Air Force,

Above: The F-16 Fighting Falcon now operates mainly as an air-to-surface strike-fighter, but it has made its mark in its designed function, air combat, in which role it is seen here armed with AIM-9J Sidewinder air-

to-air missiles in Belgian markings. The extra weight it has had to carry as a bomb truck has made inroads on its agility, but not its potency – witness its service for Israel and in the two Gulf Wars.

Solar Challenger

'*What makes the Solar Challenger unique is that it is the first aircraft with sufficient photovoltaic "muscle power" to enable it to fly unaided. Lightweight construction and energy-efficient design have produced the world's first truly solar-powered man-carrying aircraft.*'

MARTIN COWLE

Every day, boundless quantities of energy from the Sun reach the surface of our planet. Harnessing it has been the dream of mankind for many years.

A few flights had been made both in England and the USA using batteries charged by solar energy, but American Dr Paul MacCready set out to design an aircraft capable of powered flight using only energy drawn directly from the Sun's rays.

MacCready was already famous as a designer of successful human-powered aircraft. His Gossamer Condor won the Kremer prize for sustained flight on August 23, 1977, and Gossamer Albatross flew the English Channel on June 12, 1979. He was therefore no stranger to the ultralight construction needed to supplement the very limited power available from direct solar energy.

Because of the need to minimize weight, the Gossamer machines had been structurally marginal. By contrast, Solar Challenger was intended for far more ambitious flights, and was stressed to +5/-3g. This notwithstanding, its all-up weight, including the pilot, was no more than 294lb (133kg). Probably the most important weight-saving measure was the choice of pilot, Janice Brown, who weighed in at a mere 99lb (45kg).

Solar Challenger was, in effect, a powered glider. A long-span, high-set wing was supplemented by a large-area horizontal stabilizer mounted well back on the boom that served as a fuselage. Both surfaces gave plenty of area for the 1,628 solar cells, each about 0.75 x 2.48 x 0.01in

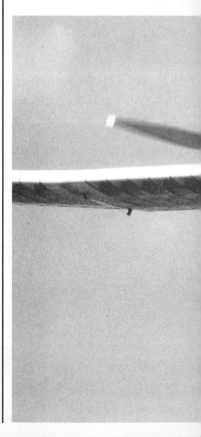

Right: The first of several flights of Solar Challenger occurred on November 20, 1980. It was the first successful aircraft capable of powered flight using only energy drawn directly from the Sun's rays.

(19mm x 63mm x 0.3mm), which provided motive power. A narrow underslung nacelle housed the cockpit, above which the boom projected forward, carrying the electric motor and a variable-pitch propeller. At the extreme rear of the boom was a raked vertical stabilizer and rudder, positioned to minimize the risk of it casting shadows across the cells, with a consequent loss of power.

By November 1980 all was ready for the first flight. Conditions had to be just right. The aircraft had to be facing into wind and aligned with the runway, with the Sun high in the sky and directly astern. On November 20 the team gathered at El Mirage, a gliding center near Shafter, California.

The clouds cleared, the Sun shone, and Janice Brown fed power to the electric motor. Solar Challenger rolled gently forward and lifted off. That first flight lasted 2 minutes 50 seconds, in which time a height of 60ft (18m) was achieved.

Other flights followed, an altitude of 14,300ft (4,358m) being reached and endurance being extended to 8 hours 19 minutes. Then, on July 7, 1981, an extensively modified Solar Challenger, piloted by Stephen Ptacek, took off from Cormeilles-en-Vexin near Paris, climbed to 12,000ft (3,657m), crossed the Channel, and landed at Manston in England just 5 hours 25 minutes later. Solar-powered flight was a reality.

Voyager

> '*The autopilot had been acting up again.... The ADI was precessing, rolling off, every now and again. Hell, I don't even want to mess with it. I want to eke out every last bit of performance even if it's just an hour or so. We're close enough to home right now that if it quit, we'd probably hand-fly it – which would be one of the most incredible feats that two people would ever have to perform. I'm looking forward to having to hand-fly this airplane like I'd look at the electric chair....*'
>
> DICK RUTAN

Voyager, designed by Burt Rutan to fly around the world non-stop and unrefueled, was a very unconventional airplane.

The best description of Voyager is a trimaran with wings. This layout was adopted to combine maximum fuel capacity with minimum necessary cruising power and drag. A small piston engine was mounted at each end of a central nacelle; two engines were needed for takeoff and climb, and flight at high weights. Later, when sufficient fuel had been burned off, the front engine could be shut down. Between the engines was a cramped cockpit and a barely adequate sleeping area.

Outboard of the nacelle were two long booms, with vertical tail surfaces mounted on them. The booms were almost entirely filled with fuel, although a small weather radar was mounted on the nose of the right one.

The booms were connected to the nacelle by a canard surface at the nose and by the wing at the halfway point. The wing itself was a *tour-de-force*; optimised for high lift and low drag, it was very long and narrow, with winglets at its extremities. It also housed fuel. Construction was of lightweight composite materials.

Right: The first unrefueled flight around the world in the atmosphere was achieved not by a multi-million dollar bomber, but by Bert Rutan's radical, private-venture Voyager, on December 14, 1986.

Planning the flight and building the aircraft occupied several years, but finally all was ready. Voyager was piloted by Dick Rutan, brother of the designer, and Jeana Yeager.

Edwards AFB, in the Mojave desert, boasts the world's longest

runway, 15,000ft (4.57km). It was here that Voyager took off on its epic flight on the morning of December 14, 1986. Disaster seemed imminent at the start. Laden with 1,200 US gallons of fuel, Voyager took 14,000ft (4.27km) of runway to become airborne, the winglets scraping the ground and breaking off. Undaunted, the Voyager crew gained height and turned west, toward the Pacific. They were on their way.

The flight was not easy. Severe turbulence could cause Voyager to break up, so it had to be detected and avoided. The autopilot needed constant adjustment to suit changing flight conditions; fuel had to be correctly balanced, and navigation monitored.

Hours turned into days as Voyager traveled steadily westwards. Beyond the Pacific, over Thailand, Sri Lanka, the shark-infested Indian Ocean; on over the continent of Africa.

Various mechanical problems arose, but fatigue was the real enemy. The autopilot gave trouble, as did one or two instruments, but Voyager flew on, across the South Atlantic to South America, across Panama, then up the west coast of the USA and finally back to Edwards, touching down after 9 days 3 minutes and 44 seconds. A distance of 24,986 statute miles (40,209km) had been covered, and just 37 US gallons of fuel remained. It had been a close-run thing indeed.

FBW Airliner

> ' *Our A320 behaved even better than expected – it is both delightfully responsive and reassuringly stable to fly, qualities which fly-by-wire brings together for the first time in an airliner. Never before have we enjoyed a first flight so much, and we are confident that airline pilots will feel the same way.* '
>
> PIERRE BAUD

The Airbus A320 is a short-to-medium-range twin-engined commercial transport developed from the earlier A300 series. Externally there is little to distinguish it from the many other short-haul airliners in service around the world, but under the skin it is very different.

The A320 features a number of airliner "firsts," including a central-ized maintenance system, gust alleviation and the extensive use of composite materials in its primary structure. Most significantly, it is the first subsonic commercial aircraft to be fitted with a fly-by-wire flight control system (FCS).

Instead of the conventional control column, the pilot and copilot each have a side-stick control similar

Below: Hong Kong-based Dragonair took delivery of its first A320 in February 1993. Its aircraft are fitted out either in a two-class layout with 12 Club and 144 economy seats, or in a 168-seat single-class configuration.

to that pioneered in the General Dynamics F-16 fighter. Pitch and roll commands are signaled to a bank of five computers, which in turn pass them to the hydraulically operated flight control surfaces. A very high degree of protection is built in. The system will not allow structural and aerodynamic limits such as design speed or g to be exceeded, while a full nose-up command will give maximum lift and no more. The aircraft will hang on the edge of the flight performance envelope without ever straying outside it. This means that the A320 cannot be stalled or over-stressed while in the automatic mode, and is thus potentially the safest aircraft in service anywhere.

As a further safety measure, the automatic FCS can be turned off and the aircraft flown manually, while back-up control is provided by a conventional mechanical system to the rudder and horizontal stabilizer trimmers.

A visit to the flight deck is instructive. Whereas, on older aircraft, the instrument panel was smothered with dials and other instruments, that of the A320 is remarkably free of clutter. It is dominated by a series of electronic flight instrumentation systems (EFIS), on which is shown (in color) all essential flight and navigation information. Another first here is that the primary flight display incorporates speed, altitude and heading. Other displays show continually monitored engine performance, warnings, and system diagrams.

Further remarkable facts about the Airbus A320 are that it is the product of 100 percent computer aided design (CAD) and 80 percent computer-assisted manufacture (CAM). The first flight was made from Toulouse on February 22, 1987, and the first deliveries, to Air France and British Caledonian (now part of BA), were made late in March 1988.

The A320 was originally built as the -100, but this was soon superseded by the -200, which has wingtip winglets, a greater maximum takeoff weight, and increased range. By the beginning of the new millennium, the A320 order book stood at 1,423 aircraft, with 880 delivered.

Below: The visible signs of advanced technology in the A320 cockpit are sidestick controllers and the all-color electronic flight instrumentation systems (EFIS) – but there's a great deal more of the FBW and other systems hidden beneath the part-composite fuselage, wing and other surfaces.

Stealth Revealed

> ' *Being a stealth pilot is one of the most labor intensive and time constrained types of flying that I know. We have very strict timing constraints: to be where you are supposed to be all the time, exactly on time, and that has to be monitored by the pilot. For example, during a bomb competition in training in the US, I dropped a weapon that landed 0.02 seconds from the desired time, and finished third!* '
>
> LT. COL. MILES POUND, USAF

In the "Invisible Man" films, the hero is able to carry out tasks that would otherwise have been impossible, because no-one can see him to stop him. The "Invisible Man" of the aviation world is the Lockheed F-117A.

It is, of course, impossible to build an invisible aircraft, but steps can be taken along the road. Ever since the Second World War, radar has assumed an increasingly dominant role, firstly in the field of detection, and secondly as a means of missile guidance and gun-laying. This being the case, electronic invisibility became a sought-after attribute.

There are two basic ways to lower the radar "signature" of an aircraft. Building it from radar-absorbent materials (RAM) is one; the other is to shape the aircraft in such a way that electronic emissions are deflected away from the receiver instead of back to it. The former method was

Right: The F-117's fuselage and wings are shaped from a combination of multi-facetted plain surfaces to dissipate radar energy away from its source. The entire airframe is sprayed with radar-absorbent material, and regular resprays ensure that the coating is kept in top condition.

Above: Surely one of the strangest shapes to fly since the 1930s – Lockheed F-117A, with steeply sloped fuselage sides to deflect radar energy.

Right: The Nighthawk generally operates in darkness, and has seen plenty of action, in Panama, the Balkans, and in the Persian Gulf.

simple; the latter was very difficult.

Various steps were taken from the 1950s onwards, but a truly low observable penetrator seemed a long way in the future.

The computers of the 1970s were not advanced enough to predict the radar cross-section (RCS) of curved surfaces with sufficient accuracy. What could be done, however, was to design an aircraft as a series of flat plates at angles calculated to deflect instead of reflect radar emissions.

This posed another problem. Conventional aerodynamics simply would not apply. The angular shape would have impossible flying characteristics, with excessive drag. By now technology was catching up. The F-16 had a digital fly-by-wire system and this, combined with suitable software, was used to tame the oddly shaped airframe. Extreme measures were also taken to minimize the airplane's infrared signature. The theory could only be proven in the air, and two scaled-down proof-

of-concept machines were built. Trials flown in 1977-78 gave promising results.

The next step was to build the full-size machine, the Lockheed F-117A, and the first flight took place on June 18, 1981. Difficulties were encountered in the development phase. Test pilot Tom Morgenfeld recalled, "It did everything but sit on its tail while it was standing on its wheels!" But finally the airplane was tamed.

Under conditions of absolute secrecy the F-117A was brought into operational service. All training missions were flown by night. This was

Right: Further evidence of the United States' stealth technology is demonstrated in the Rockwell B-1B variable-sweep strategic bomber. Careful engineering has given it a head-on radar cross-section of around 1sq m, making it a more difficult target than a small fighter. Among stealth measures are anti-radar baffles and a curved duct in the engine nacelles.

hardly surprising; the "Black Jet" (later named "Nighthawk") was too vulnerable to operate in daylight, where fighters might encounter it visually. Not until November 10, 1988, was its existence revealed. After a less-than-impressive combat debut over Panama, the stealthy strike fighter proved its worth in the Gulf War of 1991. Forty-two Nighthawks took part, flying from a base in Saudi Arabia, and repeatedly penetrating the Iraqi air defenses undetected and making precision attacks on selected targets.

Left: In designing the Northrop B-2 Spirit bomber, an RCS target of much lower even than that of the B-1B was aimed at, and it is believed that perhaps as little as 0.05sq m was achieved. It has the simplest possible front profile – two straight, moderately swept leading edges that meet at the nose.

Gargantuan

> '*I arrived over Le Bourget with* Buran *(the Russian space shuttle) on the back of my aircraft. The clouds were low, and there was drizzle. Visibility was poor, and I had to fly a steep turn beneath the clouds to line up with the runway before landing. It was no problem; I was flying with one hand only! Then to show that this airplane can go anywhere, after landing I taxied across the grass to the parking place.*'
>
> ANATOLI BULANENKO

When pilot Anatoli Bulanenko described one of *Buran's* piggy-back performances at the 1989 Paris Air Show aboard the massive, pur-pose-built Antonov An-225 Mriya, he summarized a remarkable demon-stration of the low-speed control and agility, and rough field performance, of the world's largest aircraft, and the pilot's confidence in his machine. It all sounds so easy, but in fact the circuit, made in poor visibility at what seemed barely one wingspan height above the ground, followed by a turn off the taxiway and across the soggy grass surface, impressed even the hardened aviation journalists present. The Russian space shuttle carried piggyback on the monster aircraft simply added to the effect.

The An-225 is a heavy transport designed to carry enormous loads internally or outsize loads externally. It is the biggest and heaviest aircraft ever to fly. Its overall length is 275ft (84m); the maximum takeoff weight is 590 tons (600 tonnes) and maxi-mum payload is 246 tons (250 tonnes). The engines are six Lotarev D-18T turbofans, each providing 51,590lb (229.5kN) of thrust, and range with a 197-ton (200-tonne) payload is 2,425nm (4,500km).

The An-225 was developed from what was previously the world's largest aircraft, the An-124. The fuse-lage was stretched, the rear loading doors deleted, and a new wing cen-ter section, two more turbofans and a completely new twin-fin tail unit

Right: When Russia's An-225 Mriya carried *Buran* piggy-back fashion to the Paris Air Show in June 1989, it was mimicking what NASA's 747 jumbo jet had done with the *Enterprise* Space Shuttle about ten years earlier.

Above: The An-225 was conceived specially for carrying *Buran* shuttle and Energia rocket elements from the production plant near Moscow to the Baykonur cosmodrome.

introduced. Named Mriya (Dream), the An-225 made its maiden flight on December 21, 1988. Within four months it had set 106 world and class records.

Russia was a pioneer in the field of very large aircraft. The first four-engined airplane to fly was Igor Sikorsky's *Le Grand,* on May 26, 1913, at St Petersburg. This was developed into the Il'ya Muromets, the first four-engined bomber.

After the revolution, the design of large aircraft continued. The first of these, in December 1930, was the four-engined TB-3 bomber, followed three years later by the six-engined TB-4, at that time the world's largest aircraft. The ANT-20 *Maxim Gorkii* was an eight-engined behemoth first shown to the public on May 19, 1934. Essentially a propaganda exercise, this was equipped with a cinema, a printing press and a broadcasting stu-

Above: Passengers on the promenade along the top of the fuselage of Sikorsky's Il'ya Muromets, near St Petersburg, February 1914.

dio, and carried a crew of twenty and fifty passengers. The exercise turned sour a year later when it crashed after a mid-air collision.

Even bigger aircraft were planned, the 12-engined TB-6 among them, but by then the wish had out-run the technology. The final prewar design to enter service was the TB-7 (Pe-8).

The quest for sheer size lapsed until 1957, with the debut of the Tu-114, at that time the largest commercial aircraft in the world. In 1965 the huge An-22 Anteus transport made its appearance, followed by the An-124 Ruslan in 1982. But biggest of all is Mriya.

Ultimate Fighter

> '*With the Lockheed fighter, a US pilot can enter any part of the spectrum of aerial combat against numerous contenders, with the confidence that he has the top fighter strapped to his butt. This bird of prey will kill and maim anything the enemy can get airborne and our guy will return home safely and victoriously. This is the embodiment of combat confidence.*'
>
> GEN. FRED HAEFFNER, USAF (RET.)

Fred Haeffner was no stranger to air combat. As a lieutenant colonel, on May 13, 1967, he was flying an F-4C with the 8th TFW in Vietnam, the famous Wolf Pack. Leaving the Yen Vien area after providing cover for a strike, he saw MiG-17s chasing F-105s. Diving on the North Vietnamese fighters, he launched three AIM-7 Sparrows in quick succession. The first missed by about 100ft (30m), but the second impacted just aft of the cockpit, destroying the MiG-17.

The new fighter about which Gen. Haeffner was waxing lyrical is the Lockheed Martin F-22 Raptor, selected as the USAF air-superiority fighter of the future. The requirements for the new USAF fighter were clear: it had to operate deep into hostile airspace and outfly and

Above: From this angle, the Raptor's features such as the single-piece transparency to the cockpit, including the sawtooth edges, the chined nose, and trapezoidal intakes raked laterally and vertically, can be clearly seen.

outfight the opposition; in addition, it had to be easily maintainable, operate from damaged or austere bases, and be affordable.

What makes the Raptor special? It is the result of a totally new approach to air combat, utilizing stealth and speed as never before. The essential thing is to detect without being detected, as this gives the

Left: The Raptor is the most heavily computerised fighter in the world, with fast response given by a three-stage program, compared with about 17 in most other aircraft. The flight control system is triplex digital FBW.

345

initiative. The F-22 combines state-of-the-art low observables, which make it hard to detect, with the latest detection sensors. All else being equal, it will therefore have both the initiative and the first shot.

Externally, the single-seat, twin-engined F-22 is clean and uncluttered. To minimize RCS all fuel is carried internally, as are the air-to-air missiles, which are housed in bays. It is the first US fighter to carry weapons internally since the F-106.

Speed is the other factor. Many aircraft can attain high speeds by using afterburner, but they cannot sustain them without running out of fuel. The Raptor is designed to supercruise (to cruise at supersonic speed, Mach 1.4 or more) using military power only, which means that it can supercruise for extended periods. Supercruise has other enormous advantages. Even if an opponent manages to detect the F-22, it will be very hard-pressed to reach an attacking position in the time available, and converting to the traditional astern attack position is nearly impossible. Another factor is that high speed restricts missile launch envelopes to a tremendous degree; an attacker will have to get very close to bring his missiles within range. Mach 1.4 is widely regarded as the speed which keeps a fighter's tail clear under most circumstances, and it is probable that the F-22 can supercruise at speeds significantly greater than this.

Even if close maneuver combat is joined (and the combination of speed and stealth make this unlikely unless the F-22 pilot wishes it), the Lockheed fighter, which is fitted with vectoring nozzles, lacks nothing in maneuverability, and carries a 20mm M61A-2 six-barrel rotary cannon for really close work. Handling is described as excellent; "You only have to think it and you find yourself doing it."

Although designed as the ultimate air-superiority fighter, the latest tactical thinking seems to indicate that some versions will be given the air-to-surface role, with air-to-surface ordnance including two 1,000lb Joint

Direct Attack Munitions (JDAM), as well as self-defense missiles.

Out of missiles? Disengagement? Supercruise and stealth make it easy. The F-22 appears to have no weak points.

The US Air Force plans to field 339 F-22s, and production is scheduled to run until 2013, although this could be extended by export orders.

Stealth impinged on almost every aspect of the design. A minimum of eight AAMs would be needed to give sufficient combat persistence, but these had to be carried in internal bays – six Amraam ventrally, pneumatically expelled on launch, and two Sidewinders in side bays which swung out on trapezes.

Above: Although it was the loser to the F-22 in the competition to build the US Air Force's Advanced Tactical Fighter (ATF), the Northrop/McDonnell Douglas YF-23 was the more radical design (possibly its downfall), really looking like a vision of the future. The wing planform was diamond-shaped, with 40 degrees of leading edge sweep matched by 40 degrees of forward sweep on the trailing edges, and cropped tips. In what amounted to a butterfly tail, all-moving ruddervators were splayed out at an acute angle. Trapezoidal intakes under the wing curved upward to the engine compressor face, with the engines themselves housed in overwing "humps," exhausting into shallow troughs open at the top, with sawtooth ends, vaguely reminiscent of the B-2A. The designers chose not to use thrust-vectoring nozzles, in the interests of stealth. A double internal weapons bay was located just aft of the nosewheel.

Above: Lockheed Martin were also winners in another competition (decided in October 2002) – that for the Joint Strike Fighter, a single aircraft type designed to be affordable and to satisfy the requirements of five different services, the US Air Force, US Marine Corps and US Navy, and Britain's Royal Air Force and Royal Navy. The result is the F-35, basically a single-seat, single-engined, supersonic multi-role fighter

planned for service starting in 2010. There are three distinct variants:
F-35A, conventional takeoff and landing (CTOL) version for the USAF;
the F-35C carrier-compatible CTOL aircraft mainly for the USN, but with
some for the USMC; and the more complex and more costly F-35B short
takeoff and vertical landing (STOVL) Harrier replacement for the USMC,
RAF and RN.

The Final Frontier

People began imagining the ultimate flight experience – traveling in space – centuries ago, with the Moon as the favourite destination. Dreamers and scientific writers suggested various means of propulsion into space, including waterspouts, evaporating dew, flying swans and even waxed feathers. French writer Jules Verne, in his 1865 story *From the Earth to the Moon*, chose the space cannon as the means to launch a craft to the Moon, uncannily siting it in Florida, close to where US astronauts would set out for the Moon a century later.

The truth is that only one method of space propulsion can work: only rocket motors can develop sufficient power to accelerate objects to the speed they require to overcome the Earth's gravity and get into space – at least 17,000mph (27,358kph). Only rocket motors can work in space, because they do not, like jet engines, rely on the oxygen in the atmosphere to burn their fuel. Rockets carry their own oxygen supply and so can work in airless space.

Although the rocket was invented by the Chinese in around AD1200, it was not until the latter part of the 19th century that anyone began to wonder if rocket power could be used for space travel. Russian scientist Konstantin Eduardovich Tsiolkovsky, born in 1857, became convinced of it while he was still in his twenties, and spent the next quarter of a century working out the principles of space rocket flight. In 1903, months before the Wright brothers achieved their epic flights, Tsiolkovsky set out, in an article for a scientific journal, the basic requirements.

Much more powerful rocket propellants than gunpowder, used in the military rockets of the day, would be needed for spaceflight. Also, no single rocket would be able to achieve the speed necessary to travel into space; it could never have a high

enough power-to-weight ratio. A space rocket would need to consist of a number of rocket units, or stages, joined together, and these would have to fire and separate in turn. By losing weight at each stage, the final unit could achieve the necessary speed. This is the concept of the multi-stage, or step rocket, which is used in all space launches.

A scientist most influential in developing propulsion capable of launching an object into space was the American Robert Hutchings Goddard (1882–1945), who built and fired the first rocket using liquid propellants. Although his rocket, burning gasoline and liquid oxygen, fired for only a few seconds, and rose just 185ft (56m), it paved the way for the future, being the type of rocket that has since carried men to the Moon and instruments to the planets. By 1937 Goddard's rockets were reaching speeds of 700mph (1,126kph) and heights of 1.7 miles (2.7km).

Unbeknown to him, and to most of the rest of the world, Goddard's work was being eclipsed in Germany. On the Baltic island of Peenemunde, a team under the direction of the brilliant Wernher von Braun was developing a series of advanced liquid-propellant rockets. By the time the Second World War broke out in 1939, von Braun's team were working toward a practical ballistic missile capable of delivering a high-explosive warhead over a distance of several hundred miles. The first successful firing of this weapon, designated A-4 (V-2), took place in October 1942.

At the end of the Second World War, as part of their booty, the USA and the USSR shipped unused V-2s to their respective countries, taking with them members of the German rocket development team. Wernher von Braun went to the USA and directed further rocket research at the US Army's White Sands Proving Ground in New Mexico. In 1949 his team fired the world's first multi-stage rocket, Bumper. Later flights took place from a new launch site at Cape Canaveral in Florida, a site that would develop into the famous Kennedy Space Center.

THE SPACE RACE
During the following decades of Cold War between the West and the East, many more rocket launches took place from within the USA and the USSR (at Kapustin Yar near Volvograd), leading to a race into space between the world's two greatest powers. With the Sputnik launches the Russians won the first heat, and also the second when, on April 12,

Left: The first lifting body test aircraft was built as a glider, while the Northrop/NASA X-24 was fitted with an engine. The X-24 was carried to 50,000 ft (15,240m) under the wing of a Boeing B-52 and air-launched. By using its engine the X-24 could reach over 100,000ft) (30,480m) and then glide back to its base.

Above: The prototype orbital Shuttle orbiter *Enterprise* is carried aloft on a converted jumbo jet in a captive flight test, February 1977.

1961, Russian pilot Yuri Gagarin sped into orbit to become the first astronaut, or cosmonaut as the Russians call their space travelers. He circled the Earth once in the capsule Vostok 1 on a flight lasting 108 minutes.

During the next fifteen years both countries rocketed men into space with great frequency, the highlight being the Moon landing by the lunar module of the American Apollo 11 spacecraft on July 20, 1969. The words of the first man to walk on the Moon, Neil Armstrong, are engraved in history: "That's one small step for a man," he said, "one giant leap for mankind."

The three-man crew were accommodated in a cone-shaped, pressurized command module. This was connected with a cylindrical service module housing equipment, propellants and a powerful engine. The two sections together formed the Apollo mother ship, the Command and Service Modules (CSM). The third section was the lunar module. With the crew on board, the CSM weighed close to 45 tons. To lift such a weight and

accelerate it beyond the Earth's gravity required a massive launch vehicle, the Saturn V. This leviathan of a rocket, which stood 36 storeys high on the launch pad and weighed nearly 3,000 tons, was the last in the Saturn series of heavy launch vehicles developed by von Braun's team at the Marshall Flight Center in Alabama.

Over the next two and a half years US astronauts embarked on five more successful landing missions, and there were three further missions planned, but budget cutbacks and dwindling public interest (by then a Moon shot was no longer big news) forced their cancellation. There was a lot of surplus hardware, and two further missions were dreamed up that would use this up. The first was an experimental space station called Skylab. The second was an international space mission – the Apollo-Soyuz Test Project (ASTP) –

with the Russians, who had also continued their experiments in space exploration. Any "space race" was forgotten on this 1975 mission, as a three-man American crew in an Apollo CSM met up with a two-man Russian crew in a Soyuz spacecraft. Astronauts and cosmonauts worked together in a spirit of camaraderie. This was the way to explore space: co-operation, not competition.

THE SPACE SHUTTLE

The ASTP mission was for the USA not only the end of the Apollo era but also the end of the expendable era in manned spacecraft. In the USA, experiments began with lifting body craft, such as the Northrop X-24, in which the fuselage is designed to provide aerodynamic lift It is hoped that this type will eventually be capable of entering space orbit under the power of its own engines and re-enter

Below: The Shuttle's payload bay doors are opened prior to releasing a satellite into orbit. The manipulator arm is deployed.

Above: The Space Shuttle's principal role is that of transporting satellites into space and releasing them into Earth orbit. Should a satellite develop a fault, it can be repaired in space by Shuttle mission specialists and put back to work, saving millions of dollars.

Earth's atmosphere to return to base as an aircraft. While test flights with the X-24 were progressing, NASA contracted Rockwell to design and construct the world's first reusable space craft. This new craft, the Space Shuttle, would revolutionise space travel.

The final design chosen for the Shuttle system comprised three main pieces of hardware. Crew and cargo would be housed in a delta-winged Orbiter about the size of a medium-range airliner. It would take off like a rocket, but return to Earth as a glider. The Orbiter's rocket engines would be fed with liquid oxygen propellants from an external tank. Extra thrust for lift-off would be provided by twin solid-rocket boosters (SRBs) strapped to the sides of the tank. Shortly after lift-off the SRBs would separate and be parachuted back to Earth for re-use. When the external tank emptied it would be jettisoned.

Work on the Shuttle started as the last Apollo Moon landings were taking place, but it was not until 1977 that the first Shuttle took to the air. This craft was the prototype Orbiter, named *Enterprise* to the delight of "Star Trek" fans. Flights in the atmosphere proved its aerodynamics, and work forged ahead on the first operational Orbiter, named *Columbia*.

Technical problems, particularly with the main engines and the insulating tiles that formed the heat shield of the Orbiter, wreaked havoc with the schedules, and it was not until April 12, 1981, that *Columbia* blasted off from the Kennedy Space Center on the first Shuttle mission, designated STS-1 (STS for Space Transportation System). Close to a million people watched as veteran astronaut John Young and Robert Crippen rode the new "bird" into the heavens. After a flawless mission, *Columbia*

Above: *Discovery* (OV-103) in space orbit. The manipulator arm is extended ready for satellite launch.

touched down at Edwards Air Force Base in California two days later.

Columbia was ferried back to Kennedy atop a modified Boeing 747 carrier aircraft and by November was back on the launch pad. On November 12 it was again punching its way skywards. This was the first time any craft had flown into space more than once. The following year the Orbiter

Above: A solid rocket booster emerges from the fireball that has just engulfed the *Challenger* Space Shuttle just 73 seconds after lift-off on January 28, 1986, on Shuttle mission 51-L. The seven astronauts who perish are the first in-flight victims in the US space program.

repeated the feat three more times. On the last flight (STS-5) it became officially operational, carrying two commercial satellites into orbit.

A second Orbiter, *Challenger*, went into service in April 1983, making three trips into space in the year. The following November *Columbia* was back in harness, this time carrying a science laboratory called Spacelab, built by the European Space Agency, in its payload bay. Its record crew of six included the first Euro-

pean to travel on a US spacecraft, Ulf Merbold.

It was in 1984 that the remarkable versatility of the Shuttle became apparent. In April space-walking astronauts working from the *Challenger* captured an ailing satellite named Solar Max and repaired it in the payload bay before relaunching it. They did so using a jet-propelled backpack called the Manned Manoeuvring Unit (MMU) and with the help of the Orbiter's manipulator arm. In November, on the second flight of a new Orbiter, *Discovery*, Shuttle astronauts captured two satellites that had become marooned in uselessly low orbits, and this time brought them back to Earth.

The Shuttle fleet expanded to four in 1985 when *Atlantis* became operational in October. With a fleet of four, Orbiters would soon be shuttling into orbit every few weeks, or so it seemed.

But it was not to be. On January 28, 1986, *Challenger* rose from the launch pad on its 10th and the Shuttle's 25th mission, designated 51-L. Only seventy-three seconds into the flight, the Shuttle assembly exploded in a fireball in the Florida skies. *Challenger* was blasted apart and her crew of seven died instantly, becoming the first in-flight casualties in the US space program.

The remaining Shuttle fleet was grounded as then-President Reagan set up the Rogers Commission to investigate the disaster. The immediate fault appeared to be a defective joint in one of the SRBs, which allowed hot gases to escape and torch the supporting structure. The SRB swung round and ruptured the external tank, which immediately exploded. The Rogers Commission recommended extensive modifications to the Shuttle to prevent such a thing happening again, as well as operational changes prior to launch.

The fleet remained grounded until September 1988, when *Discovery* blasted off from the launch pad on mission STS-26, spearheading the USA's "return to flight." Its four-day mission was flawless, drawing collective sighs of relief throughout the world. Nine years on, the Shuttle would be celebrating its 80th flight and preparing for its next major role in space, which was to aid the construction of the International Space Station.

On *Discovery*'s launch day in 1988 the Soviets tried to steal some of the thunder, announcing that they were about to launch a shuttle craft of their own, called *Buran* (Snowstorm). It would be an unmanned, automated

flight. A planned October launch slipped into November, and *Buran* finally made it into orbit on November 15, circling the Earth twice before landing near its launch site at the Baikonur Cosmodrome. Though outwardly a Shuttle lookalike, *Buran* did not use its own engines for lift-off. It rode into space pick-a-back on what had become the world's most powerful launch vehicle, Energia. Its own engines fired on the fringes of space to thrust it into orbit. *Buran*'s maiden flight, however, was also its last. (The only *Buran* now resides in a children's playground at Baikonur.) Plans for manned missions in this and other similar craft were eventually abandoned because of lack of funds following the break-up of the Soviet Union.

SPACE STATIONS

However, while the USA had been concentrating on developing the Space Shuttle, the Russians had been accumulating vast experience of long-duration flights in a series of space stations, building up to a continuous presence in orbit. Using automatic supply craft, they delivered fresh supplies to the crews of these stations, setting the stage for long-duration flights. In November 1978 two Soviet astronauts completed a record 139-day mission, followed in 1979 by a 175-day mission, 184 days in 1980, 211 days in 1982, and 237 days in 1984. These were all achieved in Salyut space stations.

In February 1986 a new-generation space station called *Mir* (Peace) was launched into orbit. This had a multiple-docking module at one end, with six docking ports, as well as a single port at the other. This construction hinted at the spacecraft's purpose, as the base unit for a more extensive space complex. It would house the living quarters of the crew, while the main experimental work would be carried out in the add-on units that were to follow. The first unit, Kvant 1, docked with the base unit in 1987, followed by Kvant 2 (1989), Kristall (1990), Spektr (1995) and Priroda (996). With Priroda added,

Above: The European Space Agency's concept for the re-useable space vehicle was the Hermès. Designed to be launched on top of an Ariane 5 rocket to an altitude of 31 miles (50km) it could carry a crew of three and a payload of 3,527lb (1,600kg). The cone structure at the rear of the craft contained manoeuvring engines, cooling system and docking mechanism. This Module de Resources Hermès (MRH) was jettisoned before re-entry.

the *Mir* space station was at last complete, although, at ten years old, starting to show its age.

Mir was continuously inhabited following its launch, with its cosmo-nauts continuing to smash space duration records. In December 1988 Musa Manarov and Vladimir Titov became the first space travelers to spend a year in orbit. This feat was bettered by Valeri Polyakov, returning to Earth in March 1995 after 437 days.

JOINT OPERATIONS

Another feature of missions to *Mir* have been visits by "guest" cosmonauts from many different countries. They have included European Space Agency astronauts such as Ulf Merbold (1994) and Thomas Reiter (1995) on the so-called "EuroMir" missions. In March 1995 US astronaut Norman Thagard flew on *Mir*, the prelude to the first international space link-up since the ASTP mission two decades before. This happened in June 1995 when space shuttle *Atlantis* docked with the Russian space station, a suitable spectacular to celebrate the 100th United States manned flight. It was the most extensive assembly of space hardware ever in orbit, with ten astronauts and cosmonauts coming together for the first time. There was also an exchange of crews, with two cosmonauts transferring from *Atlantis* to *Mir* and two others, along with Thagard, transferring from *Mir* to *Atlantis*.

Further Shuttle missions to *Mir* took place, to accumulate experience in joint operations as a prelude to working together in the launch, assembly and operation of the upcoming International Space Station (ISS), also known as Alpha. On later Shuttle/*Mir* missions the Shuttle ferried up astronauts for a long-term stay in *Mir*, beginning with Shannon Lucid in February 1996. She remained in orbit for 188 days, the longest any female astronaut or cosmonaut had remained in orbit.

After circling the globe 86,331 times during its fifteen-year career, *Mir* was dramatically decommissioned by bringing it back to Earth on March 23, 2001, when it created a fantastic firework display as it re-entered the Earth's atmosphere and, in a controlled maneuver, plunged into a watery grave in the South Pacific.

Above: An artist's impression of NASA's X-36 space station project. Designed to take-off and leave the earth's atmosphere to orbit under its own power, it would return to base as a glider for use again. The X-33 is probably the only lifting body space vehicle to be considered for production.

Tragedy struck the Shuttle program almost two years later, when on February 1, 2003, the Space Shuttle *Columbia* disintegrated over Texas during its re-entry into the Earth's atmosphere following a sixteen-day science mission; all seven crew were lost. Intensive early investigations as to cause produced many theories, including one that the left wing had been penetrated from the top, suggesting that a foot-square piece of the shuttle came off during orbiting flight, the day after *Columbia*'s launch. The three remaining Shuttles were grounded pending completion of the investigation.

In the immediate future the efforts of the major spacefaring nations in the sphere of manned space travel will be concentrated on the construction of the ISS. When complete, the ISS, orbiting between about 220 and 280 miles (350 and 450km), will have a mass of more than 400 tons and measure some 330ft by 250ft (100m by 75m). It will be operated by an international crew of six, with crews rotating every few months. When the all-clear is given for the resumption of Shuttle flights, the Shuttle will be the prime vehicle for assembly tasks.

When mankind reaches out to the limits of the final frontier, risk and danger (kept to an absolute minimum by scientists) may always be on the intrepid travelers' shoulders. But, if the history of spaceflight – or even of manned flight itself – has taught us anything, it is that men and women will take the risks associated with exploration, aware that dreams become a reality, and sooner than expected.

Below: Venture is a wingless lifting body concept designed by Lockheed's famous "Skunk Works." It is capable of lifting a payload of 40,000lb (18,144kg) into low orbit. Like the Space Shuttle it lands conventionally after gliding to base.

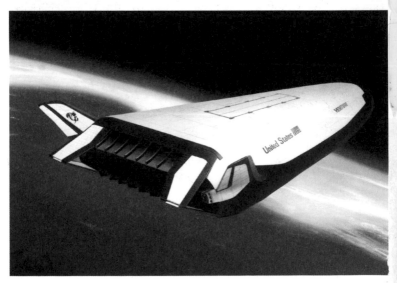